# Taste of Home
# Christmas

REIMAN MEDIA GROUP, INC.
GREENDALE, WI

# Taste of Home

## EDITORIAL

Editor-in-Chief **CATHERINE CASSIDY**
Creative Director **HOWARD GREENBERG**
Editorial Operations Director **KERRI BALLIET**

Managing Editor/Print & Digital Books **MARK HAGEN**
Associate Creative Director **EDWIN ROBLES JR.**

Editor **MICHELLE ROZUMALSKI**
Art Director **JESSIE SHARON**
Craft Editor **SHALANA FRISBY**
Layout Designers **NANCY NOVAK, CATHERINE FLETCHER**
Editorial Production Manager **DENA AHLERS**
Copy Chief **DEB WARLAUMONT MULVEY**
Copy Editors **MARY C. HANSON, JOANNE WEINTRAUB**

Chief Food Editor **KAREN BERNER**
Food Editors **JAMES SCHEND; PEGGY WOODWARD, RD**
Associate Food Editor **KRISTA LANPHIER**
Associate Editor/Food Content **ANNIE RUNDLE**
Recipe Editors **MARY KING; JENNI SHARP, RD; IRENE YEH**
Content Operations Manager **COLLEEN KING**

Test Kitchen and Food Styling Manager **SARAH THOMPSON**
Test Cooks **MATTHEW HASS, LAUREN KNOELKE**
Food Stylists **KATHRYN CONRAD (SENIOR), SHANNON ROUM, LEAH REKAU**
Prep Cooks **MEGUMI GARCIA, NICOLE SPOHRLEDER, BETHANY VANOPDORP**

Photographers **DAN ROBERTS, JIM WIELAND**
Photographer/Set Stylist **GRACE NATOLI SHELDON**
Set Styling Manager **STEPHANIE MARCHESE**
Set Stylists **MELISSA HABERMAN, DEE DEE JACQ**

Business Analyst **KRISTY MARTIN**
Billing Specialist **MARY ANN KOEBERNIK**

## BUSINESS

Vice President, Publisher **JAN STUDIN, JAN_STUDIN@RD.COM**

General Manager, Taste of Home Cooking Schools **ERIN PUARIEA**

Vice President, Brand Marketing **JENNIFER SMITH**
Vice President, Circulation and Continuity Marketing **DAVE FIEGEL**

## READER'S DIGEST NORTH AMERICA

Vice President, Business Development **JONATHAN BIGHAM**
President, Books and Home Entertaining **HAROLD CLARKE**
Chief Financial Officer **HOWARD HALLIGAN**
Vice President, General Manager, Reader's Digest Media **MARILYNN JACOBS**
Chief Marketing Officer **RENEE JORDAN**
Vice President, Chief Sales Officer **MARK JOSEPHSON**
Vice President, General Manager, Milwaukee **FRANK QUIGLEY**
Vice President, Chief Content Officer **LIZ VACCARIELLO**

## THE READER'S DIGEST ASSOCIATION, INC.

President and Chief Executive Officer **ROBERT E. GUTH**

© 2013 Reiman Media Group, Inc.
5400 S. 60th St., Greendale WI 53129

International Standard Book Number: 978-1-61765-175-5
International Standard Serial Number: 1948-8386
Component Number: 119600019H00

**COVER PHOTOGRAPHY**
Photographer **JIM WIELAND**
Food Stylist **KATHRYN CONRAD**
Set Stylist **MELISSA HABERMAN**

**PICTURED ON THE FRONT COVER:** (Bottom photo) Roast Turkey with Sausage-Cabbage Stuffing (p. 57), Orange Poppy Seed Salad (p. 107), Streusel-Topped Cherry Almond Galette (p. 137), Triple Mash with Buttered Horseradish (p. 50), Garlic Brussels Sprouts (p. 44). (Across the top) Mocha Truffle Trees (p. 112), Cinnamon Stick Candle (p. 178), Slow Cooker Caramel Apple Cider (p. 96), Cranberry-Almond Pound Cake (p. 158).

**PICTURED ON THE BACK COVER:** Chocolate Mint Delight (p. 33), Mushroom and Bacon Cheesecake (p. 93), Salt-Encrusted Prime Rib (p. 49), Fresh Green Bean Salad (p. 99).

**ADDITIONAL PHOTOGRAPHY USED:** Ornaments: Natalia Klenova/Shutterstock.com (endpapers); Ornaments and ribbon: Konstantin Chagin/Shutterstock.com (p. 1); Snowflakes: tale/Shutterstock.com (p. 4).

Printed in USA
13 5 7 9 10 8 6 4 2

# Contents

# SPREAD *good cheer* ALL SEASON LONG
## with festive new yuletide recipes, decorations, gift ideas & MORE!

*Taste of Home Christmas makes it easy to create memorable holiday celebrations for loved ones. With scrumptious dinner dishes, cookies and other favorites from home cooks like you, plus sparkling decorations and gifts, this treasury has everything you need to share the spirit of the season.*

**SMALL PLATES.** When you want merry appetizers, look here! The one- and two-bite starters in this chapter are perfect to pick up and eat while mingling. Say "cheers" with a selection of refreshing beverages, too.

**HOLIDAY DINNER IN 60.** Yes, you *can* prepare a delicious, extra-special meal for Christmas in just 1 hour. Mix and match quick-but-festive main dishes, sides and desserts to create your own distinctive menu.

**CHRISTMAS FEASTS.** These three impressive yuletide dinners—featuring main courses of turducken, prime rib and pork roast—will prove nearly impossible to choose from! A bonus recipe section gives you even more options.

**SEASONAL GET-TOGETHERS.** Gather friends and family for a canned gift exchange, a charming farmhouse-style brunch or an elegant winter-themed dinner. This chapter will show you how to host an unforgettable party.

**POTLUCK GATHERINGS.** Wow the crowd at your next bring-a-dish event with large-yield contributions full of seasonal appeal. Expect to see a long line at the buffet table for second helpings—and thirds!

**CAREFREE ENTERTAINING.** Holiday parties are fuss-free when these effortless entrees, starters and other choices are on the menu. Each one can be prepared in 30 minutes or less, giving you extra time to spend with guests.

**SIMPLY CHOCOLATE.** Indulge your chocoholic cravings with creative takes on white, dark, milk, semisweet, German and more varieties of chocolate. From desserts to beverages, these temptations are irresistible.

**YULETIDE PIES & TARTS.** For the perfect way to top off Christmas dinner, rely on these traditional and delectably different favorites. A fresh-baked pie or rustic tart always makes a comforting, home-style finale.

**SWEET SENSATIONS.** Holiday get-togethers just aren't complete without the treats of the season. Thanks to the decadent cakes, cookies, fudge and other delights in this chapter, you'll satisfy every sweet tooth.

**GIFTS FROM THE KITCHEN.** A homemade specialty is always a welcome present at Christmastime. Look here for mouthwatering goodies you can make for friends, family, neighbors, co-workers...everyone!

**DECK THE HALLS.** It's so easy and fun to decorate room after room with the simple but gorgeous craft projects in this creative chapter. In no time, you'll transform your house into a holiday home.

**GIFTS TO GIVE.** Check off each name on your list with one of these heartwarming handmade presents. From an eye-catching stamped pendant to an adorable puppet set, these do-it-yourself ideas will thrill young and old alike.

*It's all here in this exciting new edition of* Taste of Home Christmas. *Just turn the page to start experiencing the magic, beauty and joy of the holiday season like never before!*

*small*
PLATES

# Artichoke Dip Bites

Love artichoke dip? This recipe gives you the dip and dippers together in one easy-to-eat appetizer. My friends can't get enough of the creamy little cups warm from the oven.

**—NIKKOLE VANYO**
WEST FARGO, NORTH DAKOTA

**PREP:** 25 MIN.  **BAKE:** 20 MIN.
**MAKES:** 2 DOZEN

- 1   can (14 ounces) water-packed artichoke hearts, rinsed, drained and chopped
- ½   cup grated Parmesan cheese
- ½   cup mayonnaise
- ½   cup sour cream
- 2   tablespoons canned chopped green chilies
- 1   garlic clove, minced
- 1   loaf (1 pound) frozen bread dough, thawed
- 1   cup (4 ounces) shredded part-skim mozzarella cheese
  Thinly sliced green onions

**1.** In a large bowl, combine the first six ingredients; set aside.

**2.** Shape dough into twenty-four 1-in. balls. With floured fingers, press onto the bottoms and ½ in. up the sides of greased muffin cups.

**3.** Fill the cups with tablespoonfuls of the artichoke mixture; sprinkle with mozzarella cheese. Bake at 350° for 18-22 minutes or until golden brown. Garnish with green onions. Serve warm.

## Holiday Helper

When it comes to slicing green onions, I find it easier and faster to cut the onions with a kitchen scissors than with a knife. If your recipe calls for quite a few, grab a bunch at one time and snip away. You're done before you know it, and this avoids the extra cleanup of washing a cutting board.

**—LOUISE B.**
COLUMBIA, SOUTH CAROLINA

## Rosemary & Thyme Lemon Cocktail

A bubbly drink always means it's time to celebrate! Try dressing up the usual hard lemonade with sprigs of rosemary and thyme for a refreshing cocktail at Christmas or any time of year.

**—MOFFAT FRAZIER** NEW YORK, NEW YORK

**PREP:** 5 MIN. + CHILLING
**MAKES:** 15 SERVINGS

- 5    fresh rosemary sprigs
- 5    fresh thyme sprigs
- 1    bottle (1¾ liters) lemonade

**ADDITIONAL INGREDIENTS (FOR EACH SERVING)**

- 1½   ounces vodka
      Ice cubes
- 2    ounces carbonated water, chilled

**GARNISH**

    Rosemary sprig or lemon slice, optional

In a 2-qt. pitcher, muddle rosemary and thyme; add the lemonade. Cover and refrigerate overnight. Strain the lemonade; discard the herbs.

**To prepare cocktail:** *In a mixing glass or tumbler, combine ½ cup lemonade and vodka. Place ice in a highball glass; add the lemonade mixture. Top with carbonated water. Garnish as desired.*

## Steak and Blue Cheese Crescents

Grilled steak, blue cheese and bacon make these some of the heartiest, most satisfying starters you'll ever eat. I roll up the filling in refrigerated pie pastry.

**—KELLY WILLIAMS**
FORKED RIVER, NEW JERSEY

**PREP:** 30 MIN. **BAKE:** 15 MIN.
**MAKES:** 1 DOZEN

- 1    tablespoon butter, softened
- 1    teaspoon coarsely ground pepper
- ½   teaspoon seasoned salt
- 1    beef ribeye steak (12 ounces)
- ⅔   cup finely chopped walnuts
- ⅓   cup crumbled blue cheese
- 1    tablespoon minced fresh parsley
- ¼   teaspoon pepper
- 1    sheet refrigerated pie pastry
- 4    thick-sliced bacon strips, cooked and crumbled
- 1    green onion, thinly sliced
- 1    tablespoon 2% milk
- 2    teaspoons grated Parmesan cheese

**1.** In a small bowl, combine the butter, coarse pepper and seasoned salt. Rub over each side of steak.

**2.** Grill, uncovered, over medium heat or broil 4-in. from heat for 5-7 minutes on each side or until the meat reaches desired doneness (for medium-rare, a thermometer should read 145°; medium, 160°; well-done, 170°). Transfer to a cutting board; cover and let stand for 5 minutes. Cut into 12 slices.

**3.** Meanwhile, in a small bowl, combine the walnuts, blue cheese, parsley and pepper. On a lightly floured surface, roll dough into a 12-in. circle. Spread with walnut mixture; cut into 12 wedges.

**4.** Top each wedge with a steak slice, bacon and onion. Roll up wedges from the wide ends and place point side down 2 in. apart on a greased baking sheet. Curve ends to form crescents. Brush with milk; sprinkle with Parmesan cheese.

**5.** Bake, uncovered, at 425° for 14-16 minutes or until golden brown. Serve immediately.

# Philly Cheesesteak Bites

Here's a deliciously downsized version of the ever-popular Philly cheesesteak. For perfect bite-size snacks, the sandwich ingredients are layered on waffle-cut fries instead of buns.

**—TASTE OF HOME TEST KITCHEN**

**PREP:** 30 MIN. **COOK:** 5 MIN. **MAKES:** 1½ DOZEN

- 1 package (22 ounces) frozen waffle-cut fries
- 1 medium onion, halved and sliced
- ½ small green pepper, halved and sliced
- ½ small sweet red pepper, halved and sliced
- 3 tablespoons canola oil, divided
- ½ teaspoon salt, divided
- 1 beef ribeye steak (1 inch thick and ¾ pound), cut into thin strips
- ¼ teaspoon pepper
- 3 tablespoons ketchup
- 6 tablespoons process cheese sauce

**1.** Bake 18 large waffle fries according to the package directions (save remaining waffle fries for another use). Meanwhile, in a large skillet, saute onion and peppers in 1 tablespoon oil until tender. Sprinkle with ⅛ teaspoon salt. Remove and keep warm.

**2.** In the same pan, saute the steak in the remaining oil in batches for 45-60 seconds or until desired doneness. Sprinkle with pepper and remaining salt. On each waffle fry, layer the beef, onion mixture, ketchup and cheese sauce. Serve warm.

# Beef Spiedini

An Italian favorite, spiedini make savory hors d'oeuvres that are sure to tide over hungry party guests until dinnertime. The hearty skewers hold marinated steak pinwheels stuffed with a marinara-and-crumb filling.

**—DESTY LORINO** SHOREWOOD, WISCONSIN

**PREP:** 45 MIN. **BROIL:** 5 MIN./BATCH
**MAKES:** 40 APPETIZERS

- 1 beef top sirloin steak (1 inch thick and 1½ pounds)

**MARINADE**
- ½ cup olive oil
- 1 tablespoon lemon juice
- ½ teaspoon salt
- ½ teaspoon pepper

**BREADING**
- 1¼ cups seasoned bread crumbs
- ⅓ cup grated Parmesan cheese
- 2 tablespoons minced fresh parsley
- ⅛ teaspoon salt
- ⅛ teaspoon garlic powder
    Dash pepper
- ¾ cup marinara sauce

**ASSEMBLY**
- 1 medium red onion
- 40 fresh sage leaves
- ¼ cup olive oil

**1.** Thinly slice steak widthwise into 5-in. strips. In a large resealable plastic bag, combine the marinade ingredients. Add beef; seal bag and turn to coat. Refrigerate for 4 hours or overnight, turning occasionally.

**2.** Combine seasoned bread crumbs, Parmesan cheese, parsley, salt, garlic powder and pepper. Transfer half of the mixture to a shallow bowl; set aside.

**3.** For the filling, add marinara sauce to the remaining crumb mixture and mix well. Spread 1 teaspoon filling over each beef strip and roll up into pinwheels. Coat with the reserved crumb mixture.

**4.** Cut the red onion into 1-in. pieces and separate into layers. Thread a piece of red onion, a sage leaf and a beef pinwheel onto soaked wooden appetizer skewers. Drizzle lightly with oil and place on a greased 15-in. x 10-in. x 1-in. baking pan.

**5.** Broil 3-4 in. from heat for 5-7 minutes or until the beef reaches desired doneness, turning once.

## Pomegranate-Glazed Turkey Meatballs

With a splash of pomegranate juice, this recipe turns ordinary meatballs into something extraordinary for a Christmastime buffet. I love the sweet lightness of the glaze combined with the ground turkey, herbs and spices.

**—DANIELLE D'AMBROSIO** BRIGHTON, MASSACHUSETTS

**PREP:** 30 MIN.  **COOK:** 10 MIN.  **MAKES:** 3 DOZEN

1  egg, beaten
½  cup soft bread crumbs
½  cup minced fresh parsley
1  teaspoon salt
1  teaspoon smoked paprika
1  teaspoon coarsely ground pepper
¼  teaspoon garlic salt

1¼  pounds ground turkey
3  cups plus 1 tablespoon pomegranate juice, divided
½  cup sugar
1  tablespoon cornstarch

**1.** In a large bowl, combine the egg, soft bread crumbs, parsley, salt, paprika, pepper and garlic salt. Crumble the turkey over mixture and mix well. Shape into 1-in. balls.

**2.** Divide the meatballs between two ungreased 15-in. x 10-in. x 1-in. baking pans. Bake at 375° for 10-15 minutes or until a thermometer reads 165° and juices run clear.

**3.** Meanwhile, in a large skillet, combine 3 cups of pomegranate juice and sugar. Bring to a boil; cook until the liquid is reduced to about 1 cup. Combine cornstarch and remaining juice; stir into the skillet. Cook and stir for 1 minute or until thickened.

**4.** Gently stir in the meatballs and heat through. Serve in a slow cooker or chafing dish.

## Honey-Hazelnut Brie Tartines

For my French-themed dinner party, I created an appetizer using two foods I love—Brie cheese and Granny Smith apples. The topped toasts have lots of sweet-tart flavor.

—**BRIDGET KLUSMAN** OTSEGO, MICHIGAN

**PREP/TOTAL TIME:** 30 MIN.  **MAKES:** 2 DOZEN

 24  slices French bread baguette (¼ inch thick)
 ½  cup butter, softened
 ⅓  cup honey
 1  teaspoon minced fresh rosemary
 ⅓  cup chopped hazelnuts, toasted
 2  tart apples, halved and cut into ¼-inch slices
 1  round (8 ounces) Brie cheese, cut into ¼-inch slices

**1.** Place the bread on baking sheets. Broil 3-4 in. from the heat for 1-2 minutes on each side or until golden brown. In a small bowl, beat the butter, honey and rosemary until blended. Stir in hazelnuts.
**2.** Spread 1 teaspoon hazelnut mixture over each toast. Layer with the apple and Brie slices. Top with remaining hazelnut mixture. Bake at 350° for 3-5 minutes or until cheese is melted.

## Beef & Onion Piroshki

When I lived in Seattle, one of my favorite places was a small stand that sold piroshki—Russian stuffed pocket sandwiches. Whenever I'm missing my former city, I make my own batch.

—**JULIE MERRIMAN** COLD BROOK, NEW YORK

**PREP:** 30 MIN. + COOLING  **BAKE:** 15 MIN.
**MAKES:** 32 APPETIZERS

 1  pound lean ground beef (90% lean)
 1  cup finely chopped sweet onion
 2  garlic cloves, minced
 ½  teaspoon salt
 ¼  teaspoon pepper
 1  cup chopped fresh spinach
 1  cup (4 ounces) Havarti cheese
 ¼  cup sour cream
 2  tablespoons snipped fresh dill
 1  package (17.3 ounces) frozen puff pastry, thawed
 1  egg
 1  tablespoon water

**1.** In a large skillet, cook the beef, onion, garlic, salt and pepper over medium heat until the meat is no longer pink; drain. Cool to room temperature.
**2.** Stir spinach, cheese, sour cream and dill into the beef mixture. On a lightly floured surface, roll a puff pastry sheet into a 12-in. square. Cut into sixteen 3-in. squares. Repeat with remaining sheet.
**3.** Spoon 1 tablespoon beef mixture onto the center of each square. Fold the dough over the filling, forming a triangle; press the edges with a fork to seal. Transfer to greased baking sheets. Whisk the egg and water; brush over the tops. Bake at 400° for 14-16 minutes or until golden brown.

## Salmon Mousse Canapes

It's so easy to accent crunchy cucumber slices with a smooth and creamy salmon filling. Guests rave about the elegant presentation, contrasting textures and refreshing taste.

—**BARB TEMPLIN** NORWOOD, MINNESOTA

**PREP/TOTAL TIME:** 30 MIN.  **MAKES:** ABOUT 3 DOZEN

 2  English cucumbers
 1  package (8 ounces) cream cheese, softened
 ½  pound smoked salmon or lox
 1  tablespoon 2% milk
 1  teaspoon lemon-pepper seasoning
 1  teaspoon snipped fresh dill
    Salt and pepper to taste
 ½  cup heavy whipping cream
    Additional snipped fresh dill

**1.** Peel strips from the cucumbers to create a decorative edge; cut the cucumbers into ½-in. slices.
**2.** For the mousse, place the cream cheese, salmon, milk, lemon-pepper seasoning and dill in a food processor; cover and process until blended. Transfer to a small bowl and season with salt and pepper. In another bowl, beat the heavy whipping cream until stiff peaks form. Fold into the salmon mixture.
**3.** Pipe or dollop mousse onto cucumber slices; garnish with dill. Refrigerate until ready to serve.

## Wire Card Holders

Want to dress up your holiday table? Create these elegant wire spirals using long-nose pliers, wire cutters and 12-gauge wire in any color you like (available at most craft stores).

To start, cut a 12-inch piece of wire. Hold one end of the wire with long-nose pliers and use your other hand to bend the wire into a flat spiral around the held end, forming the base spiral. Continue until the base spiral is 4 to 5 rows across.

Next, curve the remaining long end of wire up about 1½ inches, forming a stem. Use the long-nose pliers to grasp the end of the stem, then curve the wire into a small spiral perpendicular to the base spiral. The small spiral should be 2 to 3 rows across.

To finish, simply insert a paper card in the small spiral. Use the wire holders as place card holders or as a markers to identify the foods on a buffet table.

## Fish Taco Bites

I think these appetizers are better than any regular-size fish tacos I've had as an entree. The creamy, citrusy salsa drizzle is fantastic not only on these, but also on other Southwestern dishes.

**—CARMELL CHILDS** FERRON, UTAH

**PREP:** 30 MIN.  **BAKE:** 20 MIN.
**MAKES:** 3 DOZEN

- ½   cup salsa verde
- 4   ounces cream cheese, softened
- 2   tablespoons lime juice, divided
- 2   tablespoons minced fresh cilantro
- 1   teaspoon honey
     Dash salt
- 12  frozen breaded fish sticks
- 1   tablespoon taco seasoning
- 36  tortilla chip scoops
- 1½  cups coleslaw mix
- ¾   cup cubed avocado
- ¾   cup chopped seeded tomato
     Lime wedges and additional minced fresh cilantro, optional

**1.** In a blender, combine the salsa, cream cheese, 1 tablespoon lime juice, cilantro, honey and salt. Cover and process until smooth; set aside.

**2.** Place fish sticks on a baking sheet. Bake at 425° for 10 minutes. Sprinkle with half of the taco seasoning. Turn fish sticks over; sprinkle with the remaining taco seasoning. Bake 7-9 minutes longer or until crisp.

**3.** Meanwhile, place chips on a serving platter. In a small bowl, combine the coleslaw mix, avocado, tomato, remaining lime juice and ½ cup salsa mixture. Spoon into chips. Cut each fish stick into three pieces. Place a fish piece in each chip; top each with about ½ teaspoon salsa mixture. Garnish with lime wedges and additional cilantro if desired.

## Bacon-Wrapped Cheese-Stuffed Dates

Each bite of these simple baked appetizers has a wonderful contrast of tastes and textures. You'll get crunchy almonds, soft dates, salty bacon, creamy blue cheese and sweet honey.

**—NANCY LATULIPPE** SIMCOE, ONTARIO

**PREP:** 25 MIN. **BAKE:** 10 MIN. **MAKES:** 32 APPETIZERS

- 16 center-cut bacon strips
- 32 pitted dates
- ⅓ cup crumbled blue cheese
- 32 blanched almonds
- 2 tablespoons honey
- ½ teaspoon coarsely ground pepper

**1.** Cut bacon strips in half widthwise. In a large skillet, cook bacon over medium heat until partially cooked but not crisp. Remove to paper towels to drain; keep warm.

**2.** Cut a lengthwise slit down the center of each date, being careful not to cut through completely. Fill each with ½ teaspoon blue cheese and 1 almond. Wrap with 1 piece bacon; secure with a toothpick.

**3.** Place in foil-lined 15-in. x 10-in. x 1-in. baking pans. Brush tops with honey. Bake at 375° for 9-11 minutes or until bacon is crisp. Sprinkle with pepper.

## Buffalo Chicken Empanadas with Blue Cheese Sauce

For the popular taste of Buffalo wings in easy-to-eat little pockets, try my golden-brown empanadas. Using rotisserie chicken and refrigerated pastry speeds up the preparation. If you like, freeze the unbaked empanadas for up to 2 months, then bake them for 12-16 minutes as directed in the recipe.

**—MELISSA MILLWOOD** LYMAN, SOUTH CAROLINA

**PREP:** 35 MIN. **BAKE:** 10 MIN./BATCH
**MAKES:** 8 DOZEN (1 CUP SAUCE)

- 1 small onion, chopped
- 1 small green pepper, chopped
- 4½ teaspoons canola oil
- 2 garlic cloves, minced
- 3 cups finely chopped rotisserie chicken
- 1½ cups (6 ounces) shredded part-skim mozzarella cheese
- ½ cup Buffalo wing sauce
- ¼ teaspoon salt
- ¼ teaspoon pepper
- 5 sheets refrigerated pie pastry
- 2 eggs
- 2 tablespoons water
- 1 cup heavy whipping cream
- 1 cup (4 ounces) crumbled blue cheese

**1.** In a small skillet, saute the onion and green pepper in oil until crisp-tender. Add garlic; cook 1 minute longer.

**2.** In a large bowl, combine the chicken, mozzarella cheese, Buffalo wing sauce, salt and pepper. Stir in the onion mixture.

**3.** On a lightly floured surface, unroll one pastry. Roll out into a 12-in. circle. Cut with a floured 3-in. biscuit cutter. Remove excess dough and reroll the scraps. Repeat with remaining pastry.

**4.** Beat eggs and water; brush over edges of pastry circles. Place heaping teaspoonfuls of filling in the centers. Fold dough over filling. Press edges with a fork to seal.

**5.** Place 2 in. apart on greased baking sheets. Brush with remaining egg mixture. Bake at 400° for 9-12 minutes or until golden brown.

**6.** Meanwhile, in a small saucepan, bring cream to a boil. Reduce heat; simmer, uncovered, for 5-7 minutes or until slightly thickened, stirring occasionally. Add blue cheese; cook and stir 2 minutes longer or until cheese is melted and sauce thickens. Serve with empanadas.

# Eggplant Pizzas

Baked and breaded slices of eggplant provide the crust for these unusual but yummy pizzas. Smother them with mozzarella cheese, veggies, sausage or any other toppings you like.

—PATTI FURNARI SHASTA, CALIFORNIA

**PREP:** 35 MIN. **BAKE:** 20 MIN.
**MAKES:** 2 DOZEN

- 1 cup all-purpose flour
- 4 eggs, beaten
- 2½ cups Italian-style panko (Japanese) bread crumbs
- 1 medium eggplant, peeled and cut into ¼-inch slices
  Olive oil-flavored cooking spray
- 1 pound bulk Italian sausage
- 1 small onion, chopped
- 1 small green pepper, chopped
- 3 garlic cloves, minced
- ½ pound sliced fresh mushrooms
- 1 small zucchini, chopped
- 1 tablespoon olive oil
- 1½ cups garden-style spaghetti or marinara sauce
- 1½ cups chopped fresh spinach
- 1½ cups (6 ounces) shredded part-skim mozzarella cheese

**1.** Place flour, eggs and bread crumbs in separate shallow bowls. Dip the eggplant in flour, eggs and then coat in crumbs. Place on greased baking sheets; coat tops with cooking spray. Bake at 400° for 15-18 minutes or until tender and golden brown.
**2.** Meanwhile, in a large skillet, cook the sausage, onion, pepper and garlic over medium heat until meat is no longer pink. Drain and transfer to a bowl; keep warm. In the same skillet, saute mushrooms and zucchini in oil until tender. Return sausage to the skillet; stir to combine.
**3.** Spread the spaghetti sauce on the eggplant rounds. Top with sausage mixture, spinach and mozzarella cheese. Bake 4-6 minutes longer or until the cheese is melted.

# Crispy Goat Cheese Appetizers

Here's a memorable party starter for the holidays. I cover goat cheese with seasoned crumbs, fry it until golden brown and finish it off with tomato, basil, balsamic vinegar and pine nuts.

—JULIA NOUSS RICHMOND, VIRGINIA

**PREP:** 35 MIN. **COOK:** 5 MIN./BATCH
**MAKES:** ABOUT 2½ DOZEN

- 4 logs (4 ounces each) herbed fresh goat cheese
- ½ cup all-purpose flour
- 2 eggs, beaten
- 1 cup panko (Japanese) bread crumbs
- 1 teaspoon dried thyme
- ½ teaspoon garlic powder
- ⅛ teaspoon kosher salt
- ½ cup canola oil
- 1 cup cherry tomatoes, halved
- 1 cup fresh basil leaves
- ¼ cup balsamic vinegar
- 1 tablespoon pine nuts

**1.** Freeze the cheese for 15 minutes. Unwrap and cut into ¼-in. slices.
**2.** Place flour and eggs in separate shallow bowls. In another shallow bowl, combine the bread crumbs, thyme, garlic powder and salt. Dip cheese slices in the flour, eggs, then bread crumb mixture.
**3.** In an electric skillet, heat the oil to 375°. Fry cheese slices, a few at a time, for 2-3 minutes on each side or until golden brown. Drain on paper towels.
**4.** Garnish each appetizer with a tomato half and basil leaf. Drizzle with balsamic vinegar; top with pine nuts. Serve warm.

# Cranberry-Beef Mini Burgers

Cranberry tapenade brings a deep red color and sweet-sour zing to these fun little bacon cheeseburgers. Serve them at Christmas and prepare to hear raves!

—**PRISCILLA YEE** CONCORD, CALIFORNIA

**PREP:** 30 MIN. **COOK:** 10 MIN./BATCH
**MAKES:** 16 APPETIZERS

**CRANBERRY TAPENADE**
- ⅔ cup dried cranberries
- ¼ cup pitted Greek olives, chopped
- 1 tablespoon balsamic vinegar
- 1 tablespoon olive oil
- 1 garlic clove, minced
- 1 teaspoon minced fresh rosemary
- 1 teaspoon minced fresh thyme

**BURGERS**
- 2 pounds ground beef
- 1 teaspoon salt
- 1 teaspoon pepper
- 4 slices provolone cheese, quartered
- ¾ cup mayonnaise
- 16 dinner rolls, split and toasted
- 2 cups fresh arugula
- 3 plum tomatoes, cut into 16 slices
- 8 bacon strips, halved and cooked

**1.** In a food processor, place the first six ingredients; pulse until berries are finely chopped. Transfer to a small bowl; stir in thyme. In a large bowl, combine the beef, salt and pepper. Shape into 16 patties, about ½ inch thick.

**2.** In a large nonstick skillet, cook patties in batches over medium heat for 3-4 minutes on each side or until a thermometer reads 160° and juices run clear, topping with cheese during last minute of cooking.

**3.** Spread mayonnaise over the cut sides of buns. Layer the bottoms with arugula, tomatoes, burgers, bacon and tapenade; replace tops.

## Hawaiian Crab Canapes

Here's a refreshing taste of paradise—an appetizer featuring crab, macadamia nuts, pineapple preserves and coconut. The sweet, crunchy canapes are a breeze to make and eat.

**—JAMIE MILLER** MAPLE GROVE, MINNESOTA

**PREP/TOTAL TIME:** 20 MIN.  **MAKES:** ABOUT 4 DOZEN

- 1 **carton (8 ounces) spreadable chive and onion cream cheese**
- 1 **package (3.2 ounces) teriyaki rice crackers**
- 1 **can (6 ounces) lump crabmeat, drained**
- 1 **jar (12 ounces) pineapple preserves**
- ¾ **cup flaked coconut, toasted**
- ½ **cup chopped macadamia nuts, toasted**
- 2 **tablespoons minced chives**

Spread the cream cheese over crackers. Top with the crab, preserves, coconut, nuts and chives.

## Honey-Pear Iced Tea

Take summery iced tea into fall and winter by stirring in pear nectar and adding a fresh pear slice to each glass as a garnish. A little honey provides an extra touch of sweetness.

**—TASTE OF HOME TEST KITCHEN**

**PREP:** 15 MIN. + CHILLING  **MAKES:** 6 SERVINGS

- 6 **individual green chai tea bags**
- 3 **cups boiling water**
- 3 **cups pear nectar**
- ⅓ **cup lemon juice**
- ⅓ **cup honey**
  **Thin pear slices**

**1.** Steep tea in boiling water for 3 minutes; discard tea bags. Cool. Refrigerate until chilled.

**2.** In a pitcher, combine the pear nectar, lemon juice, honey and chilled tea. Garnish each serving with a pear slice.

# Vegetable Samosas

My family enjoys the wonderful Indian flavors of a traditional samosa. Baked instead of fried, this version has fewer calories but keeps all of the authentic appeal we love.

—AMY SIEGEL CLIFTON, NEW JERSEY

**PREP:** 45 MIN.  **BAKE:** 20 MIN.  **MAKES:** ABOUT 3 DOZEN

- 2 large potatoes, peeled and cubed
- 1 medium onion, chopped
- 2 tablespoons olive oil
- 2 garlic cloves, minced
- 1 teaspoon salt
- 1 teaspoon curry powder
- ½ teaspoon ground cumin
- ¼ teaspoon pepper
- 1 cup canned garbanzo beans or chickpeas, rinsed, drained and mashed
- 1 cup frozen peas, thawed
- 2 tablespoons minced fresh cilantro
- 1 package (16 ounces, 14-inch x 9-inch sheet size) frozen phyllo dough, thawed
  Cooking spray

**1.** Place the potatoes in a large saucepan and cover with water. Bring to a boil. Reduce heat; cover and cook for 15-20 minutes or until tender. Drain. Mash potatoes; set aside.

**2.** In a large skillet, saute the onion in oil until tender. Add the garlic, salt, curry powder, cumin and pepper; cook 1 minute longer. Remove from the heat. Stir in the mashed potatoes, garbanzo beans, peas and cilantro.

**3.** Place one sheet of phyllo dough on a work surface with a short end facing you. (Keep remaining phyllo covered with plastic wrap and a damp towel to prevent it from drying out.) Spray sheet with cooking spray; repeat with one more sheet of phyllo, spraying the sheet with cooking spray. Cut into two 14-in. x 4½-in. strips.

**4.** Place 2 tablespoonfuls of filling on lower corner of each strip. Fold the dough over the filling, forming a triangle. Fold triangle up, then fold triangle over, forming another triangle. Continue folding, like a flag, to the end of strip.

**5.** Spritz end of dough with spray and press onto triangle to seal. Turn triangle and spritz top with spray. Repeat with remaining phyllo and filling.

**6.** Place triangles on greased baking sheets. Bake at 375° for 20-25 minutes or until golden brown. Serve warm.

# Parisian Chicken Bites

When a friend of mine returned from a trip to Paris, she raved about the food she had and described one of her favorite meals. It inspired me to create a similar hors d'oeuvre.

—NOELLE MYERS GRAND FORKS, NORTH DAKOTA

**PREP/TOTAL TIME:** 30 MIN.  **MAKES:** 4 DOZEN

- ½ pound boneless skinless chicken breasts, cut into ¼-inch cubes
- ¼ teaspoon salt
- ¼ teaspoon pepper
- ½ cup chopped fennel bulb
- 2 teaspoons olive oil
- 1 tablespoon chopped green onion
- ½ teaspoon minced fresh rosemary
- 1 medium apple, chopped
- ¼ cup chopped pecans
- 1 tablespoon minced fresh parsley
- 1 tablespoon lime juice
- 3 heads Belgian endive, separated into leaves
- 1 cup (6 ounces) dark chocolate chips
- ⅓ cup seedless blackberry spreadable fruit
- ¼ cup balsamic vinegar

**1.** Sprinkle the chicken with salt and pepper. In a large skillet, saute the chicken and fennel in oil until chicken is no longer pink. Add the green onion and rosemary; cook 1 minute longer. Remove from the heat.

**2.** In a large bowl combine apple, pecans, parsley and lime juice. Stir in chicken mixture; spoon into endive leaves.

**3.** In a microwave, melt the chocolate chips; stir until smooth. Stir in the spreadable fruit and balsamic vinegar. Drizzle over appetizers.

1. In a small bowl, combine the first 10 ingredients. Cover and refrigerate 1 cup sauce for thickening; set aside the remaining sauce for basting.

2. Cut roast in quarters and place on a rack in a shallow roasting pan; pour 1 in. of water into bottom of pan. Spoon half of the remaining sauce mixture over roast. Cover and bake at 350° for 1½ hours, basting occasionally with the remaining sauce.

3. Increase heat to 400°; bake, uncovered, 15 minutes longer, basting occasionally. Remove roast; cool slightly. Shred pork with two forks.

4. Place the reserved sauce mixture in a small saucepan. Bring to a boil. Combine the cornstarch and water until smooth; gradually stir into the pan. Bring to a boil; cook and stir for 2 minutes or until thickened; stir in pork.

5. In each of twenty-four 3-oz. glasses or mini dessert bowls, layer the rice and pork; sprinkle with cashews and green onions.

## Ham-Apple Mushrooms

If you like stuffed mushrooms, you'll want to try a filling that features chopped ham, apple and toasted pecans. The sweet and savory combination is unusual but delicious.

—**CHARLENE CHAMBERS** ORMOND BEACH, FLORIDA

**PREP:** 30 MIN. **BAKE:** 10 MIN.
**MAKES:** 34 STUFFED MUSHROOMS

- 34 **medium fresh mushrooms**
- 3 **tablespoons olive oil**
- ½ **medium Gala apple, peeled and finely chopped**
- 2 **tablespoons finely chopped shallot**
- 4 **teaspoons unsalted butter**
- 1 **cup finely chopped fully cooked ham steak**
- ½ **cup French bread baguette crumbs**
- 2 **tablespoons finely chopped pecans, toasted**
- 1 **tablespoon minced fresh parsley**
- 2 **teaspoons Dijon mustard**
- ⅛ **teaspoon pepper**

1. Remove the stems from the mushrooms; finely chop stems. In a large bowl, toss mushroom caps with olive oil to coat; set aside.

2. In a large skillet, saute the mushroom stems, apple and shallot in butter until tender. Stir in ham, bread crumbs, pecans, parsley, mustard and pepper; heat through.

3. Stuff into mushroom caps. Place on a greased 15-in. x 10-in. x 1-in. baking pan. Bake at 350° for 9-11 minutes or until lightly browned.

## Chinese Barbecued Pork Parfaits

Layered in small glasses, these Asian-style parfaits are sure to wow partygoers. The tender pork, rice and tongue-tingling sauce may tempt you to serve larger portions as an entree!

—**TASTE OF HOME TEST KITCHEN**

**PREP:** 30 MIN. **BAKE:** 1¾ HOURS **MAKES:** 2 DOZEN

- ½ **cup rice vinegar**
- ½ **cup reduced-sodium soy sauce**
- ½ **cup hoisin sauce**
- ⅓ **cup honey**
- ⅓ **cup black bean sauce**
- 9 **garlic cloves, minced**
- 4½ **teaspoons minced fresh gingerroot**
- 3 **to 4 teaspoons Chinese five-spice powder**
- 3 **teaspoons grated orange peel**
- ¾ **teaspoon pepper**
- 1 **boneless pork shoulder butt roast (2 pounds)**
- 2 **teaspoons cornstarch**
- 1 **tablespoon water**
- 3 **cups hot cooked long grain rice**
- ½ **cup lightly salted cashews**
- ½ **cup thinly sliced green onions**

## Bacon-Wrapped Scallops with Pear Sauce

I enjoy cooking for my parents, and my bacon-wrapped scallops recipe is one of their favorites. For a variation, replace the pear preserves with preserves—or jam—of a different flavor.

—ETHAN HALL KING, NORTH CAROLINA

**PREP:** 25 MIN. **COOK:** 10 MIN.
**MAKES:** 1 DOZEN

- 12 **bacon strips**
- ¾ **cup pear preserves**
- 2 **tablespoons reduced-sodium soy sauce**
- 1 **tablespoon brown sugar**
- ¼ **to ½ teaspoon crushed red pepper flakes**
- 12 **sea scallops (about ¾ pound)**
- ⅛ **teaspoon salt**
- ⅛ **teaspoon pepper**
- 1 **teaspoon olive oil**

**1.** Place the bacon in an ungreased 15-in. x 10-in. x 1-in. baking pan. Bake at 375° for 7-10 minutes or until partially cooked but not crisp. Remove to paper towels to drain; keep warm.

**2.** Meanwhile, in a small saucepan, combine the pear preserves, soy sauce, brown sugar and pepper flakes. Bring to a boil. Reduce heat; simmer, uncovered, for 3-5 minutes or until thickened.

**3.** Wrap a bacon strip around each scallop; secure with toothpicks. Sprinkle with salt and pepper. In a large skillet, cook bacon-wrapped scallops in oil over medium-high heat for 5-7 minutes or until scallops are firm and opaque, turning once. Serve with pear sauce.

## Cheese Tartlets with Fig Jam

These rich tartlets look time-consuming to fix, but they go together in less than half an hour thanks to the convenience of frozen phyllo tart shells. Your guests will think you spent hours in the kitchen! Top off each little appetizer with a fresh thyme leaf for a festive touch.

—MARY ANN LEE CLIFTON PARK, NEW YORK

**PREP/TOTAL TIME:** 25 MIN.
**MAKES:** 2½ DOZEN

- 1 **large onion, chopped**
- 3 **tablespoons olive oil**
  **Salt and pepper to taste**
- ⅓ **cup fig preserves**
- 2 **packages (1.9 ounces each) frozen miniature phyllo tart shells, thawed**
- ⅓ **cup crumbled blue cheese**
- ⅓ **cup crumbled goat cheese**
- 1 **egg yolk**
- ¼ **teaspoon crushed red pepper flakes**
  **Fresh thyme leaves, optional**

**1.** In a large skillet, saute the onion in oil until softened. Reduce the heat to medium-low; cook for 8-10 minutes or until onion is deep golden brown, stirring occasionally.

**2.** Sprinkle the onion with salt and pepper. Stir in the fig preserves. Place the phyllo tart shells on an ungreased baking sheet; fill with the onion mixture.

**3.** In a small bowl, combine cheeses, egg yolk and red pepper flakes. Spoon over the tops. Bake at 350° for 5-8 minutes or until heated through. Top with thyme if desired.

### Holiday Helper

I've found that a small funnel is handy for separating egg whites from the yolks. Simply break the egg into the wide end of the funnel. The white will run through while the yolk remains inside.

—ALICE N. REED CITY, MICHIGAN

# Mushroom Cheesecake Appetizers

I'm a fan of both cheesecake and mushrooms, so I decided to pair the two in a savory appetizer. These individual cakes are rich and satisfying—great with toasted baguette slices.

**—DONNA MARIE RYAN** TOPSFIELD, MASSACHUSETTS

**PREP:** 25 MIN. **BAKE:** 15 MIN. **MAKES:** 1 DOZEN

- 2 teaspoons butter
- ½ cup soft bread crumbs
- 1 carton (8 ounces) whipped cream cheese
- 2 eggs
- ¼ cup sour cream
- 2 tablespoons minced fresh thyme or 2 teaspoons dried thyme, divided
- ½ teaspoon salt
- ½ teaspoon pepper
- ½ cup shredded fontina cheese

**TOPPING**
- ½ pound sliced baby portobello mushrooms
- 3 tablespoons butter
- 1 garlic clove, minced
  Toasted French bread baguette slices

**1.** Grease the bottoms and halfway up the sides of muffin cups with butter. Press bread crumbs onto the bottoms and halfway up the sides of prepared cups.

**2.** In a small bowl, beat cream cheese until smooth. Beat in eggs, sour cream, 1 tablespoon thyme, salt and pepper. Divide among prepared muffin cups; sprinkle with the fontina cheese and remaining thyme. Bake at 350° for 12-15 minutes or until set.

**3.** Meanwhile, in a large skillet, saute the mushrooms in butter until tender. Add the garlic; saute 1 minute longer. Top the cheesecakes with mushroom mixture. Serve with baguette slices.

# Parsnip Latkes with Lox and Horseradish Creme

Horseradish-flavored creme fraiche lends zip to these crispy homemade latkes, which get a bit of sweetness from parsnips. Add fresh dill sprigs as the finishing touch.

**—TODD SCHMELING** GURNEE, ILLINOIS

**PREP:** 30 MIN. **COOK:** 5 MIN./BATCH
**MAKES:** ABOUT 3 DOZEN

- 1 pound potatoes, peeled
- 1 pound parsnips, peeled
- ⅔ cup chopped green onions
- 2 eggs, lightly beaten
- 1 teaspoon salt
- ½ teaspoon pepper
  Oil for deep-fat frying
- 1 package (3 ounces) smoked salmon or lox, cut into ½-inch-wide strips
- 1 cup creme fraiche or sour cream
- 1 tablespoon snipped fresh dill
- 1 tablespoon prepared horseradish
- ¼ teaspoon salt
- ⅛ teaspoon white pepper
  Fresh dill sprigs

**1.** Coarsely grate potatoes and parsnips. Place grated vegetables on a double thickness of cheesecloth; bring up corners and squeeze out any liquid. Transfer to a large bowl; stir in the onions, eggs, salt and pepper.

**2.** In an electric skillet, heat ⅛ in. of oil to 375°. Drop potato mixture by heaping tablespoonfuls into hot oil. Flatten to form patties. Fry until golden brown; turn and cook the other side. Drain on paper towels.

**3.** Roll salmon to form rose shapes; set aside. Combine the creme fraiche, dill, horseradish, salt and pepper. Top the latkes with a dollop of creme fraiche mixture and a salmon rose. Garnish with dill.

## Making Salmon Roses

Make Parsnip Latkes with Lox and Horseradish Creme (recipe above right) especially festive for the holidays by creating pretty roses.

Lay the smoked salmon or lox on a cutting board. It should be about ⅛ in. thick. Cut the salmon into ½-in. strips, then cut the strips into 3-in. lengths.

Starting at one short end, roll the salmon—tightly for about 1 in., then more loosely—around the center of the rose. Pinch the bottom of the rose tightly to secure. If necessary, use the tip of the knife to open the rose.

Then just follow the recipe to finish the latkes with flavored creme fraiche, a rose and fresh dill.

## Best Bacon Bruschetta

Here's my twist on the traditional BLT sandwich. The bite-size bruschetta pieces make it easy for party guests to munch while they mingle.

**—CHARIS O'CONNELL**
MOHNTON, PENNSYLVANIA

**PREP/TOTAL TIME:** 30 MIN.
**MAKES:** 32 APPETIZERS

- 6 **bacon strips, chopped**
- 4 **ciabatta rolls**
- 2 **tablespoons olive oil**
- 2 **medium tomatoes, seeded and chopped**
- ¼ **teaspoon salt**
- ⅛ **teaspoon pepper**
- ¾ **cup crumbled feta cheese**
- 16 **fresh basil leaves, thinly sliced**
- ½ **cup balsamic vinaigrette**

**1.** In a large skillet, cook bacon over medium heat until crisp. Remove to paper towels to drain.

**2.** Split rolls in half; cut each half into quarters. Lightly brush both sides with oil. Place in an ungreased 15-in. x 10-in. x 1-in. baking pan. Broil 3-4 in. from the heat for 2-3 minutes on each side or until golden brown.

**3.** Meanwhile, in a small bowl, combine the tomatoes, salt and pepper.

**4.** Top each piece of toasted bread with bacon, tomato mixture, cheese and basil; drizzle with vinaigrette. Serve immediately.

### Holiday Helper

To make long, even strips of leafy herbs and vegetables such as basil, sage and spinach, try this technique. First, stack the leaves neatly in the same direction, then roll the stack lengthwise into a tight cigar shape.

Next, simply slice across the rolled leaves to form strips as thin as you need. You'll have a bunch of leaves cut in no time.

## Sesame Chicken with Creamy Satay Sauce

These exotic skewers taste like they came from a Thai restaurant. I marinate the chicken in a sesame salad dressing.

**—KATHI JONES-DELMONTE**
ROCHESTER, NEW YORK

**PREP:** 20 MIN. + MARINATING
**GRILL:** 10 MIN. **MAKES:** 4 SERVINGS

- ¾ **cup Asian toasted sesame salad dressing**
- 1 **pound boneless skinless chicken breast halves, cut into 1-inch strips**
- ½ **cup reduced-fat cream cheese**
- ¼ **cup coconut milk**
- 3 **tablespoons creamy peanut butter**
- 2 **tablespoons lime juice**
- 1 **tablespoon reduced-sodium soy sauce**
- ½ **teaspoon crushed red pepper flakes**
- 1 **tablespoon minced fresh cilantro**

**1.** Pour salad dressing into a large resealable plastic bag. Add the chicken; seal bag and turn to coat. Refrigerate for 4 hours or overnight.

**2.** Drain and discard marinade. Thread chicken onto metal or soaked wooden skewers. Moisten a paper towel with cooking oil; using long-handled tongs, lightly coat grill rack.

**3.** Grill skewers, covered, over medium heat or broil 4 in. from the heat for 10-15 minutes or until no longer pink, turning once.

**4.** Meanwhile, in a small bowl, combine the cream cheese, coconut milk, creamy peanut butter, lime juice, soy sauce and pepper flakes; sprinkle with cilantro. Serve chicken with the sauce.

# Bacon-Cheddar Potato Croquettes

Instead of throwing out leftover mashed potatoes, turn them into little baked bites served with your favorite dipping sauce on the side. For make-ahead convenience, freeze the unbaked croquettes on baking sheets, then transfer them to resealable plastic bags and freeze until you're ready to use them. Bake as directed in the recipe for 20-25 minutes.

—**PAMELA SHANK** PARKERSBURG, WEST VIRGINIA

**PREP:** 20 MIN. + CHILLING  **BAKE:** 20 MIN.
**MAKES:** ABOUT 5 DOZEN

- 4 cups cold mashed potatoes (with added milk and butter)
- 6 bacon strips, cooked and crumbled
- ½ cup shredded cheddar cheese
- 2 eggs, lightly beaten
- ¼ cup sour cream
- 1 tablespoon minced chives
- ½ teaspoon salt
- ¼ teaspoon pepper
- 40 butter-flavored crackers, crushed
- ¼ cup butter, melted
- 1 teaspoon paprika
  Barbecue sauce, Dijon-mayonnaise blend or ranch salad dressing

**1.** In a large bowl, combine the first eight ingredients. Shape mixture by tablespoonfuls into balls. Roll each in cracker crumbs. Place on parchment paper-lined baking sheets. Cover and refrigerate for 2 hours or overnight.
**2.** Combine butter and paprika; drizzle over croquettes. Bake at 375° for 18-20 minutes or until golden brown. Serve with dipping sauce of your choice.

# Pork Spring Rolls

When we discovered that my daughter needed to avoid gluten, I experimented in the kitchen to create some new foods that would fit her diet. My mild pork rolls were a hit with all of our friends and family members who sampled them.

—**LOUISE MARTIN** SAN RAMON, CALIFORNIA

**PREP:** 45 MIN. + CHILLING  **MAKES:** 1½ DOZEN

- 1½ pounds ground pork
- 1 medium carrot, shredded
- 3 green onions, finely chopped
- 3 garlic cloves, minced
- 1 tablespoon grated fresh gingerroot
- 1 teaspoon ground coriander
- 1 teaspoon ground cumin
- 1 teaspoon sesame oil
- ½ teaspoon crushed red pepper flakes
- ½ teaspoon salt
- ¼ teaspoon pepper
- 2 tablespoons water
- 2 tablespoons reduced-sodium soy sauce
- 1 teaspoon sugar
- ½ package (8.8 ounces) vermicelli-style thin rice noodles
- 18 rice papers (8 inches)
  Torn romaine
  Sweet chili sauce

**1.** In a large skillet, cook pork over medium heat until no longer pink; drain. Stir in carrot, onions, garlic, ginger, coriander, cumin, oil, red pepper flakes, salt and pepper until blended.
**2.** Add the water, soy sauce and sugar. Bring to a boil. Reduce heat; simmer, uncovered, for 3-5 minutes or until liquid is evaporated. Transfer to a bowl; cool. Cover and refrigerate for 1 hour or until chilled.
**3.** Cook the noodles according to the package directions. Drain and rinse in cold water; drain well. Fill a shallow bowl with water. Soak a rice paper in the water just until pliable, about 30-45 seconds (depending on thickness of rice papers); remove, allowing excess water to drip off.
**4.** Place on a flat surface. Layer meat mixture and noodles down the center; top with romaine. Fold both ends over the filling; fold one long side over the filling, then roll up tightly. Place seam side down on a serving platter. Repeat with the remaining rice papers, meat mixture, noodles and romaine.
**5.** Cover with damp paper towels until serving. Cut rolls diagonally in half and serve with sweet chili sauce.

## Croque Monsieur Toast Cups

Ooh la la! Bring the flair of France to your next Christmastime party with bubbly toast cups inspired by Croque Monsieur—a French grilled sandwich featuring ham and cheese.

—TASTE OF HOME TEST KITCHEN

**PREP:** 45 MIN. **BROIL:** 5 MIN./BATCH
**MAKES:** 4 DOZEN

- 12 slices white bread, crusts removed
- ½ cup butter, melted
- **FILLING**
- 2 teaspoons butter
- 2 teaspoons all-purpose flour
- ¼ teaspoon salt
  Dash white pepper
  Dash ground nutmeg
- ⅔ cup 2% milk
- ¼ cup Dijon mustard
- 1 cup (4 ounces) shredded Gruyere or Swiss cheese
- ½ pound thinly sliced deli ham, julienned
  Minced chives

**1.** Flatten the bread with a rolling pin; cut each slice into four squares. Brush both sides of bread with butter; press into miniature muffin cups. Bake at 325° for 14-16 minutes or until golden brown.

**2.** Meanwhile, in a small saucepan melt the butter; whisk in flour and seasonings until smooth. Gradually whisk in milk. Bring to a boil; cook and stir 2 minutes or until thickened.

**3.** Place ¼ teaspoon mustard in each toast cup. Sprinkle half of the cheese into cups. Layer each with ham, sauce and remaining cheese. Broil 4-6 in. from the heat for 2-3 minutes or until bubbly. Sprinkle with chives.

## Orange Cranberry Splash

For a festive finishing touch during the holidays, garnish each glass of this tangy cocktail with fresh cranberries.

—RALPH FLORIO NEW YORK, NEW YORK

**PREP/TOTAL TIME:** 10 MIN.
**MAKES:** 6 SERVINGS

- 3 cups lemon-lime soda
- ¾ cup orange-flavored vodka
- ½ cup cranberry juice
- 6 tablespoons Triple Sec
  Ice cubes
- **GARNISH**
  Fresh cranberries

In a pitcher, combine the soda, vodka, cranberry juice and Triple Sec. Serve over ice. Garnish with cranberries.

28

31

34

*holiday*
# DINNER IN 60

# Turkey Tenderloins with Shallot Berry Sauce

Thanks to this quick recipe, your family can sit down to a holiday-worthy main course in just 35 minutes. The turkey tenderloins are draped with a tongue-tingling sauce featuring shallots, balsamic vinegar and raspberry jam.

—**KENDRA DOSS** COLORADO SPRINGS, COLORADO

**PREP:** 15 MIN.   **COOK:** 20 MIN.   **MAKES:** 8 SERVINGS

| | |
|---|---|
| 4 | turkey breast tenderloins (12 ounces each) |
| ½ | teaspoon salt |
| ½ | teaspoon pepper |
| 1 | tablespoon olive oil |
| ¼ | cup chicken broth |

**SAUCE**

| | |
|---|---|
| 1 | tablespoon olive oil |
| 5 | shallots, thinly sliced |
| ¼ | teaspoon salt |
| ¼ | teaspoon pepper |
| ½ | cup chicken broth |
| ¼ | cup balsamic vinegar |
| 3 | tablespoons seedless raspberry jam |

**1.** Sprinkle the turkey tenderloins with salt and pepper. In a large skillet, heat oil over medium heat. Brown the turkey on all sides in batches. Cover and cook 4-5 minutes longer or until thermometer reads 165°. Remove turkey to a platter; keep warm.

**2.** In the same skillet, add the chicken broth, stirring to loosen browned bits from pan; set aside.

**3.** Meanwhile, in a large skillet, heat oil over medium-high heat. Add the shallots, salt and pepper; cook and stir until tender. Add the chicken broth, stirring to loosen browned bits from pan. Stir in vinegar and jam. Bring to a boil; cook 4-5 minutes or until slightly thickened. Serve with turkey and pan juices.

## Holiday Helper

Want to give your green salad a homemade touch for the holidays—without spending too much time in the kitchen? Pair your favorite bagged greens with a made-from-scratch topper like Blue Cheese Salad Dressing (recipe above right). It comes together in just 10 minutes with sour cream, mayonnaise, seasonings and other everyday ingredients.

Blue Cheese Salad Dressing and other dairy-based dressings—as well as those prepared with fresh ingredients such as chopped hard-cooked egg, fresh herbs or chopped onion—will keep in the refrigerator for up to 1 week. Generally, vinaigrettes can be kept refrigerated for up to 2 weeks.

# Blue Cheese Salad Dressing

Here's a terrific finishing touch for any combination of fresh greens. At our house, the thick and creamy salad dressing does double duty—I serve it as a dip for vegetables, too.

—**CHRISTY FREEMAN** CENTRAL POINT, OREGON

**PREP/TOTAL TIME:** 10 MIN.   **MAKES:** 3 CUPS

| | |
|---|---|
| 2 | cups mayonnaise |
| 1 | cup (8 ounces) sour cream |
| ¼ | cup white wine vinegar |
| ¼ | cup minced fresh parsley |
| 1 | garlic clove, crushed |
| ½ | teaspoon ground mustard |
| ½ | teaspoon salt |
| ¼ | teaspoon pepper |
| 4 | ounces crumbled blue cheese |

Place all the ingredients in a blender; cover and process until smooth. Store in the refrigerator.

**Blue Cheese Bacon Dressing:** *After processing the dressing, stir in 6 crumbled cooked bacon strips.* **Makes: 3¼ cups.**

## Creamed Green Beans

A family favorite, this special bean recipe is easy to double and can be assembled ahead of time. My nephews love it so much, it's an absolute must when they come for dinner.
—**BETTY SHAW** WEIRTON, WEST VIRGINIA

**PREP/TOTAL TIME:** 30 MIN.  **MAKES:** 6-8 SERVINGS

- 3 **tablespoons butter, divided**
- ½ **cup cornflakes, crumbled**
- 1 **tablespoon all-purpose flour**
- ¼ **teaspoon salt**
- ¼ **teaspoon pepper**
- 1 **teaspoon dried minced onion**
- 1 **teaspoon sugar**
- 1 **cup (8 ounces) sour cream**
- 4 **to 6 cups French-style green beans, cooked and drained**
- 1 **cup (4 ounces) shredded sharp cheddar or Swiss cheese**

**1.** In a small saucepan, melt 1 tablespoon butter; stir in the cornflakes and set aside. Melt the remaining butter in a large saucepan. Stir in the flour, salt, pepper, onion and sugar; heat and stir until bubbly. Reduce heat; add sour cream and stir until smooth. Cook and stir over low heat for 2 minutes (do not boil). Fold in the beans.

**2.** Spoon into a greased 1½-qt. baking dish. Sprinkle with cheese and cornflake mixture. Bake, uncovered, at 400° for 20 minutes or until heated through.

## Cheesy Sliced Potatoes

Running out of room in the oven? Pop these sliced potatoes in the microwave. Sour cream and cheddar cheese turn them into a rich, satisfying side dish for any holiday feast.
—**JEANNINE RICKETSON** SAUGERTIES, NEW YORK

**PREP/TOTAL TIME:** 30 MIN.  **MAKES:** 8 SERVINGS

- 6½ **cups thinly sliced potatoes (about 1 pound)**
- ⅓ **cup water**
- 2 **tablespoons dried minced onion**
- 2 **teaspoons chicken bouillon granules**
- 1 **tablespoon all-purpose flour**
- ½ **teaspoon salt**
- ⅛ **teaspoon garlic powder**
- ¾ **cup milk**
- ¾ **cup sour cream**
- ½ **cup shredded cheddar cheese**
  **Coarsely ground pepper, optional**

**1.** Place the potatoes, water, onion and chicken bouillon in an ungreased microwave-safe 2½-qt. dish. Cover and microwave on high for 12-14 minutes until potatoes are tender and bouillon is dissolved, stirring once.

**2.** In a small bowl, combine flour, salt and garlic powder; stir in milk until smooth. Pour over potatoes. Microwave, uncovered, on high for 4 minutes or until thickened, stirring twice. Stir in sour cream; sprinkle with cheese. Cook 3 minutes longer or until cheese is melted. Sprinkle with pepper if desired.

## Artichoke Beef Steaks

Bright red pimientos and green artichokes make these steaks perfect for Christmas. If the weather permits, cook them on the grill and fix the topping in a skillet as directed.
**—TASTE OF HOME TEST KITCHEN**

**PREP/TOTAL TIME:** 25 MIN.  **MAKES:** 4 SERVINGS

1    jar (6½ ounces) marinated artichoke hearts
4    beef ribeye steaks (¾ inch thick and about
     8 ounces each)
½    teaspoon salt
2    tablespoons butter
1    small onion, sliced and separated into rings
1    garlic clove, minced
1    jar (2 ounces) sliced pimientos, drained

**1.** Drain the artichokes, reserving 1 tablespoon marinade. Coarsely chop the artichokes and set aside. Sprinkle the steaks with salt.

**2.** In a large skillet, cook steaks in butter over medium-high heat for 4 minutes on each side or until meat reaches desired doneness (for medium-rare, a meat thermometer should read 145°; medium, 160°; well-done, 170°). Remove to a serving platter; keep warm.

**3.** In same skillet, saute the onion and garlic in reserved marinade for 3 minutes. Add artichokes and pimientos; heat through. Serve with steaks.

# Round Cheese Bread

Who says homemade bread has to take a lot of time to make? Requiring just 10 minutes of prep work, this savory loaf gives you fresh-baked, buttery goodness in a flash.

—**DEBORAH BITZ** MEDICINE HAT, ALBERTA

**PREP:** 10 MIN. **BAKE:** 20 MIN. + COOLING
**MAKES:** 6-8 SERVINGS

- 1½ **cups biscuit/baking mix**
- 1 **cup (4 ounces) shredded part-skim mozzarella cheese**
- ¼ **cup grated Parmesan cheese**
- ½ **teaspoon dried oregano**
- ½ **cup 2% milk**
- 1 **egg, lightly beaten**
- 2 **tablespoons butter, melted**
  **Additional Parmesan cheese**

**1.** In a large bowl, combine the biscuit mix, mozzarella cheese, Parmesan cheese, oregano, milk and egg (batter will be thick).

**2.** Spoon into a greased 9-in. round baking pan. Drizzle with butter; sprinkle with additional Parmesan cheese.

**3.** Bake at 400° for 20-25 minutes or until a toothpick inserted near the center comes out clean. Cool for 10 minutes. Cut into wedges. Serve warm.

# Caesar Salad

Here's a classic combination of romaine, Parmesan cheese and croutons with a from-scratch dressing. The burst of fresh flavor is a great way to balance a heavy main course.

—**SCHELBY THOMPSON** CAMDEN WYOMING, DELAWARE

**PREP/TOTAL TIME:** 10 MIN. **MAKES:** 6-8 SERVINGS

- 1 **large bunch romaine, torn**
- ¾ **cup olive oil**
- 3 **tablespoons red wine vinegar**
- 1 **teaspoon Worcestershire sauce**
- ½ **teaspoon salt**
- ¼ **teaspoon ground mustard**
- 1 **large garlic clove, minced**
- ½ **fresh lemon**
  **Dash pepper**
- ¼ **to ½ cup shredded Parmesan cheese**
  **Caesar-flavored or garlic croutons**

**1.** Place the lettuce in a large salad bowl. Combine the next six ingredients in a blender; process until smooth. Pour over the lettuce and toss to coat.

**2.** Squeeze lemon juice over the lettuce. Sprinkle with pepper, Parmesan cheese and croutons.

# Lemon Broccoli

A twist of lemon juice and grated peel bring a delightful hint of citrus to broccoli. Simply cook the florets until crisp-tender, add the remaining ingredients, and you're done!

—**TONYA FARMER** IOWA CITY, IOWA

**PREP/TOTAL TIME:** 15 MIN. **MAKES:** 8 SERVINGS

- 3 **pounds fresh broccoli, cut into florets**
- ¼ **cup butter**
- 2 **tablespoons diced onion**
- 2 **tablespoons diced pimientos**
- 3 **to 4 teaspoons lemon juice**
- 2 **teaspoons grated lemon peel**
- ½ **teaspoon seasoned salt**
  **Dash pepper**

Add 1 in. of water to a large saucepan; add broccoli. Bring to a boil. Reduce heat; cover and simmer for 5-8 minutes or until crisp-tender. Meanwhile, melt the butter; stir in the remaining ingredients. Drain broccoli; add butter mixture and toss to coat.

## Napkin Place Card Holder

**1.** Fold a napkin in half twice to make a square and lay it flat with the open corners facing you. Fold up each open corner one at a time, staggering them about 1 inch.

**2.** Fold up the bottom edge (the edge under the folded open corners) about 1 inch to make a holder for a place card.

**3.** Turn the napkin over and fold it into thirds, tucking one corner under the other to secure.

**4.** Turn the napkin over, lay it on a plate and tuck a place card inside the bottom fold.

JOHN

## All-Star Apple Pie

Here's a busy cook's dream—a home-style apple pie that takes advantage of canned filling and a store-bought crust. Pecans, oats and coconut lend a special touch for the holidays.
**—CINDY GLICK** BRADFORD, NEW YORK

**PREP:** 10 MIN. **BAKE:** 15 MIN. + COOLING
**MAKES:** 6-8 SERVINGS

- 1 **can (21 ounces) apple pie filling**
- 1 **tablespoon lemon juice**
- ¼ **teaspoon ground cinnamon**
- 1 **pastry shell (9 inches), baked**
- ¼ **cup all-purpose flour**
- ¼ **cup packed brown sugar**
- 2 **tablespoons cold butter**
- ¼ **cup chopped pecans or walnuts**
- ¼ **cup quick-cooking oats**
- 2 **tablespoons flaked coconut**

**1.** In a large bowl, combine apple pie filling, lemon juice and cinnamon; spoon into the pastry shell. In a small bowl, combine the flour and brown sugar; cut in the butter until crumbly. Stir in the nuts, oats and coconut; sprinkle over pie filling.

**2.** Bake at 400° for 12-15 minutes or until the topping is golden brown, covering edges loosely with foil to prevent overbrowning if necessary. Cool on a wire rack.

# Chocolate Mint Delight

Sweeten your Christmastime menu with individual desserts featuring velvety chocolate pudding, peppermint candies, crushed cookies and whipped topping. Yum!

—**JEAN ANN PERKINS** NEWBURYPORT, MARYLAND

**PREP/TOTAL TIME:** 15 MIN.  **MAKES:** 4 SERVINGS

- **1** package (3.9 ounces) instant chocolate pudding mix
- **2** cups cold milk
- **28** miniature cream-filled chocolate sandwich cookies, crushed, divided
- **¼** cup crushed miniature candy canes or peppermint candy
  **Frozen whipped topping, thawed**
  **Additional miniature candy canes or peppermint candy**

**1.** Prepare pudding with milk according to the package directions. Divide among individual dessert dishes.

**2.** Reserve 2 tablespoons crushed cookies; sprinkle the remaining cookies over the pudding. Top with crushed candy. Spoon whipped topping over the candy. Sprinkle with reserved crushed cookies. Serve with additional peppermint candies.

# Mocha Eggnog

A little coffee and chocolate milk give traditional eggnog a decadent twist, much to the delight of my family. We always stir up this yummy beverage to sip while opening Christmas presents. For an added treat, grate a chocolate bar and sprinkle some on each glass.

—**BETH ANN HILL** DAYTON, OHIO

**PREP/TOTAL TIME:** 10 MIN.
**MAKES:** 2½ QUARTS

- 5 **cups chocolate milk**
- 4 **cups eggnog**
- 1 **cup heavy whipping cream, divided**
- 2 **tablespoons instant coffee granules**
- 2½ **teaspoons vanilla extract**
- 1 **teaspoon rum extract**

In a large saucepan, combine the chocolate milk, eggnog, ½ cup heavy whipping cream and instant coffee granules; heat through. Remove from the heat; stir in the extracts. In a small bowl, beat the remaining whipping cream until stiff peaks form. Dollop over eggnog.

**Editor's Note:** *This recipe was tested with commercially prepared eggnog.*

## Holiday Helper

When it comes to holiday drinks, garnishes are half the fun. Here are some celebratory ideas to get you started:

- Add extra yum to chocolaty drinks by dipping rims of glasses into Irish cream or water, then into powdered hot chocolate.
- Use the same technique to make "snow-tipped" glasses: Just dip the rims into water, then superfine sugar. Or, rim drinks with very finely crushed cookies or candies.
- Use edible drink stirrers such as rock candy sticks, candy canes or red licorice sticks.

38

55

44

*christmas*
FEASTS

# Chestnut-Onion Stuffed Turducken Bundles

A friend told me about turducken, and these bundles are my best attempt at creating a simpler version. The flavors of all three birds come through and go wonderfully with the sauce.

—**BARBARA LENTO** HOUSTON, PENNSYLVANIA

**PREP:** 65 MIN. **BAKE:** 40 MIN. + STANDING
**MAKES:** 8 SERVINGS

- 2 **cups sliced onions**
- ½ **cup whole cooked and peeled chestnuts, chopped**
- 2 **teaspoons olive oil**
- 2 **teaspoons plus ½ cup butter, melted, divided**
- 2 **tablespoons Cognac**
- 1 **teaspoon sugar**
- ½ **teaspoon dried thyme**
- 4 **turkey breast cutlets (6 ounces each)**
- 4 **boneless skinless duck breast halves (4 ounces each)**
- 8 **chicken tenderloins (1 ounce each)**
- ½ **cup dry bread crumbs**
- ¼ **cup ground almonds**

**CRANBERRY-ORANGE SAUCE**

- ½ **cup sugar**
- 1 **tablespoon plus 2 teaspoons cornstarch**
- ¼ **teaspoon salt**
- ⅛ **teaspoon ground cloves**
- 1½ **cups orange juice**
- 1½ **cups fresh cranberries**
- ¼ **cup lemon juice**
- 1 **tablespoon minced fresh mint or 1 teaspoon dried mint**
- 2 **tablespoons plus 2 teaspoons butter**
- 1 **teaspoon grated orange peel**
- ½ **teaspoon grated lemon peel**

**1.** In a large skillet, saute the onions and chestnuts in oil and 2 teaspoons butter for 15-20 minutes or until golden brown; remove from the heat. Stir in the Cognac, sugar and thyme; set aside.

**2.** Flatten the turkey and duck to ¼-in. thickness; spread two tablespoons onion mixture over each turkey and duck breast. Place duck on turkey; place two chicken tenders near one end of each duck breast. Roll up jelly-roll style, starting with a long side; secure with toothpicks.

**3.** In a shallow bowl, place the remaining melted butter. Combine the bread crumbs and almonds in a separate shallow bowl. Dip the bundles in melted butter, then coat with crumb mixture. Place seam side down in a greased 13-in. x 9-in. baking dish.

**4.** Bake, uncovered, at 375° for 40-45 minutes or until a thermometer reads 170°. Let stand for 10 minutes.

**5.** Meanwhile, in a small saucepan, whisk the sugar, cornstarch, salt, cloves and orange juice until smooth. Add the cranberries. Cook and stir over medium heat for 10-12 minutes or until thickened. Remove from the heat; add the lemon juice, mint, butter and peels.

**6.** To serve, discard the toothpicks; cut each bundle into six slices. Place three slices on each serving plate; drizzle with ¼ cup sauce.

## Rolling Turducken Bundles

**1.** After topping the flattened turkey breast with the flattened duck, lay two chicken tenders next to one another near one edge of the duck.

**2.** Roll up the layers jelly-roll style, starting where the long side of a chicken tender is positioned near the edge of the duck. Secure the bundle with toothpicks.

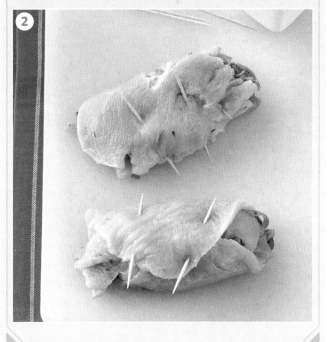

## Sherried Sweet Potato Soup

I stir up a pot of this smooth, spiced sweet potato soup when I want something out of the ordinary for guests. Using an immersion blender will result in a creamier texture.
—**CHARLENE CHAMBERS** ORMOND BEACH, FLORIDA

**PREP:** 15 MIN. **COOK:** 45 MIN. **MAKES:** 8 SERVINGS

- 4 **large sweet potatoes, peeled and cubed**
- 1 **small onion, chopped**
- 2 **tablespoons butter**
- 2 **garlic cloves, minced**
- 1 **teaspoon ground cumin**
- ½ **teaspoon salt**
- ½ **teaspoon minced fresh gingerroot**
- ½ **teaspoon ground coriander**
- ¼ **teaspoon ground cinnamon**
- ⅛ **teaspoon ground cardamom**
- 3 **cans (14 ounces each) chicken broth**
- 1 **cup heavy whipping cream**
- ⅓ **cup sherry**
- 1 **tablespoon lime juice**
- 2 **tablespoons minced fresh cilantro**

**1.** Place the sweet potatoes in a large saucepan and cover with water. Bring to a boil. Reduce heat; cover and cook for 10-15 minutes or just until tender. Drain. Mash the potatoes; set aside.

**2.** In a large saucepan, saute onion in butter until tender. Add the garlic, cumin, salt, ginger, coriander, cinnamon and cardamom; cook for 2 minutes. Stir in potatoes and broth; bring to a boil. Reduce heat; simmer, uncovered, for 25-30 minutes or until flavors are blended.

**3.** Add the cream and sherry; bring to a boil. Reduce heat; simmer, uncovered, for 5 minutes. Remove from the heat; stir in lime juice. Cool slightly. In a blender, process soup in batches until smooth. Garnish with cilantro.

# Roasted Cauliflower Mash

Here's a tempting yet lower-carb alternative to traditional holiday side dishes of spuds or rice. Guests who don't detect the cauliflower might even think it's mashed potatoes!

**—JANE MCGLOTHREN** DAPHNE, ALABAMA

**PREP:** 30 MIN.  **BAKE:** 25 MIN.
**MAKES:** 10 SERVINGS

| | |
|---|---|
| 2 | **medium heads cauliflower, broken into florets** |
| ¼ | **cup olive oil** |
| 6 | **garlic cloves, minced** |
| 2 | **teaspoons Greek seasoning** |
| 1 | **cup (4 ounces) shredded sharp cheddar cheese** |
| ⅔ | **cup sour cream** |
| ½ | **cup crumbled cooked bacon** |
| ⅓ | **cup butter, cubed** |

**1.** In a large bowl, combine the cauliflower, oil, garlic and Greek seasoning. Transfer to a greased 15-in. x 10-in. x 1-in. baking pan. Bake, uncovered, at 425° for 15-20 minutes or until tender, stirring occasionally.

**2.** Transfer cauliflower to a large bowl. Mash cauliflower with cheese, sour cream, bacon and butter. Transfer to a greased 8-in. square baking dish. Bake at 350° for 25-30 minutes or until heated through.

## Holiday Helper

I buy several pounds of bacon when it's on sale. I put the strips in a single layer on jelly-roll pans and pop them in the oven to bake at 350° for 30-45 minutes or until crisp. After draining the bacon on paper towels, I store it in a freezer container in the freezer.

This saves time later because I already have cooked bacon on hand and can easily remove any amount I need for a recipe.

**—DALE H.** HOLLAND, MICHIGAN

## Cheesecake with Caramel Apple Topping

Years ago, I decided to try dressing up my basic cheesecake by adding a topping of caramel apple slices. The rich, sweet-tart dessert is especially popular during fall and winter.

—**JOAN HUGGINS** WAYNESBORO, MISSISSIPPI

**PREP:** 30 MIN.  **BAKE:** 45 MIN. + CHILLING
**MAKES:** 8 SERVINGS (2 CUPS TOPPING)

- 1 cup graham cracker crumbs
- ⅓ cup finely chopped pecans
- ¼ cup butter, melted
- 1 tablespoon brown sugar

**FILLING**
- 2 packages (8 ounces each) cream cheese, softened
- ½ cup sugar
- ½ teaspoon vanilla extract
- ¼ teaspoon almond extract
- 2 eggs, beaten

**TOPPING**
- ¼ cup butter, cubed
- 4 medium tart apples, peeled and sliced
- 2 tablespoons lemon juice
- ¾ cup packed brown sugar
- ¾ teaspoon ground cinnamon

**1.** In a small bowl, combine the cracker crumbs, pecans, butter and brown sugar. Press onto the bottom and up the sides of a greased 9-in. pie plate; set aside.
**2.** In a large bowl, beat the cream cheese and sugar until smooth. Beat in extracts. Add eggs; beat on low speed just until combined. Pour into crust.
**3.** Bake at 325° for 45-50 minutes or until center is almost set. Cool on a wire rack for 1 hour. Refrigerate overnight.
**4.** For topping, in a large skillet, melt butter over medium heat. Add apples and lemon juice. Cook and stir for 5-7 minutes or until apples are tender. Add brown sugar and cinnamon; cook 2-3 minutes longer or until brown sugar is dissolved. Cool slightly. Serve with cheesecake.

## Caraway Cheese Biscuits

My grandchildren are always happy when I pull a pan of my cheese biscuits from the oven. The golden-brown goodies complement nearly any main course.

—**LORRAINE CALAND** SHUNIAH, ONTARIO

**PREP:** 10 MIN.  **BAKE:** 15 MIN.  **MAKES:** 10 BISCUITS

- 2 cups all-purpose flour
- 3 teaspoons baking powder
- ¾ teaspoon salt
- 6 tablespoons cold butter, cubed
- 1 cup (4 ounces) finely shredded cheddar cheese, divided
- 1½ teaspoons caraway seeds
- ¾ cup 2% milk

**1.** In a large bowl, whisk the flour, baking powder and salt. Cut in butter until mixture resembles coarse crumbs. Stir in ¾ cup cheese and caraway seeds. Add the milk; stir just until moistened.
**2.** Drop the dough by ¼ cupfuls onto ungreased baking sheets. Sprinkle with remaining cheese. Bake at 425° for 12-15 minutes or until golden brown. Serve warm.

## Wheat Berry Salad with Artichokes and Cranberries

Every year at Christmastime, I serve this hearty and colorful salad. If you like, prepare the recipe in advance—just remove it from the refrigerator 30 minutes before serving.

—**GILDA LESTER** MILLSBORO, DELAWARE

**PREP:** 10 MIN. **COOK:** 1 HOUR
**MAKES:** 12 SERVINGS (⅔ CUP EACH)

| | |
|---|---|
| 7 | **cups water** |
| 2 | **cups wheat berries** |
| 1¼ | **teaspoons salt, divided** |
| ¾ | **cup Italian salad dressing, divided** |
| 1 | **pint cherry tomatoes, halved** |
| 1 | **cup marinated quartered artichoke hearts, drained** |

| | |
|---|---|
| ½ | **cup dried cranberries** |
| ½ | **cup chopped pitted green olives** |
| ¼ | **cup sliced ripe olives** |
| 1 | **tablespoon capers, drained** |
| ½ | **cup thinly sliced fresh basil** |
| ¼ | **teaspoon pepper** |
| ½ | **cup crumbled blue cheese** |

**1.** In a large saucepan, bring water to a boil. Add wheat berries and 1 teaspoon salt. Reduce heat; simmer, covered, for 55-60 minutes or until softened. Drain.
**2.** In a large bowl, combine the wheat berries and ½ cup Italian dressing. Cool.
**3.** Add the tomatoes, artichoke hearts, cranberries, green and ripe olives, capers and basil. Pour remaining dressing over top; toss to coat. Season with pepper and remaining salt. Top with blue cheese.

# Pork Loin with Pears, Fennel and Figs

I received this recipe from a clerk at my grocery store and decided to try it when I was preparing dinner for company. When my guests sampled the seasoned pork with its fruity sauce and tender veggies, they told me, "You should have been a chef!" They never guessed how simple it was to make.

**—KENNETH HOLT** KANSAS CITY, MISSOURI

**PREP:** 45 MIN.  **BAKE:** 1¼ HOURS
**MAKES:** 10 SERVINGS (5½ CUPS SAUCE)

- 2½ teaspoons salt
- 2 teaspoons garlic powder
- 2 teaspoons mustard seed
- ¾ teaspoon pepper, divided
- 4 pounds boneless pork loin roast
- 2 garlic cloves, sliced
- 2 tablespoons canola oil
- 1 large onion, cut into 1-inch wedges
- 1 medium fennel bulb, cut into 1-inch pieces
- 1 carton (32 ounces) reduced-sodium chicken broth
- 1¼ cups plus ¼ cup apple cider, divided
- ¼ cup all-purpose flour
- 2 medium pears, cut into 1-inch pieces
- 1 cup dried figs, chopped
- ¼ cup chopped dried apricots
- 2 tablespoons butter

**1.** In a small bowl, combine salt, garlic powder, mustard seed and ¼ teaspoon pepper; rub over the pork roast. Using a sharp knife, make six to eight 1-in. slits in roast; insert the garlic.

**2.** In a large skillet, brown roast in oil on all sides. Drain. Place roast fat side up on a rack in a shallow roasting pan. Add onion and fennel. Bake, uncovered, at 325° for 1¼ to 1½ hours or until a thermometer reads 145°.

**3.** Meanwhile, in a large saucepan, bring the broth and 1¼ cups cider to a boil; cook until the liquid is reduced by half. Remove the pork and vegetables from oven; transfer drippings to a large saucepan. Tent roasting pan with foil. Let stand for 15 minutes.

**4.** Meanwhile, heat the drippings over medium. Add the reduced chicken broth mixture. Combine the flour and remaining apple cider until smooth; stir into the pan. Add the pears, figs and apricots; cook and stir until the sauce is thickened, about 15 minutes. Remove from the heat; stir in the butter and remaining pepper. Slice pork; serve with sauce and vegetables.

# Pickled Beet Salad with Warm Bacon Vinaigrette

Here's a festive, flavorful salad that goes together in a snap—perfect for time-crunched cooks. You'll love the contrasting tastes and textures of the beets, radishes, cheese and bacon.

**—TASTE OF HOME TEST KITCHEN**

**PREP:** 10 MIN.  **COOK:** 25 MIN.
**MAKES:** 16 SERVINGS (1 CUP EACH)

- 8 cups fresh baby spinach
- 1 jar (16 ounces) pickled whole beets, drained and cut into wedges
- 1 small red onion, thinly sliced
- ½ cup sliced radishes
- 1 pound bacon strips, chopped
- ⅓ cup cider vinegar
- 3 teaspoons brown sugar
- 1½ teaspoons Dijon mustard
- ½ teaspoon pepper
- ¼ teaspoon salt
- 1 cup crumbled goat cheese

**1.** In a large bowl, toss spinach, beets, onion and radishes; set aside. In a large skillet, cook bacon over medium heat until crisp, stirring occasionally. Remove with a slotted spoon; drain on paper towels.

**2.** Add vinegar, brown sugar, mustard, pepper and salt to bacon drippings; bring to a boil. Drizzle warm dressing over spinach and toss to coat. Sprinkle with cheese and bacon. Serve immediately.

## Garlic Brussels Sprouts

For a holiday side dish, I combine fresh Brussels sprouts with sauteed garlic and cook them in butter and chicken broth. If you can't find fresh sprouts, substitute frozen ones.

**—MYRA INNES** AUBURN, KANSAS

**PREP/TOTAL TIME:** 30 MIN. **MAKES:** 6 SERVINGS

1½ **pounds fresh Brussels sprouts**
4   **garlic cloves, chopped**
2   **teaspoons olive oil**
3   **teaspoons butter, divided**
½   **cup reduced-sodium chicken broth**
¼   **teaspoon salt**
⅛   **teaspoon pepper**

**1.** Trim the Brussels sprouts and cut an "X" in the core of each; set aside.
**2.** In a large saucepan, saute garlic in oil and 1 teaspoon butter for 2-3 minutes or until golden brown. Add the reserved sprouts; toss to coat.
**3.** Stir in the chicken broth, salt and pepper. Bring to a boil. Reduce the heat; cover and simmer for 8-10 minutes or until tender. Drain; add the remaining butter and toss until melted.

# Mushroom & Spinach Bread Pudding

Want a change of pace from traditional stuffing? Try this savory bread pudding loaded with cremini mushrooms and spinach. It's easy to prepare and a great way to use up leftover bread.

**—BROOKE SIFERT** BUSH, LOUISIANA

**PREP:** 25 MIN.
**BAKE:** 45 MIN. + STANDING
**MAKES:** 9 SERVINGS

| | |
|---|---|
| 6 | eggs |
| 2 | cups 2% milk |
| ¼ | cup grated Parmesan cheese, divided |
| ¾ | teaspoon salt, divided |
| ½ | teaspoon pepper, divided |
| 5 | cups cubed French bread baguette (½-inch pieces) |
| 2 | tablespoons olive oil |
| 8 | ounces sliced fresh cremini mushrooms |
| 2 | cups coarsely chopped fresh spinach |
| 2 | garlic cloves, minced |
| 1 | teaspoon dried thyme |
| 2 | cups (8 ounces) shredded mozzarella cheese |

**1.** In a large bowl, whisk eggs, milk, 2 tablespoons Parmesan cheese, ¼ teaspoon salt and ¼ teaspoon pepper until blended. Stir in French bread; let stand 10 minutes or until bread is softened.

**2.** Meanwhile, in a large skillet, heat the oil over medium heat. Add the mushrooms; cook and stir until tender. Add the spinach, garlic, thyme and remaining salt and pepper. Cook and stir until the spinach is wilted. Add to the bread mixture; stir in the mozzarella cheese.

**3.** Transfer to a greased 8-in.-square baking dish; sprinkle with remaining Parmesan cheese. Bake, uncovered, at 350° for 45-50 minutes or until golden and a knife inserted near the center comes out clean. Let stand 10 minutes before serving.

## Lighted Centerpiece

Looking to add some extra dazzle to your Christmas dinner? With this quick-and-easy idea, you can accent a flowery centerpiece with sparkling points of light.

In the arrangement shown below, Craft Editor Shalana Frisby used red submersible LED lights and white water gems (look for LED lights and water gems at craft stores). Here's how to make your own:

Following the gem manufacturer's instructions, fill a clear glass vase with enough water for the amount of gems you wish to use. Add the gems to the vase, then let them sit until the water is absorbed and they expand to fill the vase.

Turn on and place a few submersible LED lights among the gems, hiding the lights throughout. Then simply add your choice of fresh or artificial flowers to the vase as desired. Using fresh flowers? The gems will release and provide moisture to the stems.

## Spiked Pink Lady

Why reserve lemonade and strawberries for the summertime? They're just as refreshing during the holiday season. Add two more ingredients to create a crowd-pleasing cocktail.
—**SILVIA GARCIA** NEW YORK, NEW YORK

**PREP:** 15 MIN. + FREEZING
**MAKES:** 18 SERVINGS (¾ CUP EACH)

- 8 **cups pink lemonade, divided**
- 1¾ **cups vodka**
- 1 **cup frozen unsweetened strawberries**
- 4 **cups lemon-lime soda, chilled**

**1.** Pour 4 cups pink lemonade into ice cube trays; freeze until set.
**2.** Transfer the ice cubes to a punch bowl; add the vodka, strawberries and remaining lemonade. Slowly stir in the soda. Serve immediately.

# Eggnog Napoleons

These single-serving pastry desserts featuring the flavor of eggnog are Christmasy, yummy and a sweet change of pace from the usual cakes and pies on yuletide menus. A sprinkling of confectioners' sugar makes a pretty finishing touch.

**—NILA GRAHL** GURNEE, ILLINOIS

**PREP:** 25 MIN. + CHILLING  **BAKE:** 15 MIN. + CHILLING
**MAKES:** 10 SERVINGS

- ⅔ cup sugar
- ¼ cup cornstarch
- ¼ teaspoon salt
- ¼ teaspoon ground nutmeg
- 2 cups whole milk
- 2 tablespoons spiced rum
- 2 egg yolks
- 2 tablespoons butter
- 1 teaspoon vanilla extract
- 1 sheet frozen puff pastry, thawed
  Confectioners' sugar

**1.** In a small heavy saucepan, mix sugar, cornstarch, salt and nutmeg. Whisk in milk and rum. Cook and stir over medium heat until thickened and bubbly. Reduce heat to low; cook and stir 2 minutes longer. Remove from heat.

**2.** In a small bowl, whisk a small amount of hot mixture into egg yolks; return all to pan, whisking constantly. Bring to a gentle boil; cook and stir 1 minute. Immediately transfer to a clean bowl; stir in butter and vanilla. Cool slightly. Press plastic wrap onto surface of filling; refrigerate 1 hour or until cold.

**3.** On a lightly floured surface, unfold the puff pastry; roll into a 12-in. x 10-in. rectangle. Cut into fifteen 4-in. x 2-in. rectangles. Place 1 in. apart on ungreased baking sheets. Bake at 375° for 12-15 minutes or until golden brown. Remove to wire racks; cool 10 minutes. Split each pastry into two layers, making 30 layers total; cool completely.

**4.** Reserve 10 of the top pastry layers. Spread 1 rounded tablespoon filling onto each of 10 bottom layers. Top each with a second layer and another rounded tablespoon filling. Top with reserved layers. Refrigerate until serving. To serve, sprinkle with confectioners' sugar.

# Salt-Encrusted Prime Rib

This simple treatment for prime rib results in a moist, tender beef entree. It's better than any I've tasted in restaurants and makes an ideal centerpiece for Christmas dinner.

**—ROGER BOWLDS** BAKERSFIELD, CALIFORNIA

**PREP:** 15 MIN.  **BAKE:** 2¼ HOURS + STANDING
**MAKES:** 9 SERVINGS

- 1 box (3 pounds) kosher salt, divided
- 1 bone-in beef rib roast (6 to 8 pounds)
- 3 tablespoons Worcestershire sauce
- 2 tablespoons cracked ground pepper
- 2 teaspoons garlic powder
- ½ cup water

**1.** Line a shallow roasting pan with heavy-duty foil. Place 3 cups salt on foil, spreading evenly to form a ½-in. layer.
**2.** Brush roast with Worcestershire sauce; sprinkle with pepper and garlic powder. Place roast, fat side up, on top of the salt layer.
**3.** In a small bowl, combine the water and remaining salt. (Mixture should be just moist enough to hold together.) Beginning at the base, press salt mixture onto the sides and top of roast.
**4.** Bake, uncovered, at 450° for 15 minutes. Reduce heat to 325°; bake 2 to 2¼ hours longer or until thermometer reaches 130° for medium-rare; 145° for medium. (The temperature of the roast will continue to rise about 15 degrees upon standing.)
**5.** Let stand for 20 minutes. Remove and discard the salt crust, brushing away any remaining salt. Slice roast into ½-in. thick slices.

# Baked Creamy Spinach Dip

A fan of classic dishes, I often tweak them a bit to suit family members. I made this spinach dip a little lighter than most.

**—JENN TIDWELL** FAIR OAKS, CALIFORNIA

**PREP:** 25 MIN.  **BAKE:** 30 MIN.
**MAKES:** 14 SERVINGS (¼ CUP EACH)

- 2 packages (10 ounces each) frozen chopped spinach, thawed
- 1 tablespoon butter
- 2 garlic cloves, minced
- 1 tablespoon all-purpose flour
- 1 can (12 ounces) evaporated milk
- ½ cup grated Parmesan cheese, divided
- ¼ cup cream cheese
- ¼ cup ricotta cheese
- ¼ teaspoon ground nutmeg
- ½ teaspoon salt
- ¼ teaspoon pepper
  Bagel chips

**1.** Place spinach in a colander over a bowl; squeeze dry, reserving 1 cup spinach liquid.
**2.** In a large saucepan, heat the butter over medium heat. Add the garlic; cook 1 minute. Stir in flour until blended; gradually whisk in evaporated milk and reserved spinach liquid. Bring to a boil, stirring constantly; cook and stir 2-3 minutes or until thickened. Stir in ¼ cup Parmesan cheese, cream cheese, ricotta cheese, seasonings and spinach; cook and stir until blended.
**3.** Transfer to a 1½-qt. baking dish. Bake at 350° for 25-30 minutes or until bubbly and top is lightly browned. Remove from oven; top with the remaining Parmesan cheese. Bake 4-5 minutes longer or until cheese is melted. Serve with bagel chips.

## Triple Mash with Buttered Horseradish

Why settle for traditional mashed potatoes when you can enjoy three times the veggie flavor? Combine spuds with rutabaga and parsnips, plus zippy horseradish, for a taste treat.

**—LILY JULOW** GAINESVILLE, FLORIDA

**PREP:** 15 MIN. **COOK:** 35 MIN.
**MAKES:** 12 SERVINGS (⅔ CUP)

- **4 medium Yukon Gold potatoes, peeled and cubed**
- **4 medium parsnips, peeled and cubed**
- **2½ cups cubed peeled rutabaga**
- **2 teaspoons salt**
- **½ cup butter, divided**
- **1 cup soft bread crumbs**
- **2 tablespoons prepared horseradish**
- **1 cup whole milk**
- **¼ teaspoon pepper**

**1.** Place the vegetables and salt in a Dutch oven; add water to cover. Bring to a boil. Reduce the heat; cook, uncovered, 15-20 minutes or until tender.

**2.** Meanwhile, in a skillet, melt 4 tablespoons butter. Stir in the bread crumbs; toast over medium heat 3-5 minutes or until golden brown, stirring frequently. Stir in the horseradish; remove from heat.

**3.** Drain the vegetables; return to pan. Mash vegetables over low heat, gradually adding the milk, pepper and remaining butter. Spoon into serving dish; top with bread crumb mixture.

# Roasted Gremolata-Topped Broccoli

I love the challenge of transforming ordinary vegetables into something special. A crispy almond-gremolata topping, lemon and Parmesan cheese turn broccoli into a holiday-worthy side dish. If you like, prepare the topping the day before and refrigerate it, covered, until you're ready to use it.

**—LAURIE BALCOM** LYNDEN, WASHINGTON

**PREP:** 25 MIN.  **BAKE:** 20 MIN.
**MAKES:** 9 SERVINGS

### ALMOND-GREMOLATA TOPPING
- 2 slices white bread, torn
- ¼ cup salted roasted almonds
- ¼ cup lightly packed fresh parsley leaves
- 1 tablespoon grated lemon peel
- 2 garlic cloves, minced
- 4 teaspoons butter, melted

### BROCCOLI
- 2 pounds fresh broccoli florets (15 cups florets, cut from about 3 bunches)
- 2 tablespoons butter, melted
- 2 tablespoons lemon juice
- 2 tablespoons shredded Parmesan cheese

**1.** Place the first five ingredients in a food processor; pulse until the bread is coarsely chopped. Transfer to a small bowl. Drizzle with 4 teaspoons melted butter; toss to combine.

**2.** Place the broccoli in a large bowl; toss with the butter. Divide between two 15-in. x 10-in. x 1-in. baking pans coated with cooking spray. Roast 12-17 minutes or until crisp-tender.

**3.** Transfer all broccoli to a 13-in. x 9-in. baking dish. Drizzle with lemon juice; sprinkle with the bread crumb mixture and cheese. Bake at 450° for 5-8 minutes or until topping is crisp and cheese is melted.

# Persimmon Salad with Honey-Lemon Dressing

Sweet, bright-orange persimmons are in season during winter. Put that beautiful fruit to perfect use in a green salad featuring nuts, cranberries, onion, feta and a homemade dressing.

—TASTE OF HOME TEST KITCHEN

**PREP/TOTAL TIME:** 20 MIN.
**MAKES:** 12 SERVINGS (1 CUP EACH)

- 12 cups torn mixed salad greens
- 4 cups fresh arugula or baby spinach
- 4 persimmons, peeled and sliced
- 1 cup walnut halves, broken and toasted
- 1 cup dried cranberries
- 1 medium red onion, finely chopped
- ¼ cup lemon juice
- ¼ cup canola oil
- 2 tablespoons honey
- ½ teaspoon ground allspice
- ¼ teaspoon salt
- 1 cup crumbled feta cheese

In a large bowl, combine the mixed salad greens, arugula, persimmons, walnuts, dried cranberries and red onion. In a small bowl, whisk the lemon juice, oil, honey, allspice and salt. Drizzle over the salad; toss to coat. Sprinkle with feta cheese.

# Southern Lane Cake

I just love this Southern-style dessert, and so do dinner guests. With pecans, cherries and raisins in both the filling and topping, this cake is reminiscent of a classic fruitcake—only yummier! Plus, it looks beautiful on a Christmas table.

—MABEL PARVI RIDGEFIELD, WASHINGTON

**PREP:** 40 MIN. **BAKE:** 20 MIN. + CHILLING **MAKES:** 12 SERVINGS

- 6 egg whites
- ¾ cup butter, softened
- 1½ cups sugar
- 1 teaspoon vanilla extract
- 2¼ cups all-purpose flour
- 2½ teaspoons baking powder
- ½ teaspoon salt
- ¾ cup 2% milk

**FILLING**

- 6 egg yolks
- 1 cup sugar
- ½ cup butter, cubed
- ¼ cup bourbon
- 1 tablespoon grated orange peel
- ¼ teaspoon salt
- ¾ cup raisins
- ¾ cup flaked coconut
- ¾ cup chopped pecans
- ¾ cup coarsely chopped red candied cherries
- 1 cup heavy whipping cream, whipped and sweetened

**1.** Line the bottoms of three greased 9-in. round baking pans with parchment paper; grease paper; set aside. Place egg whites in a large bowl; let stand at room temperature for 30 minutes.

**2.** In another large bowl, cream the butter and sugar until light and fluffy. Beat in the vanilla. In another bowl, whisk the flour, baking powder and salt; add to creamed mixture alternately with the milk, beating well after each addition. Beat the egg whites until stiff peaks form; fold into batter. Transfer to prepared pans.

**3.** Bake at 325° for 20-25 minutes or until a toothpick inserted near the center comes out clean. Cool for 10 minutes before removing from pans to wire racks; remove paper. Cool completely.

**4.** For the filling, combine egg yolks and sugar in a large saucepan. Add the butter; cook and stir over medium-low heat until the sugar is dissolved and the mixture thickens (do not boil). Remove from heat. Stir in bourbon, orange peel and salt. Fold in raisins, coconut, pecans and candied cherries. Cool.

**5.** Place one cake layer on a serving plate; spread with a third of the filling. Repeat layers twice. Frost sides of cake with whipped cream. Refrigerate until serving.

## Spoon-Swirl Frosting

To decorate a cake with graceful swirls, all you need is the tip of a spoon. Start by scooping a generous amount of frosting or whipped cream onto the back of the spoon. Place the spoon on the cake with its tip in the 12 o'clock position, then swirl the spoon in a half circle to the left, ending in the 6 o'clock position. Repeat until the cake is covered with swirls.

# More Choices for Christmas Menus

If you like the three menus in this chapter but want even more options for entrees, sides and salads, page through this extra-special section. You'll find bonus recipes that make wonderful substitutions in the previous dinners. For additional dessert options, turn to any of the following taste-tempting chapters: Simply Chocolate (pg. 111), Yuletide Pies & Tarts (pg. 127) and Sweet Sensations (pg. 143).

# Herb-Crusted Rack of Lamb

For anyone who enjoys an entree of lamb, here's a delicious treatment for it. The preparation is quick and easy, too.

—**CAROLYN SCHMELING** BROOKFIELD, WISCONSIN

**PREP:** 15 MIN.  **BAKE:** 20 MIN.  **MAKES:** 4 SERVINGS

- ½  **cup fresh bread crumbs**
- 2  **tablespoons minced fresh parsley**
- 1  **tablespoon minced fresh thyme or 1 teaspoon dried thyme**
- 1  **garlic clove, minced**
- 2  **tablespoons olive oil**
- 2  **frenched racks of lamb (1½ pounds each)**
- ¼  **teaspoon salt**
- ¼  **teaspoon pepper**
- 1  **tablespoon Dijon mustard**

**1.** In a shallow dish, combine the bread crumbs, parsley, thyme and garlic. Add the oil and toss; set aside. Sprinkle lamb with salt and pepper. In a large skillet, brown meat on both sides. Brush mustard over top of meat, then roll in crumb mixture.

**2.** Place racks in a shallow baking pan side by side with bones interlaced and resting against each other. Bake at 375° for 30-40 minutes or until the meat reaches the desired doneness (for medium-rare, a thermometer should read 145°; medium, 160°; well-done, 170°). Let stand for 10 minutes before slicing.

# Sweet and Sour Red Cabbage

This nicely spiced cabbage-and-apple medley has always been a popular choice on our Christmas dinner table. We love the sweet-tangy taste and eye-catching color.

—**PAUL TACKMAN SR.** NORTH LAS VEGAS, NEVADA

**PREP:** 20 MIN. + STANDING  **COOK:** 35 MIN.
**MAKES:** 6 SERVINGS

- 1  **medium head red cabbage, shredded**
- 1  **medium apple, peeled and thinly sliced**
- ⅔  **cup sugar**
- ¾  **teaspoon salt**
- ½  **teaspoon dried rosemary, crushed**
- ⅛  **teaspoon pepper**
- 2  **bay leaves**
- 4  **whole cloves**
- ⅓  **cup cider vinegar**
- 2  **tablespoons lemon juice**

**1.** In a large skillet, combine the cabbage, apple, sugar, salt, rosemary and pepper. Place bay leaves and cloves on a double thickness of cheesecloth; bring up corners of the cloth and tie with string to form a bag. Stir into cabbage mixture. Let stand for 40 minutes or until some moisture has been drawn from cabbage.

**2.** Bring to a boil. Reduce heat; cover and simmer for 30-35 minutes or until cabbage is tender, stirring occasionally. Stir in vinegar and lemon juice; heat through. Discard spice bag. Serve with a slotted spoon.

# Ranch Green Beans

Years ago, I discovered this handwritten recipe on a note card. The ranch-flavored dish is deliciously different from typical green bean casseroles and quickly became a favorite.

—**CAROL CONN** AURORA, COLORADO

**PREP:** 15 MIN.  **COOK:** 20 MIN.  **MAKES:** 6 SERVINGS

- 1¼  **pounds fresh green beans, trimmed**
- 2  **tablespoons butter**
- 1½  **cups sliced fresh mushrooms**
- 1  **medium onion, chopped**
- 2  **garlic cloves, minced**
- 2  **tablespoons all-purpose flour**
- 1½  **cups 2% milk**
- 2  **tablespoons ranch salad dressing mix**
- ¼  **teaspoon white pepper**
- ¼  **cup soft bread crumbs, toasted**

**1.** Place green beans in a Dutch oven; add water to cover. Bring to a boil. Cook, uncovered, 3-4 minutes or just until tender. Drain.

**2.** Meanwhile, in a large skillet, heat butter over medium-high heat. Add mushrooms and onion; cook and stir 3-4 minutes or until tender. Add garlic; cook 1 minute longer.

**3.** In a small bowl, whisk flour and 2 tablespoons milk until smooth. Whisk in the remaining milk; stir into the mushroom mixture. Bring to a boil, stirring constantly. Cook and stir for 2 minutes. Stir in salad dressing mix and pepper. Add beans; heat through. Transfer to a serving bowl; sprinkle with bread crumbs.

## Romaine Salad with Apple Vinaigrette

Looking for a salad that's simple but special? This one is a hit whenever I bring it to a potluck at work. I blend apples into the homemade vinaigrette and toss them with the romaine, too.

**—MARY JUNE DONOVAN**
CLINTON, MASSACHUSETTS

**PREP/TOTAL TIME:** 30 MIN.
**MAKES:** 8 SERVINGS
(1 CUP VINAIGRETTE)

- ⅓ cup chopped peeled tart apple
- ⅓ chopped peeled ripe pear
- ¼ cup unsweetened apple juice
- 2 tablespoons cider vinegar
- 1 tablespoon lemon juice
- ¼ teaspoon salt
- ¼ teaspoon pepper
- ¼ cup canola oil

**SALAD**
- 8 cups torn romaine
- 2 medium apples, thinly sliced
- ½ cup pine nuts, toasted
- 1½ cups crumbled feta cheese

**1.** In a blender, combine the first seven ingredients. Cover and process for 30 seconds or until smooth. While processing, gradually add the oil in a steady stream.

**2.** In a serving bowl, combine the romaine, apples and nuts. Drizzle with the vinaigrette; sprinkle with feta cheese.

### Holiday Helper

When choosing the best apples for recipes, keep in mind that different varieties of apples offer different flavors:

- Granny Smith—Tart
- McIntosh—Tart, tangy
- Rome Beauty—Mildly tart
- Pink Lady—Sweet-tart
- Empire—Sweet-tart
- Golden Delicious—Mildly sweet
- Red Delicious—Sweet
- Gala—Sweet
- Fuji—Very sweet

## Wild Rice-Stuffed Acorn Squash

I tried many variations of ingredients for the stuffing in my acorn squash. Here's the version I liked best—a rustic medley of rice, maple syrup, cherries and more.

**—MICHELLE SPRINGER** SPRING, TEXAS

**PREP:** 1 HOUR **BAKE:** 45 MIN.
**MAKES:** 8 SERVINGS

- 4 small acorn squash
- 3 tablespoons olive oil, divided
- ¾ teaspoon salt, divided
- 2 teaspoons ground coriander, divided
- ½ teaspoon ground nutmeg, divided
- 1 pound fresh carrots, peeled and cut into ½-in. cubes
- ¾ cup pecan halves, coarsely chopped
- ¾ cup dried cherries, coarsely chopped
- 10 fresh sage leaves, chopped
- 2 garlic cloves, minced
- 2 tablespoons maple syrup

**FILLING**
- 1 cup uncooked wild rice
- 1 tablespoon olive oil
- ¾ cup finely chopped sweet onion
- ¼ teaspoon ground cinnamon
- 2 cups vegetable broth

**1.** Cut squash lengthwise in half; remove and discard seeds. Brush with 2 tablespoons oil; sprinkle with ¼ teaspoon salt, ½ teaspoon coriander and ¼ teaspoon nutmeg. Place squash in a 15-in. x 10-in. x 1-in. baking pan, cut sides up. Bake at 375° for 35-45 minutes or until easily pierced with a fork.

**2.** In a small bowl, combine the carrots and remaining oil, salt, coriander and nutmeg. Bake for 15-20 minutes or just until tender, stirring occasionally. Stir in pecans, cherries, sage, garlic and maple syrup. Bake 10 minutes longer.

**3.** Rinse wild rice thoroughly; drain. In a small saucepan, heat the oil over medium heat. Add onion; cook and stir 2-3 minutes or until softened. Stir in rice and cinnamon, then add broth. Bring to a boil. Reduce heat; cover and simmer for 40-50 minutes or until rice is fluffy and tender. Drain if necessary.

**4.** Combine rice and carrot mixtures. Arrange squash on a serving platter, cut sides up. Fill with rice mixture. Serve warm.

# Bacon-Wrapped Stuffed Tenderloins

I'm always looking for new ways to use blue cheese. It creates a savory filling for pork tenderloins when I mix it with toasted almonds, red onion, herbs and spices. If you like, add more zip to your entree with red pepper flakes.

—**KATHRYN ORR** ARVADA, COLORADO

**PREP:** 45 MIN.  **COOK:** 10 MIN.
**MAKES:** 3 STUFFED TENDERLOINS (4 SERVINGS EACH)

- 3   pork tenderloins (1 pound each)
- 2   cups crumbled blue cheese
- ¾   cup slivered almonds, toasted
- ½   cup finely chopped red onion
- 2   tablespoons minced fresh rosemary or 2 teaspoons dried rosemary, crushed
- 2   garlic cloves, minced
- ½   teaspoon crushed red pepper flakes, optional
- ½   teaspoon salt
- ¼   teaspoon pepper
- 6   bacon strips

**1.** Make a lengthwise slit through the center of each pork tenderloin to within ½ in. of the bottom. Open tenderloin so it lies flat; cover with plastic wrap. Flatten to ½-in. thickness. Remove plastic.

**2.** In a small bowl, combine the blue cheese, almonds, red onion, rosemary, garlic and red pepper flakes if desired. Divide among tenderloins. Close tenderloins and sprinkle with salt and pepper. Wrap each with two bacon strips; secure with toothpicks.

**3.** In a large skillet, brown the pork on all sides in batches until the bacon is almost crisp. Place on a rack in a shallow roasting pan. Bake, uncovered, at 425° for 8-12 minutes or until a thermometer inserted in pork reads 145°.

**4.** Let stand for 5 minutes. Discard the toothpicks before slicing.

# Roast Turkey with Sausage-Cabbage Stuffing

Here's a holiday staple in our family. The golden-brown bird is moist, flavorful and impressive. Guests often rave about it and never even realize that it contains cabbage!

—**ALMA WINBERRY** GREAT FALLS, MONTANA

**PREP:** 30 MIN.  **BAKE:** 3 HOURS + STANDING
**MAKES:** 12 SERVINGS (ABOUT 8 CUPS STUFFING)

- ⅓   cup unsalted butter, softened
- 3   tablespoons minced fresh thyme
- 1   teaspoon salt
- ¼   teaspoon pepper
- 1   turkey (12 to 14 pounds)

**STUFFING**

- 1   pound bulk Italian sausage
- 3   cups chopped cabbage
- 1   large carrot, shredded
- 1   celery rib, chopped
- 1   small onion, chopped
- 2   tablespoons half-and-half cream
- ¾   teaspoon poultry seasoning
- ¼   teaspoon salt
- ⅛   teaspoon pepper
- 3   cups seasoned stuffing cubes
- 1   egg, lightly beaten
- ⅔   to ¾ cup chicken broth

**1.** In a small bowl, mix the butter, thyme, salt and pepper. Place turkey on a rack in a shallow roasting pan, breast side up. With your fingers, carefully loosen skin from the turkey breast; rub half of the butter mixture under the skin. Rub remaining butter mixture over turkey. Tuck wings under turkey; tie drumsticks together.

**2.** Bake at 325° for 3 to 3¾ hours or until a thermometer inserted in thigh reads 180°. Baste occasionally with pan drippings.

**3.** For stuffing, in a Dutch oven, cook sausage over medium heat for 6-8 minutes or until no longer pink, breaking into crumbles. Remove with a slotted spoon; drain on paper towels. Discard drippings, reserving 1 tablespoon.

**4.** Add the cabbage, carrot, celery and onion to reserved drippings; cook and stir over medium heat until tender. Stir in cream, poultry seasoning, salt and pepper.

**5.** Add stuffing cubes, egg and sausage; toss to combine. Stir in enough broth to reach desired moistness; transfer to a greased 11-in. x 7-in. baking dish. Bake, covered, for 30 minutes. Uncover and bake 10-15 minutes longer or until lightly browned.

**6.** Remove turkey from oven; cover loosely with foil and let stand for 20 minutes before carving. Serve with stuffing.

## Chickpea Pancetta Salad with Cran-Orange Vinaigrette

When it comes to holiday-worthy salads, this one really fills the bill. The colorful mix of dried cranberries, orange segments, salad greens and red pepper looks beautiful on the table.

—**TERESA SMITH** SANTA ROSA, CALIFORNIA

**PREP:** 20 MIN. + CHILLING  **COOK:** 10 MIN.
**MAKES:** 8 SERVINGS

- ½  cup white cranberry juice
- 2  tablespoons white balsamic vinegar
- ¼  cup dried cranberries
- 1  tablespoon minced fresh basil
- 1  tablespoon minced fresh parsley
- 2  teaspoons grated orange peel
- ¼  teaspoon salt
- ¼  teaspoon coarsely ground pepper
- ⅓  cup olive oil

**SALAD**

- 1  can (15 ounces) chickpeas or garbanzo beans, rinsed and drained
- 1  small sweet red pepper, chopped
- ½  cup dried cranberries
- 2  green onions, chopped
- 2  tablespoons minced fresh basil
- 2  tablespoons minced fresh parsley
- 6  ounces diced pancetta or bacon
- 8  cups spring mix salad greens
- ⅓  cup chopped walnuts, toasted
- 16  orange segments

**1.** Place the first eight ingredients in a blender; cover and pulse until smooth. While processing, gradually add oil in a steady stream.

**2.** In a small bowl, combine the beans, red pepper, dried cranberries, green onions, basil and parsley. Pour ⅓ cup dressing over bean mixture; refrigerate for at least 1 hour. Refrigerate remaining dressing.

**3.** In a large skillet, cook pancetta over medium heat until crisp. Remove to paper towels with a slotted spoon; drain.

**4.** In a large bowl, combine the salad greens and ¼ cup dressing; toss to coat. Divide among eight salad plates. Top with bean mixture, pancetta and walnuts. Top with oranges. Serve with remaining dressing.

## Herbed Parmesan Bread

I've been baking my Parmesan bread for so many years, I can no longer remember where the recipe came from. Thanks to a convenient mix, I can get a loaf in the oven fast.

—**LESLEY ARCHER** CHAPALA, MEXICO

**PREP:** 10 MIN.  **BAKE:** 35 MIN. + COOLING
**MAKES:** 1 LOAF (12 SLICES)

- 3¾  cups biscuit/baking mix
- 1  cup plus 2 tablespoons grated Parmesan cheese, divided
- 1  teaspoon Italian seasoning
- ½  teaspoon salt
- 1  egg
- 1  can (5 ounces) evaporated milk
- ¾  cup water

**1.** In a large bowl, combine the biscuit mix, 1 cup cheese, Italian seasoning and salt. In a small bowl, whisk the egg, milk and water. Stir into the dry ingredients just until moistened. Transfer to a greased 8-in. x 4-in. loaf pan. Sprinkle with remaining cheese.

**2.** Bake at 350° for 35-40 minutes or until a toothpick inserted near the center comes out clean. Cool for 10 minutes before removing from pan to a wire rack.

# Garlicky Cheddar Cheese Bisque

I came up with a cheddar cheese soup awhile ago and decided to give it a boost with a variety of root vegetables. Crushed pita chips and fresh parsley make great garnishes.
—**PATRICIA HARMON** BADEN, PENNSYLVANIA

**PREP:** 30 MIN. **COOK:** 40 MIN. **MAKES:** 6 SERVINGS

- 1 tablespoon butter
- 1 tablespoon canola oil
- 1 medium leek (white portion only), sliced
- ½ cup chopped carrot
- ½ cup chopped celery
- ½ cup chopped peeled parsnip
- 1 teaspoon salt
- ½ teaspoon pepper
- 6 garlic cloves, minced
- 2 cans (14½ ounces each) chicken broth
- ⅔ cup dry white wine
- 2 tablespoons cornstarch
- ¼ cup cold water
- 1 can (12 ounces) evaporated milk
- 2 cups (8 ounces) shredded sharp white cheddar cheese
  Crushed baked pita chips
  Minced fresh parsley

**1.** In a large saucepan, heat butter and oil over medium heat. Add vegetables, salt and pepper; cook and stir for 7-8 minutes or until vegetables are crisp-tender. Add garlic; cook 1-2 minutes longer.
**2.** Stir in the broth and wine; bring to a boil. Reduce heat; simmer, uncovered, 15-20 minutes or until vegetables are tender. Remove from heat; cool slightly. Meanwhile, in a small bowl, mix cornstarch and water until smooth.

**3.** Process the soup in batches in a food processor until smooth. Return all to the pan. Stir in the evaporated milk and cornstarch mixture; bring to a boil. Reduce heat; simmer, uncovered, until thickened and bubbly, stirring frequently. Add the cheese; cook and stir until cheese is blended. Top servings with crushed chips and parsley.

# Frozen Christmas Salad

My mom's use of red and green cherries to decorate dishes at Christmastime inspired me to create a yuletide gelatin mold. It's cool, creamy and fun to serve guests.
—**PAT HABIGER** SPEARVILLE, KANSAS

**PREP:** 25 MIN. + FREEZING **MAKES:** 10 SERVINGS

- 1 can (20 ounces) crushed pineapple, drained
- 2 cups miniature marshmallows
- 1 package (8 ounces) cream cheese, softened
- ½ cup mayonnaise
- 12 red maraschino cherries, chopped and patted dry
- 12 green maraschino cherries, chopped and patted dry
- ½ cup chopped walnuts
- 1 cup heavy whipping cream

**1.** In a small bowl, combine the pineapple and miniature marshmallows. Set aside until the marshmallows are softened, about 15 minutes.
**2.** Meanwhile, in a small bowl, beat the cream cheese and mayonnaise until smooth. Stir into the marshmallow mixture. Fold in cherries and walnuts.
**3.** In a small bowl, beat the cream until soft peaks form. Fold into the pineapple mixture. Spoon into a 6-cup mold; freeze overnight. Let stand at room temperature for 15-20 minutes; unmold onto a serving plate.

## Roasted Butternut Penne

To use up my bumper crop of winter squash, I tossed it into a rich, creamy pasta dish. The meatless main course combines restaurant elegance with home-cooked convenience.

**—VERONICA CALLAGHAN**
GLASTONBURY, CONNECTICUT

**PREP:** 20 MIN.  **BAKE:** 15 MIN.
**MAKES:** 4 SERVINGS

- ½  **pound uncooked penne pasta**
- 2  **cups cubed peeled butternut squash**
- 2  **shallots, quartered**
- 1  **tablespoon olive oil**
- ½  **teaspoon salt, divided**
- ¼  **teaspoon pepper**
- ¾  **cup half-and-half cream**
- ¾  **cup sour cream**
- ½  **cup crumbled blue cheese**
- ¼  **teaspoon cayenne pepper**
- ¼  **cup coarsely chopped pistachios**

**1.** Cook pasta according to package directions. Meanwhile, place squash and shallots in a greased 15-in. x 10-in. x 1-in. baking pan. Drizzle with oil and sprinkle with ¼ teaspoon salt and pepper. Toss to coat.

**2.** Bake, uncovered, at 400° for 15-20 minutes or until tender, stirring occasionally. When cool enough to handle, finely chop shallots.

**3.** In a small saucepan, combine the cream and sour cream. Bring to a gentle boil. Remove from the heat. Stir in the blue cheese, cayenne and remaining salt.

**4.** Drain the pasta; transfer to a large bowl. Add sauce mixture and roasted vegetables; toss to combine. Sprinkle with pistachios.

## Green Salad with Vanilla-Citrus Vinaigrette

Just thinking about this refreshing medley makes my mouth water! The citrusy salad is a variation of a recipe my mother shared with me years ago.

**—MARY SHENK** DEKALB, ILLINOIS

**PREP/TOTAL TIME:** 30 MIN.
**MAKES:** 8 SERVINGS
(1⅔ CUPS VINAIGRETTE)

**VANILLA-CITRUS VINAIGRETTE**
- ⅔  **cup orange juice**
- 3  **tablespoons lemon juice**
- 2  **tablespoons honey**
- 1  **tablespoon lime juice**
- 2½  **teaspoons grated orange peel**
- 1  **teaspoon grated lemon peel**
- ¾  **teaspoon grated lime peel**
- ¾  **teaspoon vanilla extract**
- ¼  **teaspoon coarsely ground pepper**
- ⅛  **teaspoon salt**
- ⅔  **cup canola oil**

**CARAMELIZED PECANS**
- ¼  **cup chopped pecans**
- 1  **teaspoon butter**
- 2  **tablespoons sugar**

**SALAD**
- 8  **cups spring mix salad greens**
- 1⅓  **cups chopped celery**
- 1⅓  **cups orange segments**
- ⅓  **cup chopped red onion**
- ⅓  **cup minced fresh cilantro**

**1.** Place the first ten ingredients in a blender. While processing, gradually add the oil in a steady stream. Store vinaigrette in an airtight container in the refrigerator.

**2.** In a small heavy skillet, cook pecans in butter over medium heat until toasted, about 3 minutes. Sprinkle with sugar. Cook and stir 1-2 minutes longer or until sugar is melted. Spread on foil to cool completely.

**3.** Just before serving, combine the greens, celery, oranges, onion and cilantro in a large bowl. Drizzle with ¾ cup vinaigrette; toss to coat. Refrigerate remaining vinaigrette for later use. Sprinkle with pecans.

75

69

66

*seasonal*
GET-TOGETHERS

# Canned Gift Exchange

Gather fellow gardeners who love to can and welcome them to a harvest-inspired holiday party—a gift exchange of canned treats. It's a refreshing change of pace from the usual cookie exchange and a wonderful way to share preserved produce. For inspiration, page through this section packed with scrumptious recipes.

# Giardiniera

Sweet and tangy, this classic Italian condiment is loaded with veggies. Serve it alongside pickles or olives on a relish tray.

—TASTE OF HOME TEST KITCHEN

**PREP:** 1 HOUR  **PROCESS:** 10 MIN./BATCH  **MAKES:** 10 PINTS

| | |
|---|---|
| 6 | cups white vinegar |
| 3½ | cups sugar |
| 3 | cups water |
| 4½ | teaspoons canning salt |
| 1 | tablespoon dried oregano |
| 1 | tablespoon fennel seed |
| 2 | small heads cauliflower, broken into small florets (about 12 cups) |
| 4 | large carrots, sliced |
| 4 | celery ribs, cut into ½-inch slices |
| 48 | pearl onions, peeled and trimmed (about 1¼ pounds) |
| 4 | large sweet red peppers, cut into ½-inch strips |
| 4 | serrano peppers, seeds removed and thinly sliced |
| 10 | bay leaves |
| 20 | whole peppercorns |
| 10 | garlic cloves, thinly sliced |

**1.** In a large kettle, combine the vinegar, sugar, water, canning salt, oregano and fennel seed. Bring to a boil. Add cauliflower, carrots, celery and onions; return to a boil. Remove from the heat; add peppers.

**2.** Carefully ladle hot mixture into hot 1-pint jars, leaving ½ in. headspace. Add a bay leaf, 2 peppercorns and a few slices of garlic to each jar. Remove air bubbles; wipe the rims and adjust the lids. Process for 10 minutes in a boiling-water canner.

**Editor's Note:** *The processing time listed is for altitudes of 1,000 feet or less. For altitudes up to 3,000 feet, add 5 minutes; 6,000 feet, add 10 minutes; 8,000 feet, add 15 minutes; 10,000 feet, add 20 minutes.*

# Apricot & Maraschino Cherry Preserves

This chunky spread is so colorful and festive—like fruitcake in a jar! The fruits are readily available year-round.

—**JUDY TINSLEY** BOLIVAR, MISSOURI

**PREP:** 2 HOURS  **PROCESS:** 10 MIN.  **MAKES:** 5 HALF-PINTS

| | |
|---|---|
| 2⅔ | cups water |
| 2 | cups dried apricots or dried peaches, halved |
| 1 | can (20 ounces) unsweetened pineapple chunks, undrained |
| 2½ | cups sugar |
| 3 | tablespoons lemon juice |
| 1 | jar (6 ounces) red maraschino cherries, halved and patted dry |
| 1 | jar (6 ounces) green maraschino cherries, halved and patted dry |

**1.** Place the water and apricots in a Dutch oven. Bring to a boil. Reduce heat; simmer, uncovered, for 30 minutes or until the liquid is almost evaporated. Stir in the pineapple, sugar and lemon juice. Cook and stir for 35-40 minutes or until thickened.

**2.** Using a potato masher, mash the fruit. Add maraschino cherries; bring to a boil. Remove from the heat; skim off foam if necessary.

**3.** Carefully ladle the hot mixture into hot half-pint jars, leaving ¼ in. headspace. Remove air bubbles; wipe the rims and adjust the lids. Process for 10 minutes in a boiling-water canner.

**Editor's Note:** *The processing time listed is for altitudes of 1,000 feet or less. Add 1 minute to the processing time for each 1,000 feet of additional altitude.*

# Honey Lemon Jelly

I love honey and lemon, so I combined them into a doubly delightful jelly. Spread it on your favorite bagels, English muffins or scones for a sweet-tart breakfast treat.

**—RAMONA POWELL** BARLOW, KENTUCKY

**PREP:** 50 MIN.  **PROCESS:** 5 MIN.  **MAKES:** 3 HALF-PINTS

- 2½ cups honey
- ¾ cup lemon juice
- 6 tablespoons grated lemon peel
- 1 pouch (3 ounces) liquid fruit pectin

**1.** In a Dutch oven, combine the honey, lemon juice and lemon peel. Bring to a full rolling boil over high heat, stirring constantly. Stir in the fruit pectin. Boil for 1 minute, stirring constantly.

**2.** Remove from the heat; skim off foam if necessary. Carefully ladle hot mixture into hot sterilized half-pint jars, leaving ¼ in. headspace. Remove air bubbles; wipe the rims and adjust the lids. Process for 5 minutes in a boiling-water canner.

**Editor's Note:** *The processing time listed is for altitudes of 1,000 feet or less. Add 1 minute to the processing time for each 1,000 feet of additional altitude.*

# Gift Card Snow Globes

Have extra mason jars? Put them to fun use by turning them into waterless snow globes containing gift cards. They make playful presents for family and friends.

Start with a clean wide-mouth jar. Remove the insert from the lid, then cut a 3-in. white Styrofoam ball in half and use tacky glue to glue the flat side of one half to the inside of the insert. Let it dry, then use one edge of the gift card to make a 1-in.-deep slit in the glued foam.

Avoiding the slit, use a craft knife to carve flat areas in the foam for any miniature plastic figures you want inside the globe. To add a mini tree, remove the base from the tree, then insert the wire trunk into the foam. Glue all figures and trees in place and let them dry.

Place the gift card in the slit and add a dimensional glue dot in back to secure it to the foam.

If you wish, base-coat the outside of the lid ring with metal priming paint, let it dry and then paint it with acrylic craft paint.

Put a few pinches of artificial snow in the jar. Place the decorated lid insert back into the lid ring. Holding the lid ring and insert together, turn it upside down and place the lid back on the jar, screwing the lid on tightly. Turn the jar over, allowing the snow to fall, and shake it gently to position the snow evenly over the figures.

If you like, tie a ribbon around the lid ring—or add other embellishments—for a pretty finishing touch.

## Spicy Bavarian Beer Mustard

Here's a gift with bite! Include a tag with serving ideas—for example, the spicy mustard is great with bratwurst.

—TASTE OF HOME TEST KITCHEN

**PREP:** 15 MIN. + CHILLING  **PROCESS:** 15 MIN.
**MAKES:** 7 HALF-PINTS

|   |   |
|---|---|
| 2 | cups dark beer |
| 2 | cups brown mustard seed |
| 2 | cups ground mustard |
| 1½ | cups packed brown sugar |
| 1½ | cups malt vinegar |
| ½ | cup balsamic vinegar |
| 3 | teaspoons salt |
| 2 | teaspoons ground allspice |
| ½ | teaspoon ground cloves |
| 2 | teaspoons vanilla extract |

**1.** In a small bowl, combine the beer and mustard seeds. Cover and refrigerate overnight.

**2.** Place the seed mixture in a blender. Cover and process until chopped and slightly grainy. Transfer to a Dutch oven. Add the ground mustard, brown sugar, vinegars, salt, allspice and cloves. Bring just to a boil. Remove from the heat; stir in vanilla.

**3.** Carefully ladle the hot mixture into hot half-pint jars, leaving ½ in. headspace. Remove air bubbles; wipe the rims and adjust the lids. Process for 10 minutes in a boiling-water canner.

**Editor's Note:** *The processing time listed is for altitudes of 1,000 feet or less. For altitudes up to 3,000 feet, add 5 minutes; 6,000 feet, add 10 minutes; 8,000 feet, add 15 minutes; 10,000 feet, add 20 minutes.*

## Pickled Sweet Onions

These slightly crunchy pickled onions are not only a tasteful gift for Christmas, but also a welcome contribution to a backyard barbecue as a relish for burgers and hot dogs.

—LAURA WINEMILLER DELTA, PENNSYLVANIA

**PREP:** 30 MIN. + STANDING  **PROCESS:** 10 MIN.
**MAKES:** 4 HALF-PINTS

|   |   |
|---|---|
| 8 | cups thinly sliced sweet onions |
| 2 | tablespoons canning salt |
| 1¾ | cups white vinegar |
| 1 | cup sugar |
| 1 | teaspoon dried thyme |

**1.** Place sweet onions in a colander over a plate; sprinkle with canning salt and toss. Let stand for 1 hour. Rinse and drain onions, squeezing to remove excess liquid.

**2.** In a Dutch oven, combine the vinegar, sugar and thyme; bring to a boil. Add the onions and return to a boil. Reduce heat; simmer, uncovered, for 10 minutes. Remove from the heat.

**3.** Carefully ladle the hot mixture into hot half-pint jars, leaving ½ in. headspace. Remove air bubbles; wipe rims and adjust lids. Process for 10 minutes in a boiling-water canner. Refrigerate remaining relish for up to 1 week.

**Editor's Note:** *The processing time listed is for altitudes of 1,000 feet or less. For altitudes up to 3,000 feet, add 5 minutes; 6,000 feet, add 10 minutes; 8,000 feet, add 15 minutes; 10,000 feet, add 20 minutes.*

# Champagne Jelly

When I hosted a Christmas open house, I sent each guest home with a batch of my blush-colored jelly. It was a hit! The recipe requires just three ingredients—Champagne, sugar and fruit pectin.

**—GAIL SHEPPARD** SOMERVILLE, ALABAMA

**PREP:** 15 MIN.  **PROCESS:** 10 MIN.
**MAKES:** 4 HALF-PINTS

- 3 **cups sugar**
- 2 **cups pink Champagne**
- 1 **pouch (3 ounces) liquid fruit pectin**

1.  In a Dutch oven, combine the sugar and Champagne. Bring to a full rolling boil over high heat, stirring often. Stir in pectin. Boil for 1 minute, stirring constantly.

2.  Remove from the heat; skim off foam if necessary. Carefully ladle the hot mixture into hot half-pint jars, leaving ¼ in. headspace. Remove air bubbles; wipe rims and adjust lids. Process for 10 minutes in a boiling-water canner.

**Editor's Note:** *The processing time listed is for altitudes of 1,000 feet or less. Add 1 minute to the processing time for each 1,000 feet of additional altitude.*

## Holiday Helper

Here's a quick and easy way to put pretty fabric toppers on gift jars of jelly, jam or other canned items. Just put the fabric over the top of the jar and use a rubber band to hold it in place. Then tie a coordinating ribbon around the jar and snip off the rubber band.

**—CHARLOTTE S.**
HARRISONBURG, VIRGINIA

# Gingered Pear & Currant Chutney

Living on a small farm, my husband and I always shared the chores, including canning our harvest. One of our favorite condiments, this chutney is especially good with pork roast.
—**ELLEN MOORE** SPRINGFIELD, NEW HAMPSHIRE

**PREP:** 2¾ HOURS  **PROCESS:** 15 MIN.  **MAKES:** 6 PINTS

| | |
|---|---|
| 3 | cups sugar |
| 3 | cups cider vinegar |
| 2 | small lemons, thinly sliced and seeds removed |
| 1 | large onion, chopped |
| 1 | cup dried currants |
| ⅓ | cup minced fresh gingerroot |
| 2 | garlic cloves, minced |
| 1 | teaspoon ground allspice |
| 20 | large pears (about 6 pounds), peeled and chopped |

**1.** In a Dutch oven, combine the first eight ingredients. Bring to a boil over medium heat, stirring occasionally. Reduce heat; simmer, uncovered, for 15-20 minutes or until mixture becomes syrupy.

**2.** Stir in the pears. Return to a boil. Reduce heat; simmer, uncovered, for 1¾ hours or until the fruit is tender and the mixture has thickened, stirring occasionally.

**3.** Remove from the heat. Carefully ladle the hot mixture into hot 1-pint jars, leaving ½ in. headspace. Remove air bubbles; wipe rims and adjust lids. Process for 15 minutes in a boiling-water canner.

**Editor's Note:** *The processing time listed is for altitudes of 1,000 feet or less. For altitudes up to 3,000 feet, add 5 minutes; 6,000 feet, add 10 minutes; 8,000 feet, add 15 minutes; 10,000 feet, add 20 minutes.*

# Host a Canned Gift Exchange

## *Guests will relish the experience!*

Share your canned bounty with friends—and give them the chance to do the same. Here are tips from the Washington State Fruit Commission, the Northwest Cherry Growers and others on how to throw a preservation-themed party:

## Choose your canned gifts

From sweet jams and marmalades to tangy pickles, the sky's the limit. Want some new recipes to try? Consider Gingered Pear & Currant Chutney (left), Champagne Jelly (pg. 66), Giardiniera (pg. 63), Apricot & Maraschino Cherry Preserves (pg. 63), Honey Lemon Jelly (pg. 64), Spicy Bavarian Beer Mustard (pg. 65) and Pickled Sweet Onions (pg. 65).

## Send invitations

Give guests an idea of how many canned items to bring. To provide inspiration, let them know what foods of your own you'll be contributing to the gift exchange. Remind them to label their jars with the contents and canning date, and encourage them to bring a sturdy box, crate or laundry basket to make it easier to tote their treats home.

## Create enough space

Make sure you have plenty of empty counter or table space for setting out everyone's canned creations. Remember to leave enough room around jars to make it easy to read labels.

## Snack on canned treats

When planning the party menu, take a look at the preserved items in your pantry. Have extras? Feature them on your buffet table to give guests a taste of your garden-grown harvest during the event. For example, offer your signature salsa with chips, or spread jelly over cream cheese for topping crackers.

## Jam out!

Karaoke with a canning theme? Sure! Stir some of these tunes into your holiday playlist: *Cherry, Cherry* (Neil Diamond), *Blueberry Hill* (Chubby Checker), *I Heard It Through the Grapevine* (Marvin Gaye) and *Strawberry Fields Forever* (The Beatles).

## Get 'em crafting

For another fun party activity, gather the group for a canning-inspired craft project—Gift Card Snow Globes (pg. 64). They're fun and easy to make (with or without the gift cards inside)!

# Winter Wonderland Dinner Party

Celebrate winter's beauty with a dinner table trimmed in the icy blues, shiny silvers and snowy whites of the season. The elegant menu here will ensure a memorable occasion. For dessert, choose from the treats in the Simply Chocolate (pg. 111), Yuletide Pies & Tarts (pg. 127) and Sweet Sensations (pg. 143) chapters.

# Artichoke-Stuffed Beef Tenderloin

This bacon-topped roast is perfect for Christmas or any holiday. A big slice is almost a meal in itself!

—**JAMIE JONES** MADISON, GEORGIA

**PREP:** 30 MIN. **BAKE:** 40 MIN. + STANDING
**MAKES:** 10 SERVINGS

- 1 **medium onion, chopped**
- 3 **garlic cloves, minced**
- ¼ **cup butter, cubed**
- 1 **can (14 ounces) water-packed artichoke hearts, rinsed, drained and chopped**
- 2 **cans (6 ounces each) sliced mushrooms, drained**
- 1½ **cups chicken broth**
- 1 **package (6 ounces) stuffing mix**
- 1 **beef tenderloin roast (3 to 3½ pounds)**
- 4 **bacon strips, halved**

**1.** In a large skillet, saute the onion and garlic in the butter until tender. Stir in the artichokes, mushrooms and chicken broth. Bring to a boil. Remove from the heat. Stir in stuffing mix; cool slightly.

**2.** Cut a lengthwise slit down the center of the tenderloin to within ½ in. of the bottom. Open tenderloin so it lies flat. On each half, make another lengthwise slit down the center to within ½ in. of the bottom; open tenderloin and cover with plastic wrap. Flatten to ½-in. thickness. Remove plastic.

**3.** Spread stuffing mixture over meat. Roll up jelly-roll style, starting with a long side. Tie the roast at 2-in. intervals with kitchen string. Place on a rack in a shallow roasting pan; arrange bacon pieces over roast.

**4.** Bake at 425° for 40-50 minutes or until the meat reaches the desired doneness (for medium-rare, a meat thermometer should read 145°; medium, 160°; well-done, 170°). Let stand for 10 minutes before slicing.

## Stuffing the Tenderloin

Artichoke-Stuffed Beef Tenderloin (recipe at left) may look like a complicated entree but is actually easier to prepare than it appears. You'll need only 30 minutes of prep time before this succulent roast goes in the oven.

After stirring up the stuffing mix, use the simple how-to photos here as a guide for cutting and stuffing the tenderloin. In no time, you'll have a showstopping main course that's sure to win raves at your Christmas dinner table.

**1.** Cut a lengthwise slit down the center of the tenderloin to within ½ in. of the bottom.

**2.** Down the center of each half, make another lengthwise slit to within ½ in. of the bottom.

**3.** Cover the tenderloin with plastic wrap. Use a meat mallet to flatten the meat to ½-in. thickness.

**4.** Remove the plastic wrap. Spread the stuffing over the tenderloin, not quite to the edges.

**5.** After rolling up the tenderloin jelly-roll style, tie it at 2-in. intervals with kitchen string.

# Tropical Cooler

With only four ingredients, this festive punch is easy to stir up in 10 minutes. I served it at a party for my son, and guests liked the slightly tart flavor.

**—ROBIN WERNER**
BRUSH PRAIRIE, WASHINGTON

**PREP/TOTAL TIME:** 10 MIN.
**MAKES:** 12 SERVINGS (¾ CUP EACH)

- 1 bottle (32 ounces) cranberry juice, chilled
- 1 liter ginger ale, chilled
- 1 cup chilled tropical fruit punch
- 1 cup chilled orange juice

Just before serving, combine all ingredients in a punch bowl.

## Holiday Helper

Chill all punch ingredients before preparing the recipe so that you don't have to dilute it with ice to get it cold. Or consider garnishing a cold punch with an ice ring (which lasts longer than cubes). To make an ice ring, fill a ring mold with extra punch or punch ingredients and freeze until solid.

# Martini Cheese Dip

After tasting a delicious cheese dip at a get-together, I experimented at home and came up with my own version. For an extra-special touch, present it in a martini glass and add an olive garnish.

**—CRYSTAL BRUNS** ILIFF, COLORADO

**PREP:** 10 MIN. + CHILLING
**MAKES:** 1¼ CUPS

- 1 package (8 ounces) cream cheese, softened
- 1 tablespoon mayonnaise
- ¼ cup sliced green olives with pimientos, drained and chopped
- 2 to 3 tablespoons vodka
- 2 tablespoons olive juice
- ¼ teaspoon coarsely ground pepper
  Assorted fresh vegetables

In a large bowl, beat the cream cheese and mayonnaise until blended. Stir in the green olives, vodka, olive juice and pepper. Refrigerate for at least 2 hours. Spoon into a martini glass if desired. Serve with vegetables.

# Creamy Seafood Bisque

This deceptively simple bisque makes a memorable first course or even a casual meal with a salad or breadsticks. I top bowlfuls with shredded Parmesan cheese and sliced green onions.

**—WANDA ALLENDE** ORLANDO, FLORIDA

**PREP:** 25 MIN. **COOK:** 25 MIN.
**MAKES:** 8 SERVINGS (2½ QUARTS)

| | |
|---|---|
| ½ | cup butter, cubed |
| 1 | medium red onion, chopped |
| 1 | cup sliced fresh mushrooms |
| 2 | garlic cloves, minced |
| ½ | cup all-purpose flour |
| 1 | teaspoon salt |
| 1 | teaspoon coarsely ground pepper |
| 2 | tablespoons tomato paste |
| 1 | carton (32 ounces) chicken broth |
| 2 | cups whole baby clams, drained |
| ½ | pound uncooked medium shrimp, peeled and deveined |
| 2 | cups lump crabmeat, drained |
| 2 | cups heavy whipping cream |
| ½ | cup shredded Parmesan cheese |
| 2 | green onions, thinly sliced |

**1.** In a Dutch oven, heat the butter over medium-high heat. Add the red onion and mushrooms; saute for 4-5 minutes or until tender. Add the garlic; cook 1 minute longer. Stir in flour, salt and pepper until blended; add tomato paste. Gradually whisk in broth; bring to a boil. Reduce heat; cover and simmer for 5 minutes.

**2.** Add the clams and shrimp; return to a boil. Reduce the heat; simmer, uncovered, 5-10 minutes longer or until the shrimp turn pink, stirring occasionally. Stir in crab and cream; heat through (do not boil). Serve with cheese and green onions.

# Holiday Salad

When I plan holiday meals, I ask each family member for their requests. My daughter always wants a green salad with red apples, blue cheese, walnuts and a tangy dressing.

—**PAT SCHMELING** GERMANTOWN, WISCONSIN

**PREP:** 25 MIN. + CHILLING  **MAKES:** 12 SERVINGS

- ⅓ **cup white wine vinegar**
- 1 **tablespoon Dijon mustard**
- ¾ **teaspoon dill weed**
- ¾ **teaspoon ground nutmeg**
- ¼ **teaspoon salt**
- ¼ **teaspoon pepper**
- ¾ **cup olive oil**

- 4 **large Red Delicious apples, thinly sliced**
- ½ **cup crumbled blue cheese**
- ⅓ **cup walnut halves**
- 9 **cups torn romaine**
- 3 **cups chopped watercress (about 1½ bunches)**

**1.** In a small bowl, whisk the first six ingredients; gradually whisk in the oil until blended. In a large bowl, combine the apples, cheese, walnuts and 3 tablespoons dressing; toss to coat. Cover and refrigerate for up to 4 hours. Cover and refrigerate remaining dressing.

**2.** Just before serving, combine romaine and watercress in a large bowl; drizzle with the reserved dressing and toss to coat. Divide among 12 salad plates; top with the apple mixture.

## Orange-Glazed Baby Carrots

Here's a wonderful accompaniment to just about any entree, whether on a Christmas menu or not. The carrots are sauteed in an orange butter sauce with a unique blend of spices.

**—ANGELA BARTOW** CATO, WISCONSIN

**PREP/TOTAL TIME:** 30 MIN.
**MAKES:** 4 SERVINGS

| | |
|---|---|
| 1 | pound fresh baby carrots |
| 3 | tablespoons butter |
| 3 | tablespoons thawed orange juice concentrate |
| ¼ | teaspoon dried thyme |
| ¼ | teaspoon paprika |
| ¼ | teaspoon ground cumin |
| ⅛ | teaspoon salt |
| ⅛ | teaspoon pepper |

In a large skillet, saute the baby carrots in butter for 8 minutes. Stir in the remaining ingredients; cook 2 minutes longer. Reduce heat; cover and simmer for 8-10 minutes or until carrots are tender.

## Golden Crescents

Rolls made with store-bought dough just can't compare to the homemade kind. When my grandchildren take one of these slightly sweet, tender crescents from the basket, they say, "Grandma, you're the world's best cook." It makes my time in the kitchen worth the while!

**—BERTHA JOHNSON** INDIANAPOLIS, INDIANA

**PREP:** 25 MIN. + RISING  **BAKE:** 10 MIN.
**MAKES:** 2 DOZEN

| | |
|---|---|
| 2 | packages (¼ ounce each) active dry yeast |
| ¾ | cup warm water (110° to 115°) |
| ½ | cup sugar |
| 2 | eggs |
| ¼ | cup butter, softened |
| 2 | tablespoons shortening |
| 1 | teaspoon salt |
| 4 | to 4½ cups all-purpose flour |
| 2 | tablespoons melted butter plus additional as needed, divided |

**1.** In a large bowl, dissolve yeast in warm water. Add the sugar, eggs, softened butter, shortening, salt and 2 cups flour; beat until smooth. Add enough of the remaining flour to form a soft dough. Turn onto a floured surface; knead until smooth and elastic, about 6-8 minutes.
**2.** Place in a greased bowl, turning once to grease the top. Cover with plastic wrap and let rise in a warm place until doubled, about 1½ hours.
**3.** Punch dough down; divide in half. Roll each portion into a 12-in. circle. Brush each with 1 tablespoon melted butter and cut into 12 wedges. Roll up wedges from the wide end and place point side down 2 in. apart on greased baking sheets. Curve ends to form crescents. Cover and let rise until doubled, about 45 minutes.
**4.** Bake at 375° for 8-10 minutes or until golden. Brush with additional melted butter if desired.

# Farmhouse-Style Breakfast

Ring the dinner bell for a hearty, down-home breakfast during the holiday season. You'll satisfy even the biggest appetites at the table when you serve up delicious, filling dishes such as Sunday Brunch Casserole, Maple-Glazed Sausages, Caramel-Pecan Apple Slices and Bacon Cinnamon Buns. What a way to start the day!

# Sunday Brunch Casserole

My husband and sons frequently ask for this popular baked dish. But when making their request, they refer to it as "egg pie!" The cheesy casserole is nice enough for a holiday brunch yet satisfying enough for a weeknight dinner.
—**PATRICIA THROLSON** BECKER, MINNESOTA

**PREP:** 20 MIN.  **BAKE:** 35 MIN.  **MAKES:** 8 SERVINGS

- ½ pound sliced bacon, chopped
- ½ cup chopped onion
- ½ cup chopped green pepper
- 12 eggs, lightly beaten
- 1 cup 2% milk
- 1 teaspoon salt
- ½ teaspoon pepper
- ¼ teaspoon dill weed
- 1 package (16 ounces) frozen shredded hash brown potatoes, thawed
- 1 cup (4 ounces) shredded cheddar cheese

**1.** In a large skillet, cook bacon over medium heat until crisp. Remove with a slotted spoon; drain on paper towels. Discard drippings, reserving 2 tablespoons.

**2.** In the same skillet, saute the onion and green pepper in the reserved bacon drippings until tender; remove with a slotted spoon.

**3.** In a large bowl, whisk the eggs, milk and seasonings. Stir in the hash browns, cheddar cheese, onion mixture and bacon.

**4.** Transfer to a greased 13-in. x 9-in. baking dish. Bake, uncovered, at 350° for 35-45 minutes or until a knife inserted near the center comes out clean.

# Maple-Glazed Sausages

It's so easy to simmer up a sugar-and-spice syrup to coat a skillet full of breakfast sausages. The glazed links go well with French toast, omelettes, pancakes—just about anything.
—**TRUDIE HAGEN** ROGGEN, COLORADO

**PREP/TOTAL TIME:** 20 MIN.  **MAKES:** 10 SERVINGS

- 2 packages (6.4 ounces each) brown-and-serve sausage links
- 1 cup maple syrup
- ½ cup packed brown sugar
- 1 teaspoon ground cinnamon

In a large skillet, brown the sausage links. In a small bowl, combine the syrup, brown sugar and cinnamon; pour over sausages. Bring to a boil. Reduce heat; simmer, uncovered, until sausages are glazed.

# Salt & Pepper Shaker Crate

With this easy idea, a mini wood crate becomes a cute way to corral salt and pepper shakers. All you'll need to make it are acrylic craft paints and a few other supplies.

Select a 2½-in.-high crate or a size that suits your shakers. Lightly sand the crate and wipe away any dust.

Base-coat the crate with ivory paint, using as many coats as needed for complete coverage and letting it dry between coats. With a sponge brush, apply a crackle finish paint (such as One Step Crackle by DecoArt) following the manufacturer's instructions. Let it dry.

Mix equal parts brown and gold paint and use a flat brush to apply it over the crackle. Immediately wipe off the excess as you go, leaving it mainly in cracked areas. Repeat until the entire surface is covered. Let it dry.

Dip a dry flat brush in ivory paint, wipe off as much excess paint as possible and lightly dry-brush the entire crate. When it's dry, add your salt and pepper shakers.

# Glazed Cranberry Biscuits

My family loves biscuits for breakfast. One Sunday, I decided to make those golden goodies extra special by adding white baking chips, dried cranberries and a simple orange glaze.

**—LORI DANIELS** BEVERLY, WEST VIRGINIA

**PREP:** 30 MIN. **BAKE:** 15 MIN.
**MAKES:** ABOUT 1 DOZEN

- 2 **cups all-purpose flour**
- 2 **teaspoons baking powder**
- ½ **teaspoon salt**
- ½ **teaspoon grated orange peel**
- ½ **teaspoon ground cinnamon**
- ¼ **cup shortening**
- ¼ **cup cold butter**
- ¾ **cup 2% milk**
- ¼ **cup orange juice**
- 1 **cup dried cranberries**
- ½ **cup white baking chips**

**DRIZZLE**
- 1½ **cups confectioners' sugar**
- 2 **tablespoons orange juice**
- ¼ **teaspoon orange extract**

**1.** In a large bowl, combine the first five ingredients. Cut in shortening and butter until mixture resembles coarse crumbs. Stir in the milk and orange juice just until moistened. Stir in cranberries and baking chips.

**2.** Turn onto a lightly floured surface; knead gently 8-10 times. Pat or roll out to ¾-in. thickness; cut with a floured 2½-in. biscuit cutter.

**3.** Place 2 in. apart on a greased baking sheet. Bake at 400° for 12-16 minutes or until lightly browned. In a small bowl, combine confectioners' sugar, orange juice and extract; drizzle over biscuits. Serve warm.

## Caramel-Pecan Apple Slices

Here's a warm and comforting side dish for a winter brunch. Ready to enjoy in only 15 minutes, the apples are also good alongside a pork entree or spooned over vanilla ice cream.
—**CAROL GILLESPIE** CHAMBERSBURG, PENNSYLVANIA

**PREP/TOTAL TIME:** 15 MIN.  **MAKES:** 6 SERVINGS

- ⅓ **cup packed brown sugar**
- 2 **tablespoons butter**
- 2 **large apples, cut into ½-inch slices**
- ¼ **cup chopped pecans, toasted**

1. In a large skillet, cook and stir the brown sugar and butter over medium heat until the sugar is dissolved. Add the apples; cook, uncovered, over medium heat for 5-7 minutes or until tender, stirring occasionally. Stir in pecans. Serve warm.

**Editor's Note:** *To toast nuts, spread in a 15-in. x 10-in. x 1-in. baking pan. Bake at 350° for 5-10 minutes or until lightly browned, stirring occasionally. Or, spread in a dry nonstick skillet and heat over low heat until lightly browned, stirring occasionally.*

## Creamy Caramel Mocha

Indulge in a coffeehouse-quality drink at Christmastime or any time at all. Topped with whipped cream and a decadent butterscotch-caramel drizzle, this chocolaty treat will perk up even the sleepiest person at the table.
—**TASTE OF HOME TEST KITCHEN**

**PREP/TOTAL TIME:** 20 MIN.  **MAKES:** 6 SERVINGS

- ½ **cup heavy whipping cream**
- 1 **tablespoon confectioners' sugar**
- 1 **teaspoon vanilla extract, divided**
- ¼ **cup Dutch baking cocoa**
- 1½ **cups half-and-half cream**
- 4 **cups hot strong brewed coffee**
- ½ **cup caramel flavoring syrup**
  **Butterscotch-caramel ice cream topping**

1. In a small bowl, beat the whipping cream until it begins to thicken. Add the confectioners' sugar and ½ teaspoon vanilla; beat until stiff peaks form.
2. In a large saucepan over medium heat, whisk the cocoa and half-and-half cream until smooth. Heat until bubbles form around sides of pan. Whisk in coffee, caramel syrup and remaining vanilla. Top servings with whipped cream; drizzle with butterscotch topping.

**Editor's Note:** *This recipe was tested with Torani brand flavoring syrup. Look for it in the coffee section.*

## Bacon Cinnamon Buns

I absolutely love bacon! Adding it to traditional cinnamon buns creates a sweet and savory, finger-licking-good treat.
—**DANIELLE WILLIAMS** NEWPORT, RHODE ISLAND

**PREP:** 50 MIN. + RISING  **BAKE:** 20 MIN.  **MAKES:** 1 DOZEN

- 1 **package (¼ ounce) active dry yeast**
- 1 **cup warm whole milk (110° to 115°)**
- ¼ **cup sugar**
- ¼ **cup butter, softened**
- 1 **egg yolk**
- 1½ **teaspoons vanilla extract**
- ¾ **teaspoon salt**
- ½ **teaspoon ground nutmeg**
- 2¾ **to 3 cups all-purpose flour**

**FILLING**
- 5 **bacon strips, chopped**
- ½ **cup packed brown sugar**
- 1 **tablespoon maple syrup**
- 2 **teaspoons ground cinnamon**
- ½ **teaspoon ground nutmeg**

**ICING**
- 2 **cups confectioners' sugar**
- ½ **cup butter, softened**
- 2 **tablespoons whole milk**
- 1 **tablespoon maple syrup**

**1.** In a small bowl, dissolve yeast in warm milk. In a large bowl, combine the sugar, butter, egg yolk, vanilla, salt, nutmeg, yeast mixture and 1 cup flour; beat on medium speed for 2 minutes. Stir in enough remaining flour to form a soft dough (dough will be sticky).

**2.** Turn dough onto a floured surface; knead until smooth and elastic, about 6-8 minutes.

**3.** Place dough in a greased bowl, turning once to grease the top. Cover with plastic wrap and let rise in a warm place until doubled, about 1 hour.

**4.** In a small skillet, cook bacon over medium heat until crisp. Remove with a slotted spoon; drain on paper towels. Discard drippings, reserving 2 tablespoons.

**5.** Wipe skillet clean if necessary. Combine brown sugar, syrup, cinnamon, nutmeg and reserved bacon drippings in skillet; cook and stir over medium heat until blended. Cool to room temperature.

**6.** Punch the dough down. Roll into an 18-in. x 12-in. rectangle. Spread bacon mixture to within ½ in. of edges. Roll up jelly-roll style, starting with a short side; pinch seams to seal. Cut into 12 rolls.

**7.** Place the rolls, cut side down, in a greased 13-in. x 9-in. baking dish. Cover and let rise in a warm place until doubled, about 45 minutes. Bake at 400° for 18-20 minutes or until golden brown.

**8.** In a small bowl, beat icing ingredients until smooth. Spread over warm rolls. Serve warm.

81

89

82

*potluck*
GATHERINGS

# Cinnamon Apple-Nut Salad

This sensational salad boasts so much color, taste and texture, you'll want to enjoy it year-round. The cinnamon in the dressing is the perfect complement to the crisp apples.

**—JESSICA LIN** WEST HARTFORD, CONNECTICUT

**PREP:** 25 MIN. + CHILLING  **MAKES:** 12 SERVINGS

- 3  **medium red apples, chopped**
- 3  **medium Granny Smith apples, chopped**
- 1  **cup chopped pecans, toasted**
- ½  **cup dried cranberries**
- 2  **green onions, chopped**
- ¼  **cup plus 1½ teaspoons mayonnaise**
- 3  **tablespoons cider vinegar**
- 3  **tablespoons honey**
- 1  **tablespoon plus 1½ teaspoons orange juice**
- 1  **tablespoon grated orange peel**
- ¾  **teaspoon ground cinnamon**
- ¼  **teaspoon pepper**

In a large bowl, combine the apples, pecans, cranberries and green onions. In a small bowl, whisk the remaining ingredients until blended. Pour over apple mixture; toss to coat. Refrigerate for 1 hour before serving.

**Editor's Note:** *To toast nuts, spread them in a 15-in. x 10-in. x 1-in. baking pan. Bake at 350° for 5-10 minutes or until lightly browned, stirring occasionally. Or, spread in a dry nonstick skillet and heat over low heat until lightly browned, stirring occasionally.*

## Cheese Soup with a Twist

One of my favorite childhood memories is of my Aunt Claire ladling up big bowlfuls of her famous cheese-and-veggie soup for us. She would serve each hearty, bacon-topped helping with a slice of warm buttered bread. Her recipe has become a must-have item on our annual holiday buffet.

**—ROB FEEZOR** ALEXANDRIA, VIRGINIA

**PREP/TOTAL TIME:** 30 MIN. **MAKES:** 8 SERVINGS (2 QUARTS)

| | |
|---|---|
| 5 | bacon strips, diced |
| ½ | cup chopped celery |
| ½ | cup chopped onion |
| ½ | cup chopped green pepper |
| ¼ | cup all-purpose flour |
| ¼ | teaspoon coarsely ground pepper |
| 4 | cups reduced-sodium chicken broth |
| 2 | cups milk |
| 3 | cups cubed process cheese (Velveeta) |
| ½ | cup sliced pimiento-stuffed olives |
| ½ | cup grated carrots |
| 2 | tablespoons sherry, optional |
| | Minced fresh parsley |

**1.** In a Dutch oven, cook bacon over medium heat until crisp. Using a slotted spoon, remove to paper towels to drain. In the drippings, saute the celery, onion and green pepper until tender.

**2.** Stir in flour and pepper until blended; gradually add chicken broth and milk. Bring to a boil; cook and stir for 1-2 minutes or until thickened.

**3.** Add the cheese, olives, carrots and sherry if desired; cook and stir until cheese is melted. Sprinkle servings with parsley and bacon.

## Hot Antipasto

My husband's family always requests this baked Italian-style appetizer for our Christmas Eve potluck. Everyone loves that the antipasto has so much to nibble on, from sausages and mushrooms to cherry peppers and olives.

**—SUSAN LEIGHTON** PORTLAND, CONNECTICUT

**PREP:** 25 MIN. **BAKE:** 25 MIN.
**MAKES:** 28 SERVINGS (½ CUP EACH)

| | |
|---|---|
| 1 | pound sweet Italian sausage links, cut into ½-inch slices |
| 1 | pound hot Italian sausage links, cut into ½-inch slices |
| 1 | jar (16 ounces) pepperoncini, drained |
| 1 | jar (16 ounces) pickled hot cherry peppers, drained |
| 1 | can (16 ounces) kidney beans, rinsed and drained |
| 1 | can (15 ounces) garbanzo beans or chickpeas, rinsed and drained |
| 1 | jar (8 ounces) marinated whole mushrooms, drained |
| 1 | jar (7½ ounces) marinated quartered artichoke hearts, drained |
| 1 | jar (7 ounces) pimiento-stuffed olives, drained |
| 1 | can (6 ounces) pitted ripe olives, drained |
| 1 | package (3½ ounces) sliced pepperoni |
| 2 | cups (8 ounces) shredded Italian cheese blend |

**1.** In a large skillet, cook sausages over medium heat until no longer pink; drain and place in a large bowl.

**2.** Stir in pepperoncinis, peppers, beans, mushrooms, artichokes, olives and pepperoni. Transfer to an ungreased 13-in. x 9-in. baking dish (dish will be full).

**3.** Bake, uncovered, at 350° for 20 minutes. Sprinkle with cheese. Bake 4-5 minutes longer or until cheese is melted.

**Editor's Note:** *Look for pepperoncinis (pickled peppers) in the pickle and olive section of your grocery store.*

1. Cut roast into thirds. Combine the ground coffee, salt and pepper; rub over roast. In a large skillet, brown meat in oil on all sides; drain.

2. Transfer meat to a 5-qt. slow cooker. Add celery, carrot, onion, chicken stock, brewed coffee, parsley, coriander seeds, cumin, peppercorns, cinnamon stick and bay leaf; pour over roast.

3. Cover and cook on low for 8-10 hours or until meat is tender. When cool enough to handle, shred meat. Skim fat from cooking juices. Strain cooking juices, discarding the vegetables, cinnamon stick and bay leaf.

4. Spoon about ½ cup pulled pork onto each bun; top with cheese. Serve with cooking juices.

## Chicken and Olive Mole Casserole

Looking for a potluck dish that has a little kick to it? Try my Southwestern chicken casserole. The mole sauce lends an authentic touch, and guests are always pleasantly surprised to detect a hint of sweetness from chocolate.

—**BARBARA WHITE** LIVINGSTON, TEXAS

**PREP:** 50 MIN.  **BAKE:** 40 MIN. + STANDING  **MAKES:** 8 SERVINGS

| | |
|---|---|
| 2 | large onions, finely chopped, divided |
| 3 | tablespoons olive oil |
| 3 | garlic cloves, minced |
| 1 | teaspoon salt |
| 1 | teaspoon dried oregano |
| 1 | teaspoon ground cumin |
| ¼ | teaspoon ground cinnamon |
| 5 | tablespoons chili powder |
| 3 | tablespoons all-purpose flour |
| 4½ | cups reduced-sodium chicken broth |
| ½ | ounce semisweet chocolate, coarsely chopped |
| 6 | cups shredded cooked chicken |
| 12 | corn tortillas (6 inches), warmed |
| 1 | cup sliced pimiento-stuffed olives |
| 4 | cups (16 ounces) shredded Monterey Jack cheese |

1. In a large saucepan, saute 1 cup onion in oil until tender. Reduce heat to low. Add the garlic, salt, oregano, cumin and cinnamon; cover and cook for 10 minutes. Stir in chili powder and flour until blended. Gradually stir in chicken broth. Bring to a boil. Cook until the mixture is reduced to 3 cups, about 35 minutes. Remove from the heat; stir in chocolate.

2. In a large bowl, combine the chicken and ½ cup sauce mixture. Spread ½ cup sauce mixture into a greased 13-in. x 9-in. baking dish. Layer with half of the tortillas, chicken mixture, remaining onion and olives; top with 1 cup sauce and 2 cups cheese. Repeat layers.

3. Cover and bake at 375° for 30 minutes. Uncover; bake 10-15 minutes longer or until cheese is melted. Let stand for 10 minutes before serving.

## Coffee-Braised Pulled Pork Sandwiches

Coffee adds such a deep, robust flavor to meat. This recipe is a cinch to get started in the morning before I leave for work. By the time I get home, the pork is tender and delicious.

—**JACQUELYNN SANDERS** BURNSVILLE, MINNESOTA

**PREP:** 30 MIN.  **COOK:** 8 HOURS  **MAKES:** 10 SERVINGS

| | |
|---|---|
| 1 | boneless pork shoulder butt roast (3 to 3½ pounds) |
| ⅓ | cup ground coffee beans |
| ½ | teaspoon salt |
| ½ | teaspoon pepper |
| 2 | tablespoons canola oil |
| 2 | celery ribs, chopped |
| 1 | large carrot, chopped |
| 1 | medium onion, chopped |
| 2 | cups chicken stock |
| 1½ | cups strong brewed coffee |
| 2 | tablespoons minced fresh parsley |
| 1 | teaspoon coriander seeds |
| 1 | teaspoon ground cumin |
| 1 | teaspoon whole peppercorns, crushed |
| 1 | cinnamon stick (3 inches) |
| 1 | bay leaf |
| 10 | hoagie or kaiser buns, split |
| 10 | slices pepper jack cheese |

# Five-Cheese Spinach & Artichoke Dip

Whenever I'm invited to a party, the host asks me to bring my hot spinach-and-artichoke dip loaded with mozzarella, feta, Asiago, provolone and cream cheeses. I serve it straight from the slow cooker, so setup and cleanup are a breeze.

**—NOELLE MYERS** GRAND FORKS, NORTH DAKOTA

**PREP:** 20 MIN.  **COOK:** 2½ HOURS
**MAKES:** 16 SERVINGS (¼ CUP EACH)

- 1  jar (12 ounces) roasted sweet red peppers
- 1  jar (6½ ounces) marinated quartered artichoke hearts
- 1  package (10 ounces) frozen chopped spinach, thawed and squeezed dry
- 8  ounces fresh mozzarella cheese, cubed
- 1½  cups (6 ounces) shredded Asiago cheese
- 2  packages (3 ounces each) cream cheese, softened and cubed
- 1  cup (4 ounces) crumbled feta cheese
- ⅓  cup shredded provolone cheese
- ⅓  cup minced fresh basil
- ¼  cup finely chopped red onion
- 2  tablespoons mayonnaise
- 2  garlic cloves, minced
   Assorted crackers

**1.** Drain the peppers, reserving 1 tablespoon liquid; chop peppers. Drain artichokes, reserving 2 tablespoons liquid; coarsely chop artichokes.

**2.** In a 3-qt. slow cooker coated with cooking spray, combine the spinach, cheeses, basil, onion, mayonnaise, garlic, artichoke hearts and peppers. Stir in the reserved pepper and artichoke liquids. Cook, covered, on high for 2 hours. Stir the dip; cook, covered, 30-60 minutes longer. Stir before serving; serve with crackers.

## Peanut Butter Brownie Pie

Love the combination of chocolate and peanut butter? Here's a luscious way to indulge in that ever-popular pairing. If you like, make the pie a day ahead and store it in the refrigerator.
—NANCY DONATO UNIONTOWN, OHIO

**PREP:** 20 MIN. **BAKE:** 20 MIN. + CHILLING **MAKES:** 10 SERVINGS

- 1 package (10¼ ounces) fudge brownie mix (8-inch square pan size)
- ¼ cup water
- ¼ cup canola oil
- 1 egg

**FILLING**
- 1 package (3 ounces) cook-and-serve vanilla pudding mix
- 1¾ cups 2% milk
- ⅓ cup creamy peanut butter
- 1 carton (8 ounces) frozen whipped topping, thawed
- 2 tablespoons chopped salted peanuts

**1.** In a large bowl, combine the fudge brownie mix, water, oil and egg until blended. Spread the batter into a greased 9-in. pie plate.

**2.** Bake at 325° for 12 minutes. Using a metal spatula, spread batter up the sides of pie plate. Bake 8-13 minutes longer or until toothpick inserted near the center comes out clean. Cool completely on a wire rack.

**3.** Meanwhile, in a small saucepan, combine the pudding mix and milk. Cook and stir over medium heat until the mixture comes to a boil. Cook and stir 1-2 minutes longer or until thickened. Remove from the heat; stir in peanut butter until blended. Transfer to a small bowl. Cover and refrigerate until chilled.

**4.** Pour the filling into the brownie crust. Spread with whipped topping; sprinkle with peanuts. Chill for 2 hours before serving.

**Editor's Notes:** *If you prefer, use instant pudding for the cooked pudding. Beat the milk, pudding mix and peanut butter together for 1 minute; let stand for 5 minutes. Pour into the cooled brownie crust and proceed as recipe directs.*

## Maple Brandy Punch

Reminiscent of an old-fashioned brandy punch, this smooth, maple-infused beverage is sure to liven up yuletide events. Pour it over sliced apples and lemon for a festive touch.
—TASTE OF HOME TEST KITCHEN

**PREP:** 20 MIN. + COOLING **MAKES:** 20 SERVINGS

- 1⅓ cups maple syrup
- 2 cups apple brandy
- 2 cups Cognac
- 2 cups spiced rum
- ¼ cup lemon juice
- 2 teaspoons bitters
- 2 bottles (1 liter each) carbonated water, chilled
  Ice cubes
  Thinly sliced apples and lemon twists

**1.** Place syrup in a small saucepan. Bring to a boil. Reduce heat; simmer, uncovered, for 5 minutes. Remove from the heat and set aside to cool.

**2.** Combine the brandy, Cognac, rum, lemon juice and bitters in a punch bowl; stir in the maple reduction. Add the carbonated water. Serve over ice with apple slices and lemon twists.

### Holiday Helper

My pumpkin pie is often requested for potlucks, so I've gotten in the habit of doubling the recipe when I'm preparing it for my family. I wrap the extra baked pies three times in plastic wrap and once in aluminum foil, then pop them in the freezer.

The wrapping makes transporting the frozen pies easy. At the potluck, I simply unwrap and thaw them for a convenient and crowd-pleasing dessert.

—ELISABETH W. SPENCER, INDIANA

# Riesling and Swiss Cheese Fondue

Cheese lovers can't get enough of this rich fondue accented with riesling wine. It makes a savory, no-fuss appetizer for the holidays. Try sliced smoked sausage and bread cubes as dippers.

**—ANGELA SPENGLER** CLOVIS, NEW MEXICO

**PREP/TOTAL TIME:** 20 MIN.
**MAKES:** 3 CUPS

- 4 **cups (16 ounces) shredded Swiss cheese**
- 2 **tablespoons all-purpose flour**
- 1 **cup dry riesling wine**
- 1 **garlic clove, minced**
- 2 **tablespoons sherry**
- 1 **tablespoon lemon juice**
- ⅛ **teaspoon ground nutmeg**
  **Sliced smoked sausage and cubed French bread baguette**

**1.** In a large bowl, combine the cheese and flour. In a large saucepan, heat wine and garlic over medium heat until bubbles form around sides of pan (do not boil).

**2.** Reduce the heat to medium-low. Add ½ cup cheese mixture; stir constantly until almost completely melted. Continue adding the cheese mixture, ½ cup at a time, allowing cheese to melt almost completely between additions. Stir in the sherry, lemon juice and nutmeg.

**3.** Transfer to a heated fondue pot; keep fondue bubbling gently. Serve with sausage and bread cubes. If fondue becomes too thick, stir in a little additional wine.

## Portobello Beef Burgundy

Rely on the convenience of your slow cooker for a main dish that has hearty, stick-to-your-ribs goodness. Tender cubes of beef and sliced portobello mushrooms are draped in a rich Burgundy sauce and served over noodles. It's guaranteed to have potluck guests going back for seconds!

—**MELISSA GALINAT** LAKELAND, FLORIDA

**PREP:** 30 MIN.  **COOK:** 7½ HOURS  **MAKES:** 6 SERVINGS

- ¼ **cup all-purpose flour**
- ½ **teaspoon salt**
- ½ **teaspoon seasoned salt**
- 1½ **teaspoons minced fresh thyme or ½ teaspoon dried thyme**
- ¾ **teaspoon minced fresh marjoram or ¼ teaspoon dried thyme**
- ½ **teaspoon pepper**
- 2 **pounds beef sirloin tip steak, cubed**
- 2 **bacon strips, diced**
- 3 **tablespoons canola oil**
- 1 **garlic clove, minced**
- 1 **cup Burgundy wine or beef broth**
- 1 **teaspoon beef bouillon granules**
- 1 **pound sliced baby portobello mushrooms**
  **Hot cooked noodles, optional**

**1.** In a large resealable plastic bag, combine the first six ingredients. Add the beef, a few pieces at a time, and shake to coat.
**2.** In a large skillet, cook the bacon over medium heat until crisp. Remove to paper towels with a slotted spoon; drain. In the same skillet, brown the beef in oil in batches, adding the garlic to the last batch; cook 1-2 minutes longer. Drain.
**3.** Transfer to a 4-qt. slow cooker. Add wine to skillet, stirring to loosen browned bits from pan. Add bouillon; bring to a boil. Stir into slow cooker. Stir in reserved bacon. Cover and cook on low for 7-9 hours or until meat is tender.
**4.** Stir in portobello mushrooms. Cover and cook on high 30-45 minutes longer or until mushrooms are tender and sauce is slightly thickened. Serve with noodles if desired.

## Crowd-Pleasing Baked Ziti

This zippy ziti casserole gets a little kick from crushed red pepper flakes. Feel free to omit them—or take the heat up a notch by using hot Italian sausage instead of sweet.

—**GERALDINE SAUCIER** ALBUQUERQUE, NEW MEXICO

**PREP:** 1¾ HOURS  **COOK:** 40 MIN.  **MAKES:** 12 SERVINGS

- ½ **pound ground beef**
- ½ **pound bulk Italian sausage**
- 1 **medium onion, chopped**
- 2 **garlic cloves, minced**
- 1 **can (28 ounces) crushed tomatoes**
- 1 **can (15 ounces) tomato sauce**
- 1 **bay leaf**
- 1 **tablespoon Italian seasoning**
- 1 **teaspoon dried basil**
- ½ **teaspoon sugar**
- ½ **teaspoon salt**
- ½ **teaspoon crushed red pepper flakes**
- ½ **teaspoon pepper**
- 1 **package (16 ounces) ziti or small tube pasta**
- 2 **cups (8 ounces) shredded part-skim mozzarella cheese**
- ½ **cup grated Romano cheese**
- ½ **cup grated Parmesan cheese**
- 1 **cup ricotta cheese**

**1.** In a large saucepan, cook the beef, sausage, onion and garlic over medium heat until the meat is no longer pink; drain. Stir in the tomatoes, tomato sauce, bay leaf, Italian seasoning, basil, sugar, salt, pepper flakes and pepper.
**2.** Bring to a boil. Reduce heat; cover and simmer for 1 hour, stirring occasionally. Uncover; simmer 15-30 minutes longer or until sauce reaches desired thickness. Discard bay leaf. Cool.
**3.** Meanwhile, cook the pasta according to the package directions; drain. In a large bowl, combine 1 cup sauce mixture, 1 cup mozzarella cheese, ¼ cup Romano cheese, ¼ cup Parmesan cheese and pasta.
**4.** Spread 1½ cups sauce mixture into a greased 13-in. x 9-in. baking dish. Dot with ½ cup ricotta cheese. Top with pasta mixture. Pour remaining sauce mixture over the top. Dot with remaining ricotta cheese. Sprinkle with remaining mozzarella, Romano and Parmesan cheeses. Cover and bake at 350° for 20 minutes. Uncover; bake 20-25 minutes longer or until bubbly.

# Curry Potato Gratin

I wanted to spice up a potato gratin dish, and curry did the trick. It gives cheesy, golden-brown spuds an extra bit of zip.

**—TEDDY DEVICO** WARREN, NEW JERSEY

**PREP:** 30 MIN.  **BAKE:** 25 MIN. + STANDING
**MAKES:** 8 SERVINGS

|   |   |
|---|---|
| 2 | pounds Yukon Gold potatoes, peeled and quartered |
| 1 | large sweet onion, finely chopped |
| 2 | tablespoons butter |
| 4 | garlic cloves, minced |
| 2 | cups heavy whipping cream |
| 5 | bay leaves |
| 1 | tablespoon curry powder |
| ½ | teaspoon salt |
| ½ | teaspoon pepper |
| ⅛ | teaspoon ground nutmeg |
| 1 | cup grated Parmesan cheese, divided |
| 2 | teaspoons minced fresh thyme |

**1.** In a food processor fitted with the slicing blade, slice potatoes; set aside. In a Dutch oven, saute onion in butter until tender. Add garlic; cook 1 minute longer. Add cream, bay leaves, curry, salt, pepper, nutmeg and potatoes. Bring to a boil. Reduce heat; simmer, uncovered, for 8-10 minutes or until potatoes are almost tender. Discard bay leaves; stir in ¾ cup cheese and thyme.

**2.** Transfer to a greased 13-in. x 9-in. baking dish. Sprinkle with remaining cheese. Bake, uncovered, at 400° for 25-30 minutes or until golden brown and potatoes are tender. Let stand for 10 minutes before serving.

## Potluck Carrier Wrap

Create a simple but convenient carrier for toting your potluck dish. Just lay a large cloth napkin flat and set the dish on top so that each point of the napkin can be brought up over one side of the dish. Then knot these opposite ends at the top to form a handle.

## Cherry Cobbler Bars

Here's old-fashioned comfort food at its best! A twist on a classic dessert, this recipe transforms cherry cobbler into easy-to-serve, easy-to-eat bars that are perfect for potlucks. The ruby-red fruit peeking out from under the topping makes a cheery addition to a Christmastime spread.

—**MARY BOGE** RED BOILING SPRINGS, TENNESSEE

**PREP:** 20 MIN. **BAKE:** 30 MIN. + COOLING **MAKES:** 2 DOZEN

- 1 **cup butter, softened**
- 1¾ **cups sugar**
- 4 **eggs**
- 1 **teaspoon vanilla extract**
- 3 **cups all-purpose flour**
- 1½ **teaspoons baking powder**
- ¼ **teaspoon salt**
- 1 **can (21 ounces) cherry pie filling**

**ICING**

- ½ **cup confectioners' sugar**
- 1 **tablespoon milk**
- ⅛ **teaspoon vanilla extract**

**1.** In a large bowl, cream butter and sugar. Add eggs, one at a time, beating well after each addition. Stir in vanilla. Combine the flour, baking powder and salt; add to the creamed mixture.

**2.** Spread 3 cups batter into an ungreased 15-in. x 10-in. x 1-in. baking pan. Spread the pie filling over batter. Drop remaining batter by teaspoonfuls over top.

**3.** Bake at 350° for 30-35 minutes or until a toothpick inserted near the center comes out clean. Cool on a wire rack. Combine the confectioners' sugar, milk and vanilla; stir until smooth. Drizzle over bars.

## Simple Italian Pasta Salad

A colorful pasta salad always gets lots of attention on a buffet table. I toss in artichokes, sun-dried tomatoes, pepperoni and three kinds of cheese for a hearty, Italian-style medley.

—**JOANNE WRIGHT** NILES, MICHIGAN

**PREP/TOTAL TIME:** 25 MIN.
**MAKES:** 12 SERVINGS (¾ CUP EACH)

- 1 **package (16 ounces) tricolor spiral pasta**
- 1 **small onion, chopped**
- 2 **teaspoons olive oil**
- 1 **garlic clove, minced**
- 1 **jar (7½ ounces) marinated quartered artichoke hearts**
- 1 **jar (7 ounces) oil-packed sun-dried tomatoes**
- ½ **pound fresh mozzarella cheese, cubed**
- 1½ **cups (6 ounces) crumbled feta cheese**
- ½ **cup shredded Parmesan cheese**
- ¼ **cup sliced pepperoni, chopped**
- 2 **tablespoons minced fresh basil or 2 teaspoons dried basil**
- 1 **teaspoon minced fresh oregano or ½ teaspoon dried oregano**

**1.** Cook the pasta according to the package directions. Meanwhile, in a small skillet, saute the onion in oil until tender. Add garlic; cook 1 minute longer. Set aside.

**2.** Drain the artichoke hearts and sun-dried tomatoes, reserving the liquids. Chop the artichokes and tomatoes; set aside.

**3.** Drain the pasta. In a large bowl, combine pasta, cheeses, pepperoni, basil, oregano, onion mixture, artichokes and tomatoes. In a small bowl, combine the reserved liquids. Drizzle over the salad and toss to coat. Chill until serving.

## Slow-Cooked Calico Beans

My sister-in-law gave me her recipe for meaty, slow-cooked beans. They're on the menu at all of our family events—by popular demand! The combination of ground beef and bacon creates a satisfying side that complements many main courses, from holiday roasts and steaks to grilled burgers and hot dogs.

**—DONNA ADAM** PERTH, ONTARIO

**PREP:** 30 MIN. **COOK:** 6 HOURS
**MAKES:** 10 SERVINGS

- 1 **pound ground beef**
- 2 **cans (16 ounces each) baked beans**
- 1 **can (16 ounces) kidney beans, rinsed and drained**
- 1 **can (15 ounces) white kidney or cannellini beans, rinsed and drained**
- 1 **can (20 ounces) unsweetened crushed pineapple, drained**
- 1 **medium onion, finely chopped**
- ½ **cup packed brown sugar**
- ½ **cup ketchup**
- 2 **tablespoons cider vinegar**
- 1 **tablespoon Dijon mustard**
- ½ **pound bacon strips, cooked and crumbled**

**1.** In a large skillet, cook the beef over medium heat until no longer pink; drain. Transfer to a 4-qt. slow cooker. Add the beans, pineapple, onion, brown sugar, ketchup, cider vinegar and mustard.
**2.** Cover and cook on low 6-8 hours or until heated through. Just before serving, stir in bacon.

## Dutch Apple Pie Tartlets

These miniature apple-pie pastries make a delightful addition to a buffet or treat platter. Using convenient frozen phyllo shells, they go together in only 15 minutes. Dust the tartlets with a little confectioners' sugar after baking for an extra-special presentation.

**—MARY ANN LEE** CLIFTON PARK, NEW YORK

**PREP:** 15 MIN. **BAKE:** 20 MIN.
**MAKES:** 2½ DOZEN

- 1 **cup finely chopped peeled apple**
- ¼ **cup lemon curd**
- 2 **packages (1.9 ounces each) frozen miniature phyllo tart shells**

**TOPPING**
- ½ **cup all-purpose flour**
- 3 **tablespoons sugar**
- ½ **teaspoon ground cinnamon**
- ¼ **cup cold butter**
  **Confectioners' sugar**

**1.** In a small bowl, combine apples and lemon curd. Spoon into tart shells.
**2.** In another bowl, combine the flour, sugar and cinnamon; cut in butter until mixture resembles fine crumbs. Spoon over apple mixture. Place on an ungreased baking sheet.
**3.** Bake at 350° for 18-20 minutes or until golden brown. Cool on wire racks for 5 minutes. Dust with confectioners' sugar. Serve warm or at room temperature. Refrigerate leftovers.

# Italian Pineapple Trifle

Every year for our family's Christmas Eve celebration, my grandmother made a rich, decadent pineapple trifle. Now, I fix it myself to carry on the tradition. The easy, no-bake dessert is tangy and refreshing after a hearty meal.

**—ANN-MARIE MILANO**
MILTON, MASSACHUSETTS

**PREP:** 30 MIN. + CHILLING
**MAKES:** 16 SERVINGS

- 1 **carton (15 ounces) ricotta cheese**
- 2 **packages (one 8 ounces, one 3 ounces) cream cheese, softened**
- ¾ **cup sugar**
- 2 **teaspoons vanilla extract, divided**
- 2 **cups heavy whipping cream**
- 2 **cans (8 ounces each) unsweetened crushed pineapple, drained**
- 1 **can (15¾ ounces) lemon pie filling**
- 3 **packages (3 ounces each) ladyfingers, split**

**1.** In a small bowl, beat the ricotta, cream cheese, sugar and 1 tsp. vanilla until fluffy. In a large bowl, whip the heavy cream until stiff peaks form; fold into ricotta mixture.

**2.** In another bowl, combine the pineapple, pie filling and remaining vanilla. In a 3-qt. trifle bowl or glass serving bowl, arrange two packages of ladyfingers over the bottom and up the sides.

**3.** Layer a third of the ricotta mixture, a third of the pineapple mixture and half of the remaining ladyfingers. Repeat layers once. Layer the remaining ricotta and pineapple mixtures. Cover and refrigerate several hours or overnight.

# Mushroom and Bacon Cheesecake

My family loves anything that has cream cheese, so I knew a savory cheesecake appetizer would be a hit. Add mushrooms, bacon and fresh parsley on top for a hearty garnish.

—**MACEY ALLEN** GREEN FOREST, ARKANSAS

**PREP:** 50 MIN.  **BAKE:** 55 MIN. + CHILLING
**MAKES:** 16 SERVINGS

- 1¾ **cups soft bread crumbs**
- 1 **cup grated Parmesan cheese**
- 6 **tablespoons butter, melted**

**FILLING**
- 1 **cup finely chopped onion**
- 1 **cup finely chopped sweet red pepper**
- 1 **tablespoon olive oil**
- 4 **cups assorted chopped fresh mushrooms**
- 3 **packages (8 ounces each) cream cheese, softened**
- 1 **teaspoon salt**
- 1 **teaspoon pepper**
- ½ **cup sour cream**
- 4 **eggs, lightly beaten**
- 12 **bacon strips, cooked and crumbled**
- 1 **cup (4 ounces) crumbled feta cheese**
- ½ **cup minced fresh parsley**
  **Roasted sliced mushrooms, fresh parsley and additional cooked bacon strips, optional**
  **Assorted crackers**

**1.** Place a greased 9-in. springform pan on a double thickness of heavy-duty foil (about 18 in. square). Securely wrap foil around pan.
**2.** In a small bowl, combine the bread crumbs, Parmesan cheese and butter. Press onto the bottom of springform pan. Place pan on a baking sheet. Bake at 350° for 10-15 minutes or until golden brown. Cool on a wire rack.
**3.** Meanwhile, in a large skillet, saute the onion and red pepper in oil for 2 minutes. Add the mushrooms; cook and stir for 10 minutes or until the liquid has evaporated. Set aside to cool.
**4.** In a large bowl, beat the cream cheese, salt and pepper until light and fluffy. Beat in sour cream. Add eggs; beat on low speed just until combined. Fold in the bacon, feta cheese, parsley and mushroom mixture. Pour into crust. Place springform pan in a large baking pan; add 1 in. of hot water to larger pan.
**5.** Bake at 350° for 55-65 minutes or until center is just set and top appears dull. Remove springform pan from water bath. Cool on a wire rack for 10 minutes. Carefully run a knife around edge of pan to loosen; cool 1 hour longer. Refrigerate overnight.
**6.** Remove sides of pan. Top with mushrooms, parsley and additional bacon if desired. Serve with crackers.

# Sweet & Salty Cranberry Bars

Loaded with sweet and salty ingredients, these chunky bars make irresistible pop-in-your-mouth treats. They're perfect after a casual holiday lunch or dinner.

—**KARA FIRSTENBERGER** CARDIFF, CALIFORNIA

**PREP:** 15 MIN.  **BAKE:** 30 MIN. + COOLING  **MAKES:** 2 DOZEN

- 1 **package yellow cake mix (regular size)**
- 1 **egg**
- ½ **cup butter, melted**
- 1 **cup dried cranberries**
- 1 **cup coarsely chopped cashews**
- 1 **cup butterscotch chips**
- 1 **cup semisweet chocolate chips**
- 1 **can (14 ounces) sweetened condensed milk**

**1.** In a large bowl, beat the cake mix, egg and butter until combined. Press into a greased 13-in. x 9-in. baking pan. Bake at 375° for 10 minutes.
**2.** Sprinkle the dried cranberries, cashews, butterscotch chips and chocolate chips over the warm crust. Drizzle with the sweetened condensed milk. Bake 18-20 minutes longer or until golden brown. Cool completely before cutting into bars.

## Bacon-Balsamic Deviled Eggs

These yummy deviled eggs are always at the top of my family's list for our holiday appetizer buffet. Everyone loves the addition of bacon, and the balsamic vinegar is a tongue-tingling twist.

—**LAURA KLOTZ** NIXA, MISSOURI

**PREP/TOTAL TIME:** 30 MIN.
**MAKES:** 2 DOZEN

- 12 **hard-cooked eggs**
- ½ **cup mayonnaise**
- 4 **bacon strips, cooked and crumbled**
- ¼ **cup finely chopped red onion**
- 1 **tablespoon white balsamic vinegar**
- 2 **teaspoons sugar**
- ¼ **teaspoon celery salt**
- ¼ **teaspoon pepper**
  **Minced fresh parsley**

**1.** Cut the eggs in half lengthwise. Remove the yolks; set the egg whites aside. In a small bowl, mash the egg yolks. Add the mayonnaise, bacon, onion, vinegar, sugar, celery salt and pepper; mix well.
**2.** Stuff or pipe into the egg whites. Refrigerate until serving. Sprinkle with parsley.

### Holiday Helper

Here's my fuss-free way to make deviled eggs: I place the cooked yolks and all of the other filling ingredients in a large resealable plastic bag, seal it and knead everything together by hand. Then I snip a corner off of the bag and use it like a pastry bag to squeeze the filling into the egg white halves.

It's easier than filling the eggs with a spoon, and cleanup is as easy as can be. Just toss out the bag, and you're done!

—**JULIE B.** BLUFF DALE, TEXAS

## Cranberry-Eggnog Gelatin Salad

Here's a refreshing, festive choice for a Christmastime potluck. Bursting with flavor, the molded salad features a sweet pineapple-eggnog layer that contrasts wonderfully with the tangy gelatin on top. I like the make-ahead convenience of doing the prep work the day before.

—**NANCY FOUST** STONEBORO, PENNSYLVANIA

**PREP:** 30 MIN. **COOK:** 5 MIN. + CHILLING
**MAKES:** 16 SERVINGS

- 2 **packages (3 ounces each) raspberry gelatin**
- 2 **cups boiling water**
- 1 **cup cold water**
- 1 **can (14 ounces) whole-berry cranberry sauce**
- 1 **medium navel orange, peeled and chopped**
- 1 **tablespoon grated orange peel**
- 1 **can (20 ounces) unsweetened crushed pineapple, undrained**
- 2 **envelopes unflavored gelatin**
- 1½ **cups eggnog**
- 3 **tablespoons lime juice**

**1.** In a large bowl, dissolve raspberry gelatin in boiling water. Stir in the cold water, then the cranberry sauce, chopped orange and orange peel. Pour into a 10-in. fluted tube pan or 12-cup ring mold coated with cooking spray; refrigerate for 40 minutes or until firm.
**2.** Meanwhile, drain pineapple; pour the juice into a saucepan. Sprinkle unflavored gelatin over juice and let stand for 1 minute. Cook and stir over low heat until gelatin is completely dissolved.
**3.** In a large bowl, combine eggnog and lime juice. Gradually stir in the gelatin mixture. Chill until soft-set. Fold in the pineapple. Spoon over the raspberry layer. Refrigerate salad overnight. Unmold onto a serving platter.
**Editor's Note:** *This recipe was tested with commercially prepared eggnog.*

# Golden Butternut Squash Lasagna

This saucy meatless dish features a favorite winter veggie at its finest. Covered with a rich cream topping, the deliciously different lasagna is packed with roasted butternut squash, two kinds of cheese and plenty of seasonings.

**—LISA SHEETS** CARMEL, INDIANA

**PREP:** 55 MIN. **BAKE:** 40 MIN. + STANDING
**MAKES:** 12 SERVINGS

- 1 **medium butternut squash (3 pounds), peeled, seeded and cut into ½-inch cubes**
- 3 **tablespoons canola oil**
- 9 **lasagna noodles**
- 3½ **cups 2% milk**
- ¼ **cup fresh rosemary leaves**
- 3 **garlic cloves, minced**
- 2 **tablespoons butter**
- 2 **tablespoons all-purpose flour**
- 1 **teaspoon salt**
- ¼ **teaspoon pepper**
- 8 **ounces fontina cheese, thinly sliced**
- 1½ **cups grated Parmesan cheese, divided**
- ½ **cup heavy whipping cream**

**1.** Divide squash between two greased 15-in. x 10-in. x 1-in. baking pans. Drizzle with oil and toss to coat. Bake, uncovered, at 425° for 20-25 minutes or until tender, stirring occasionally.

**2.** Meanwhile, cook lasagna noodles according to the package directions. In a small saucepan, combine the milk and rosemary. Bring to a boil. Reduce heat; simmer, uncovered, for 10 minutes. Strain, reserving milk and set aside. Discard rosemary.

**3.** In a Dutch oven, saute garlic in butter for 1 minute. Stir in the flour, salt and pepper until blended. Gradually add milk. Bring to a boil. Cook and stir for 2 minutes or until thickened. Set aside 1 cup sauce. Stir the squash into the remaining sauce.

**4.** Drain lasagna noodles. Spread reserved 1 cup sauce into a greased 13-in. x 9-in. baking dish. Layer with three noodles, half of the squash mixture, half of the fontina cheese and ½ cup Parmesan cheese. Repeat layers. Top with the remaining noodles. Beat the cream until soft peaks form. Spread over top. Sprinkle with remaining Parmesan cheese.

**5.** Cover and bake at 375° for 30 minutes. Uncover; bake 10-15 minutes longer or until bubbly and golden brown. Let stand for 15 minutes before serving.

## Slow Cooker Caramel Apple Cider

Slow-cooked with cinnamon and allspice, this heartwarming sipper is guaranteed to chase away the chill of winter. Serve brimming mugs of the hot beverage alongside a platter of Christmas cookies at your next holiday get-together.

**—TASTE OF HOME TEST KITCHEN**

**PREP:** 5 MIN.  **COOK:** 2 HOURS
**MAKES:** 12 SERVINGS (¾ CUP EACH)

| | |
|---|---|
| 8 | **cups apple cider or juice** |
| 1 | **cup caramel flavoring syrup** |
| ¼ | **cup lemon juice** |
| 1 | **vanilla bean** |
| 2 | **cinnamon sticks (3 inches)** |
| 1 | **tablespoon whole allspice** |
| | **Whipped cream, hot caramel ice cream topping and cinnamon sticks (3 inches), optional** |

**1.** In a 3-qt. slow cooker, combine the apple cider, caramel syrup and lemon juice. Split the vanilla bean and scrape seeds; add the seeds to the cider mixture. Place the bean, cinnamon sticks and allspice on a double thickness of cheesecloth; bring up corners of cloth and tie with string to form a bag. Add to cider mixture.

**2.** Cover and cook on low for 2-3 hours or until heated through. Discard spice bag. Pour cider into mugs; garnish with whipped cream, caramel topping and additional cinnamon sticks if desired.

**Editor's Note:** *This recipe was tested with Torani brand flavoring syrup. Look for it in the coffee section.*

99

106

110

*carefree*
ENTERTAINING

## Mu Shu Chicken Cones

My Asian-inspired cones make a distinctively different entree for casual holiday gatherings and game-day parties. Feel free to substitute pulled pork for the shredded chicken.

**—SUSAN ROTH** NAZARETH, PENNSYLVANIA

**PREP:** 20 MIN.  **COOK:** 15 MIN.  **MAKES:** 16 SERVINGS

- ¾   **cup sliced fresh shiitake mushrooms**
- 1   **tablespoon canola oil**
- 1½   **teaspoons minced fresh gingerroot**
- 1½   **teaspoons minced garlic**
- 3   **cups coleslaw mix**
- 2   **cups shredded rotisserie chicken**
- 3   **green onions, sliced**
- ½   **cup hoisin sauce**
- 1   **tablespoon honey**
- 1½   **teaspoons sesame oil**
- 16   **flour tortillas (6 inches), warmed**

**1.** In a large skillet, saute the mushrooms in oil over medium heat until tender. Add the ginger and garlic; cook 1 minute longer.

**2.** Stir in the coleslaw mix, chicken, green onions, hoisin sauce, honey and sesame oil; heat through.

**3.** To serve, cut the tortillas in half. Roll up each into a cone shape. Spoon 2 tablespoons filling into each cone. Arrange cones, seam side down, on a serving platter.

## Creating Tortilla Cones

To save a bit of time, stack the flour tortillas and cut the entire stack in half at once. Form each tortilla half into a cone—the bottom point of the cone will be the center of the cut edge of the tortilla.

# Chili-Lime Snack Mix

Why buy a pricey bagged snack mix when you can easily make a better-tasting one at home? Create a Southwestern sensation with chili powder, cayenne pepper and a twist of lime.
—**JULIE BECKWITH** CRETE, ILLINOIS

**PREP/TOTAL TIME:** 15 MIN.  **MAKES:** 3 QUARTS

8 **cups Corn Chex**
1 **cup cheddar-flavored snack crackers**
1 **cup corn nuts**
1 **cup corn chips**
1 **cup miniature pretzel twists**
6 **tablespoons butter, melted**
1 **tablespoon lime juice**
2 **teaspoons chili powder**
1 **teaspoon grated lime peel**
½ **teaspoon onion powder**
½ **teaspoon garlic powder**
⅛ **teaspoon cayenne pepper**

**1.** In a large microwave-safe bowl, combine the first five ingredients. In a small bowl, combine the remaining ingredients; pour over cereal mixture and toss to coat.
**2.** Microwave, uncovered, on high for 5 minutes, stirring three times. Spread onto waxed paper to cool. Store in an airtight container.
**Editor's Note:** *This recipe was tested in a 1,100-watt microwave.*

# Fresh Green Bean Salad

I had a green bean salad at a local deli and enjoyed it so much, I came up with my own version. It lasts for several days in the refrigerator, and the taste keeps getting better.
—**ALLISON BROOKS** FORT COLLINS, COLORADO

**PREP:** 25 MIN.  **COOK:** 10 MIN.
**MAKES:** 12 SERVINGS (¾ CUP EACH)

4 **cups fresh green beans, trimmed and halved**
2 **cups cherry tomatoes, halved**
1 **large English cucumber, seeded and chopped**
1 **cup fresh baby carrots, cut in half lengthwise**
1 **cup coarsely chopped fresh parsley**
**DRESSING**
½ **cup olive oil**
2 **tablespoons lemon juice**
1 **tablespoon white wine vinegar**
1 **tablespoon grated lemon peel**
1 **teaspoon Dijon mustard**
1 **garlic clove, minced**
½ **teaspoon salt**
½ **teaspoon ground mustard**
¼ **teaspoon pepper**

**1.** In a large saucepan, bring 4 cups water to a boil. Add the green beans; cook, uncovered, for 3 minutes. Drain and immediately place green beans in ice water. Drain and pat dry.
**2.** In a large bowl, combine beans, tomatoes, cucumber, carrots and parsley. For dressing, in a small bowl, whisk the dressing ingredients. Pour over the salad; toss to coat. Refrigerate until serving. Serve with a slotted spoon.

## Roasted Sweet Potato and Onion Salad

My family's love of potato salad and sweet potatoes led to this combination recipe that I serve on holidays. Maple syrup in the vinaigrette lends a pleasant hint of sweetness.

—**SUSAN JORDAN** DENVER, COLORADO

**PREP:** 20 MIN. **BAKE:** 35 MIN. **MAKES:** 6 SERVINGS

- 4  small sweet potatoes, peeled and cut into 1-inch cubes
- 1  large onion, cut into eight wedges
- 2  tablespoons olive oil
- ½  teaspoon salt
- ½  teaspoon pepper
- ¼  teaspoon garlic powder

**BALSAMIC VINAIGRETTE**

- ⅓  cup olive oil
- 2  tablespoons balsamic vinegar
- 1  teaspoon maple syrup
- 1  garlic clove, minced
- ½  teaspoon grated lemon peel
- ½  teaspoon minced chives
- ½  teaspoon minced fresh marjoram
- ¼  teaspoon salt

**1.** In a large bowl, toss the sweet potatoes, onion, oil, salt, pepper and garlic powder. Transfer to a greased 15-in. x 10-in. x 1-in. baking pan. Bake at 425° for 35-40 minutes or until potatoes are tender.

**2.** In a small bowl, whisk the vinaigrette ingredients. Drizzle vinaigrette over the potato mixture; toss to coat. Serve immediately.

## Rich Chicken Alfredo Pizza

After a nonstop day of shopping or decorating, settle in for a sure-to-please meal of homemade pizza. With a prebaked crust and simple Alfredo sauce, it's easy and delicious.

—**TAMMY HANKS** GAINSVILLE, FLORIDA

**PREP:** 30 MIN. **BAKE:** 15 MIN.
**MAKES:** 1 PIZZA (8 MAIN DISH OR 12 APPETIZER SLICES)

- 2½  teaspoons butter
- 1  garlic clove, minced
- 1½  cups heavy whipping cream
- 3  tablespoons grated Parmesan cheese
- ½  teaspoon salt
- ¼  teaspoon pepper
- 1  tablespoon minced fresh parsley
- 1  prebaked 12-inch thin pizza crust
- 1  cup cubed cooked chicken breast
- 1  cup thinly sliced baby portobello mushrooms
- 1  cup fresh baby spinach
- 2  cups (8 ounces) shredded part-skim mozzarella cheese

**1.** In a small saucepan over medium heat, melt the butter. Add the garlic; cook and stir for 1 minute. Add the heavy whipping cream; cook until the liquid is reduced by half, about 15-20 minutes. Add the Parmesan cheese, salt and pepper; cook and stir until thickened. Remove from the heat; stir in parsley. Cool slightly.

**2.** Place crust on an ungreased baking sheet; spread with cream mixture. Top with chicken, mushrooms, spinach and mozzarella cheese. Bake at 450° for 15-20 minutes or until cheese is melted and crust is golden brown.

## Sicilian Overstuffed Sandwich Wedges

For a casual lunch or supper, I frequently rely on my stuffed Italian-style sandwich. I can put it together the night before, and all I have to do the next day is cut it into wedges.

—**PAT POWELL** WOOSTER, OHIO

**PREP:** 30 MIN. + CHILLING  **MAKES:** 8 SERVINGS

| | |
|---|---|
| 1 | round loaf (1 pound) unsliced Italian bread |
| ½ | cup pitted Greek olives, sliced |
| ½ | cup chopped pimiento-stuffed olives |
| ¼ | cup minced fresh parsley |
| ¼ | cup olive oil |
| 1 | tablespoon fresh oregano leaves |
| 1 | tablespoon balsamic vinegar |
| 1 | teaspoon minced garlic |
| ½ | teaspoon coarsely ground pepper |
| ¼ | teaspoon crushed red pepper flakes |
| ½ | cup sliced pepperoncini |
| ¼ | pound thinly sliced hard salami |
| ¼ | pound sliced provolone cheese |
| 1 | jar (16 ounces) roasted sweet red pepper strips, drained |
| ¼ | pound sliced pepperoni |

**1.** Cut loaf of bread in half; hollow out the top and bottom, leaving a ¾-in. shell (discard removed bread or save for another use).

**2.** In a small bowl, combine olives, parsley, oil, oregano, vinegar, garlic, pepper and pepper flakes. Spoon half into the bread shell. Layer with pepperoncini, salami, cheese, roasted peppers, pepperoni and remaining olive mixture. Replace bread top.

**3.** Wrap in plastic wrap; refrigerate for 2-3 hours or overnight. Cut into eight wedges.

**Editor's Note:** *This recipe was tested with Vlasic roasted red pepper strips. Look for pepperoncini (pickled peppers) in the pickle and olive section of your grocery store.*

## Creamy Seafood Dip

We've had this every Christmas since I was a kid. For a lighter dip, simply substitute reduced-fat mayo and sour cream.

—**ALICE PARETI** ANKENY, IOWA

**PREP:** 15 MIN. + CHILLING  **MAKES:** 3 CUPS

| | |
|---|---|
| 2 | cups (16 ounces) sour cream |
| ⅓ | cup mayonnaise |
| 1 | can (6 ounces) crabmeat, drained, flaked and cartilage removed |
| 1 | cup (5 ounces) frozen cooked salad shrimp, thawed and chopped |
| 2 | tablespoons onion soup mix |
| ⅛ | teaspoon garlic powder |
| ⅛ | teaspoon paprika |
| | Corn chips |

**1.** In a small bowl, combine sour cream and mayonnaise. Stir in crab, shrimp, soup mix and garlic powder. Cover and refrigerate overnight.

**2.** Sprinkle with paprika. Serve with corn chips.

# Savory Mushroom Tarts

When I had drop-in company, I grabbed some mushrooms I had on hand and threw together bite-size tarts. The filling can be made a day ahead—just remove it from the refrigerator 30 minutes before spooning it into the shells.

**—LINDA ALLEMAN** FALLS CHURCH, VIRGINIA

**PREP/TOTAL TIME:** 30 MIN. **MAKES:** 2½ DOZEN

- 1 **bacon strip, chopped**
- 1½ **cups chopped fresh mushrooms**
- ¾ **cup chopped fresh shiitake mushrooms**
- 1 **tablespoon olive oil**
- 1½ **teaspoons finely chopped sun-dried tomatoes (not packed in oil)**
- 1 **teaspoon minced fresh thyme**
- ⅛ **teaspoon salt**
- ⅛ **teaspoon pepper**
- 2 **packages (1.9 ounces each) frozen miniature phyllo tart shells**
- ⅓ **cup garlic-herb spreadable cheese**

**1.** In a large skillet, cook the bacon over medium heat until crisp. Remove to paper towels; drain, reserving bacon drippings.

**2.** Saute mushrooms in oil and drippings until tender. Stir in the bacon, tomatoes, thyme, salt and pepper. Fill each phyllo tart shell with a heaping teaspoonful of filling and ½ teaspoon spreadable cheese.

**3.** Place on ungreased baking sheets. Bake at 350° for 6-8 minutes or until heated through.

# Paprika-Parmesan Puffed Cheese Sticks

My party guests never guess how easy these appetizers are to prepare. The miniature seasoned breadsticks require just five ingredients but instantly upgrade any menu.
—**MELANIE MILHORAT** NEW YORK, NEW YORK

**PREP/TOTAL TIME:** 15 MIN.  **MAKES:** 3 DOZEN

- 1 **sheet frozen puff pastry, thawed**
- ¼ **cup grated Parmesan cheese**
- ½ **teaspoon paprika**
- ¼ **teaspoon salt**
- ¼ **teaspoon dried savory**

**1.** Unfold puff pastry. On a lightly floured surface, roll pastry sheet into a 10-in. square.
**2.** In a small bowl, combine the remaining ingredients; sprinkle over the pastry. Cut pastry into 12 strips, about ¾-in. wide. Cut each strip widthwise into thirds. Place 1 in. apart on parchment paper-lined baking sheets. Bake at 375° for 5-7 minutes or until golden brown. Serve immediately.

# Crowd-Favorite Swedish Meatballs

At family potlucks, these Swedish meatballs always disappear in a flash. Using packaged meatballs and purchased Alfredo sauce saves a lot of time in the kitchen, too.
—**CAROLE BESS WHITE** PORTLAND, OREGON

**PREP:** 15 MIN.  **COOK:** 2 HOURS  **MAKES:** 11 SERVINGS

- 1 **package (32 ounces) frozen fully cooked Swedish meatballs**
- 2 **jars (15 ounces each) roasted garlic Alfredo sauce**
- 2 **cups (16 ounces) heavy whipping cream**
- 2 **cups (16 ounces) sour cream**
- ¾ **teaspoon hot pepper sauce**
- ½ **teaspoon garlic powder**
- ½ **teaspoon dill weed**
- ⅛ **teaspoon pepper**
  **Paprika**
  **Hot cooked noodles**

**1.** Place the meatballs in a 5-qt. slow cooker. Combine the Alfredo sauce, whipping cream, sour cream, pepper sauce, garlic powder, dill and pepper. Pour over meatballs. Cover and cook on low for 2-3 hours or until heated through.
**2.** Sprinkle with paprika. Serve with noodles.

# Pear Ginger Mojito

Flavored vodka, ginger beer, a pear and cinnamon syrup turn a traditional mojito into a seasonal refresher for autumn and winter. Add a lime slice to each glass for a festive garnish.
—**TASTE OF HOME TEST KITCHEN**

**PREP/TOTAL TIME:** 10 MIN.  **MAKES:** 2 SERVINGS

- 1 **medium pear, peeled and thinly sliced**
- 4 **teaspoons maple syrup**
- 4 **lime wedges**
- 1 **cup ginger beer, chilled**
- 4 **ounces pear-flavored vodka**
- 2 **tablespoons cinnamon flavoring syrup or 2 dashes ground allspice**
- 2 **dashes bitters**
- 2 **cups ice cubes**
  **Lime slices, optional**

In each of two cocktail glasses, muddle half of the pear slices with 2 teaspoons maple syrup. Squeeze one lime wedge into each glass, reserving two wedges for garnish. Divide remaining ingredients between both glasses; stir. Garnish with lime slices if desired.

with butter. Repeat with remaining phyllo, brushing each layer with remaining butter.

**3.** Place Brie in center of phyllo stack; top with ball of crab mixture. Bring up corners of dough around Brie and ball; invert and place seam side down in a greased 9-in. pie plate. Combine egg and water. Brush over dough.

**4.** Bake at 375° for 20-25 minutes or until golden brown. Let stand for 5 minutes before serving with crackers.

## Frozen Pumpkin Mousse Parfaits

Even people who don't care for pumpkin pie rave about these frosty parfaits. The creamy, nicely spiced mousse contrasts wonderfully with the toffee "crunch" pieces.

—**JANE LISKA** HARBOR SPRINGS, MICHIGAN

**PREP:** 25 MIN.  **BAKE:** 10 MIN. + FREEZING  **MAKES:** 8 SERVINGS

> 1  cup chopped walnuts
> 1  cup brickle toffee bits
> 1  tablespoon brown sugar
> 1  tablespoon butter, melted
> **MOUSSE**
> 3½  cups heavy whipping cream, divided
> 2  cups sugar
> 10  egg yolks, beaten
> 2  cans (15 ounces each) solid-pack pumpkin
> ¼  cup dark rum or 2 teaspoons rum extract
> 2  teaspoons ground cinnamon
> 2  teaspoons vanilla extract
> 1  teaspoon ground ginger
> ½  teaspoon salt
> ½  teaspoon ground nutmeg

**1.** In a small bowl, combine walnuts, toffee bits, brown sugar and butter. Press into a thin layer on a greased baking sheet. Bake at 350° for 10-13 minutes or until golden brown. Cool. Break into small pieces.

**2.** In a large saucepan, combine 1½ cups heavy whipping cream and sugar. Cook and stir over medium heat for 10-15 minutes or until slightly thickened. Remove from the heat.

**3.** Stir a small amount of hot mixture into the egg yolks; return all to the pan, stirring constantly. Bring to a gentle boil; cook and stir 2 minutes longer. Remove from the heat. Stir in the pumpkin, rum, cinnamon, vanilla, ginger, salt and nutmeg. Transfer to a large bowl. Cool to room temperature without stirring. Press waxed paper onto surface of pudding; refrigerate until chilled.

**4.** In a small bowl, beat 1 cup cream until stiff peaks form. Fold into pumpkin mixture.

**5.** In each of eight dessert dishes, layer 4 teaspoons nut mixture and ½ cup mousse; repeat layers. Freeze for at least 3 hours or overnight.

**6.** Just before serving, in a small bowl, beat remaining cream until stiff peaks form. Garnish the parfaits with whipped cream and remaining nut mixture.

## Crab-Brie Cheese Ball

This is no ordinary cheese ball! The phyllo-wrapped, baked Brie always wows the crowd at the annual parties I host for employees and customers of my business.

—**JODY ISSOD** MARLBOROUGH, MASSACHUSETTS

**PREP:** 20 MIN.  **BAKE:** 20 MIN.  **MAKES:** 8 SERVINGS

> 1  can (6 ounces) lump crabmeat, drained
> ¼  cup finely chopped sweet red pepper
> 1  green onion, finely chopped
> ½  teaspoon garlic salt
> ½  teaspoon pepper
> 16  sheets phyllo dough (14-inch x 9-inch sheet size)
> ¼  cup butter, melted
> 1  round (8 ounces) Brie cheese, rind removed
> 1  egg
> 1  tablespoon water
> Assorted crackers

**1.** In a small bowl, combine the first five ingredients. Shape into a ball; set aside.

**2.** Place one sheet of phyllo dough on a work surface. (Keep remaining dough covered with plastic wrap and a damp towel to prevent it from drying out.) Brush dough

# Italian Three-Cheese Macaroni

A self-proclaimed mac-and-cheese connoisseur, my husband says that this is his favorite version. The Italian seasoning and tomatoes really complement the pasta and cheeses.

—**ADRIANE MUMMERT** LANCASTER, PENNSYLVANIA

**PREP:** 30 MIN.  **BAKE:** 50 MIN.
**MAKES:** 12 SERVINGS (1 CUP EACH)

- 4    **cups uncooked elbow macaroni**
- ½   **cup butter, cubed**
- ¼   **cup all-purpose flour**
- 2    **teaspoons Italian seasoning**
- 1    **teaspoon salt**
- 1    **teaspoon pepper**
- 4    **cups 2% milk**
- 2    **cups (8 ounces) shredded cheddar cheese**
- ½   **cup grated Parmesan cheese**
- 2    **cans (14½ ounces each) diced tomatoes, undrained**
- 2    **cups (8 ounces) shredded part-skim mozzarella cheese**
- ½   **cup dry bread crumbs**
- 2    **tablespoons butter, melted**

**1.** Cook macaroni according to the package directions.
**2.** Meanwhile, in a small saucepan, melt the butter. Stir in the flour, Italian seasoning, salt and pepper until smooth; gradually add the milk. Bring to a boil; cook and stir for 2 minutes or until thickened. Remove from the heat; stir in the cheddar and Parmesan cheeses until melted. Drain macaroni.
**3.** Spread 1 cup cheese sauce in a greased 13-in. x 9-in. baking pan. Layer with half of the macaroni, tomatoes and cheese sauce. Repeat layers. Sprinkle with mozzarella cheese. Combine crumbs and butter; sprinkle over top.
**4.** Cover and bake at 350° for 40 minutes. Uncover and bake 10-15 minutes longer or until golden brown and bubbly. Let stand for 5 minutes before serving.

# French Apricot Cream Cheese Bars

My sister-in-law gave me her recipe for apricot cream cheese bars years ago. They're so yummy, I like to include them with the cookies and candy on my Christmas treat tray.
—**JANE MCMILLAN** DANIA BEACH, FLORIDA

**PREP:** 20 MIN. **BAKE:** 35 MIN. + CHILLING **MAKES:** 3 DOZEN

- 1 package French vanilla cake mix (regular size)
- ⅓ cup butter, melted
- 1 egg
- **FILLING**
- 1 jar (10 to 12 ounces) apricot preserves
- 1 package (8 ounces) cream cheese, softened
- ½ cup sugar
- ½ teaspoon vanilla extract
- 1 egg, lightly beaten

**1.** In a large bowl, combine the cake mix, butter and egg until crumbly. Remove 1½ cups and set aside. Press the remaining crumb mixture into a greased 13-in. x 9-in. baking dish.

**2.** Bake at 350° for 10 minutes. Spread apricot preserves over warm crust.

**3.** In a small bowl, beat cream cheese, sugar and vanilla until smooth. Add the egg; beat on low speed just until combined. Drop by spoonfuls and spread over the crust; sprinkle with reserved crumb mixture.

**4.** Bake at 350° for 25-30 minutes or until center is almost set and topping is golden brown. Cool on a wire rack for 1 hour. Refrigerate for at least 2 hours. Cut into bars.

# Caramel Orange Spritzer

Butterscotch-caramel ice cream topping and orange juice may seem like an unusual combination, but everyone enjoys this sweet sipper. Cardamom and coriander add even more flavor.
—**TASTE OF HOME TEST KITCHEN**

**PREP:** 20 MIN. + CHILLING **MAKES:** 8 SERVINGS (1 CUP EACH)

- 3 tablespoons cardamom pods, crushed
- 1 tablespoon coriander seeds
- 1 cup sugar
- 1 cup water
- 2 cups orange juice
- 2 tablespoons lemon juice
- ¼ cup butterscotch-caramel ice cream topping
- 1 bottle (1 liter) carbonated water, chilled
  Ice cubes
  Orange slices, optional

**1.** In a dry small skillet over medium heat, toast the cardamom pods and coriander seeds until aromatic, about 4-5 minutes. In a small saucepan, combine the seeds, sugar and water. Bring to a boil over medium heat; cook and stir for 1 minute. Remove from the heat; stir in juices. Cool to room temperature. Cover and refrigerate overnight.

**2.** Strain the juice mixture, discarding cardamom and coriander. Whisk in caramel topping. Pour into a large pitcher. Stir in carbonated water. Serve over ice. Garnish with orange slices if desired.

# Orange Poppy Seed Salad

In our area, olives, walnuts, pomegranates and oranges are grown locally, and I love using them in recipes. I toss all four ingredients into my simple but refreshing romaine salad.
—**FAITH SOMMERS** BANGOR, CALIFORNIA

**PREP:** 35 MIN. **MAKES:** 8 SERVINGS

- 8 cups torn romaine
- 1 can (15 ounces) mandarin oranges, drained
- ¾ cup chopped walnuts, toasted
- ⅔ cup canola or olive oil
- ½ cup sugar
- ¼ cup cider vinegar
- 1 tablespoon poppy seeds
- ½ teaspoon salt
- ½ teaspoon ground mustard
- ½ cup pomegranate seeds

In a large bowl, combine romaine, oranges and walnuts. Place the oil, sugar, vinegar, poppy seeds, salt and mustard in a jar with a tight-fitting lid; shake well. Pour desired amount over romaine mixture; toss to coat. Sprinkle with pomegranate seeds. Refrigerate remaining dressing.

## Herbed Turkey & Cranberry Sloppy Joes

These deliciously different sloppy joes pile on the flavor with herbs, spices, dried berries and more. Keep the meat mixture warm in a slow cooker and let guests spoon it onto buns.

—JAMIE MILLER MAPLE GROVE, MINNESOTA

**PREP:** 15 MIN. **COOK:** 25 MIN.
**MAKES:** 10 SERVINGS

- 2 pounds ground turkey
- 1 cup chopped sweet onion
- 1 celery rib, finely chopped
- 2 garlic cloves, minced
- 1 tablespoon olive oil
- 1 can (14½ ounces) petite diced tomatoes, undrained
- ½ cup dried cranberries
- ¼ cup chili sauce
- 1 teaspoon dried sage leaves
- 1 teaspoon dried thyme
- 1 teaspoon dried rosemary, crushed
- ¾ teaspoon salt
- ½ teaspoon pepper
- ⅔ cup jellied cranberry sauce
- ⅓ cup mayonnaise
- 2 teaspoons Dijon mustard
- 10 hamburger buns, split

**1.** In a large skillet, cook the turkey, onion, celery and garlic in oil over medium heat until meat is no longer pink; drain.

**2.** Stir in the tomatoes, dried cranberries, chili sauce, sage, thyme, rosemary, salt and pepper. Bring to a boil. Reduce heat; cover and simmer for 6-8 minutes or until flavors are blended. Stir in cranberry sauce and heat through.

**3.** Combine the mayonnaise and mustard; spread on hamburger buns. Spoon ½ cup sloppy joe mixture on each bun.

## Pork Tenderloin with Marsala Mushroom Sauce

I served this one year for Christmas Eve dinner, and the saucy entree is now a favorite. My husband likes the leftovers because he uses them for sandwiches.

—KAREN LATIMER WINNIPEG, MANITOBA

**PREP:** 15 MIN. **COOK:** 25 MIN.
**MAKES:** 6 SERVINGS

- 1 package (½ ounce) dried chanterelle mushrooms
- ½ cup hot water
- 1 teaspoon dried parsley flakes
- ½ teaspoon dried marjoram
- ½ teaspoon dried rosemary, crushed
- ½ teaspoon dried sage leaves
- ½ teaspoon dried savory
- ½ teaspoon garlic powder
- ¾ teaspoon salt, divided
- ¼ teaspoon pepper
- 2 pork tenderloins (¾ pound each)
- 3 tablespoons canola oil, divided
- ½ pound sliced baby portobello mushrooms
- ½ pound sliced fresh button mushrooms
- 4 ounces pearl onions, trimmed and peeled
- 1 cup Marsala wine
- 1 cup chicken broth
- 2 tablespoons cornstarch
- 2 tablespoons cold water
  Minced fresh parsley, optional

**1.** In a small bowl, combine dried mushrooms and hot water; set aside. In another bowl, combine the dried herbs, garlic powder, ¼ teaspoon salt and pepper. Sprinkle over pork.

**2.** In a large skillet, brown pork in 2 tablespoons oil on all sides. Remove from pan and keep warm.

**3.** In the same skillet, saute the sliced mushrooms and pearl onions in the remaining oil until the mushrooms are browned. Add the Marsala wine, chicken broth and remaining salt. Drain chanterelle mushrooms; add to the pan. Bring to a boil. Reduce heat; add pork.

**4.** Cover and cook for 15-20 minutes or until a thermometer reads 145°. Remove the pork and let stand for 5 minutes before slicing.

**5.** Combine cornstarch and water until smooth; gradually stir into the pan. Bring to a boil; cook and stir for 2 minutes or until thickened.

**6.** Slice pork and serve with sauce. Garnish with parsley if desired.

Taste of Home ❄ CHRISTMAS

# Cranberry-Pear Compote Shortcake

Here's a homestyle recipe I've shared with many of my friends and family members. Fresh pears, cranberries and cinnamon transform the usual summery shortcake into a wonderfully wintry treat.

**—PRISCILLA GILBERT**
INDIAN HARBOUR BEACH, FLORIDA

**PREP:** 30 MIN. + CHILLING
**COOK:** 20 MIN.  **MAKES:** 8 SERVINGS

⅓  cup packed brown sugar
¼  cup sugar
2  tablespoons butter
1  cinnamon stick (3 inches)
3  cups fresh or frozen cranberries, halved, divided
½  cup ginger ale
2½  cups sliced fresh pears
¼  cup light corn syrup
8  individually frozen biscuits
2  cups heavy whipping cream
1  tablespoon confectioners' sugar
2  teaspoons grated orange peel
2  tablespoons butter, softened

**1.** In a large saucepan, combine the sugars, butter and cinnamon. Cook over medium heat for 4-5 minutes or until sugars are dissolved, stirring occasionally. Gently stir in 2 cups cranberries and ginger ale.
**2.** Bring to a boil. Cook and stir for 8-10 minutes or until the mixture is thickened. Add pears; cook and stir 5-10 minutes longer or until the pears are tender. Remove from the heat. Add the corn syrup and remaining cranberries. Transfer to a small bowl; cover and refrigerate until chilled.
**3.** Prepare biscuits according to package directions. Meanwhile, in a small bowl, beat cream until it begins to thicken. Add confectioners' sugar and peel; beat until stiff peaks form.
**4.** Split warm biscuits. Spread with butter; layer with the compote and cream. Replace tops.

1. In a large heavy saucepan, combine the rice, milk, sugar, butter and salt. Bring to a boil over medium heat. Cook for 15 minutes or until thick and creamy, stirring occasionally. Remove from the heat. Stir a small amount of the hot mixture into the egg yolks; return all to the pan, stirring constantly.

2. Bring to a gentle boil; cook and stir 2 minutes longer. Remove from the heat. Stir in cherries and vanilla. Cool for 15 minutes, stirring occasionally. Transfer to dessert dishes. Cover and refrigerate for 1 hour.

3. In a small heavy saucepan, combine the sugar, cherry juice and salt. Bring to a boil.

4. Meanwhile, beat egg white and cream of tartar in a large heat-proof bowl until stiff peaks form. With mixer running on high speed, carefully add hot syrup in a slow steady stream. Continue beating until soft peaks form. Stir in extract. Dollop over the pudding. Garnish with cherries if desired.

## Maraschino Cherry Rice Pudding

As a grandmother, I've been cooking for many years and love to share my recipes. This pretty cherry pudding is a fun choice when you need a dessert for a special occasion.

—**SHARON CRIDER** JUNCTION CITY, KANSAS

**PREP:** 30 MIN. + CHILLING  **COOK:** 15 MIN.
**MAKES:** 9 SERVINGS

    3    cups cooked long grain rice
    3    cups 2% milk
    ⅓    cup sugar
    2    tablespoons butter
    ¼    teaspoon salt
    2    egg yolks, lightly beaten
    ½    cup chopped maraschino cherries
    1    teaspoon vanilla extract
**TOPPING**
    ⅓    cup sugar
    2    tablespoons maraschino cherry juice
         Dash salt
    1    egg white
    ¼    teaspoon cream of tartar
    ¼    teaspoon almond extract
         Maraschino cherries, optional

## Heirloom Tomato and Grape Bruschetta

I wanted to try something new with bruschetta, so I added red grapes, pistachios, Gorgonzola cheese and French herbs. It's an appetizer everyone enjoys.

—**TERRI CRANDALL** GARDNERVILLE, NEVADA

**PREP/TOTAL TIME:** 25 MIN.  **MAKES:** 3 DOZEN

    ½    cup pistachios
    1    package (8 ounces) cream cheese, cubed
    ½    cup crumbled Gorgonzola cheese
    ¼    teaspoon crushed red pepper flakes
    2    large heirloom tomatoes, chopped
    1    cup seedless red grapes, halved
    1    tablespoon olive oil
    2    teaspoons red wine vinegar
    1    teaspoon herbes de Provence
    ¼    teaspoon salt
    36   slices French bread baguette (¼-inch thick)

1. Place pistachios in a food processor; cover and process until chopped. Add the cream cheese, Gorgonzola and pepper flakes. Cover and process until blended; set aside.

2. In a large bowl, combine the tomatoes and grapes. In another bowl, combine oil, vinegar, herbes de Provence and salt. Pour over tomato mixture; toss to coat.

3. Place baguette slices on a baking sheet. Broil 3-4 inches from the heat for 1-2 minutes or until toasted. Spread each with the cheese mixture. Broil 2-3 minutes longer or until cheese is melted. Top with tomato mixture.

**Editor's Note:** *Look for herbes de Provence in the spice aisle.*

126

126

123

*simply*
CHOCOLATE

# Mocha Truffle Trees

I serve my layered, Kahlua-spiked dessert wedges every year at our annual yuletide party. They're so decadent, and the Pirouette-cookie tree trunks make them fun.

—**ERICA JANSSEN** LINDSTROM, MINNESOTA

**PREP:** 45 MIN. + CHILLING  **BAKE:** 10 MIN.
**MAKES:** 12 SERVINGS

- 1 **cup chocolate wafer crumbs**
- ¼ **cup sugar**
- ¼ **cup butter, melted**

### WHITE CHOCOLATE LAYER

- 6 **ounces white baking chocolate, finely chopped**
- 3 **tablespoons heavy whipping cream**
- 1 **tablespoon butter**
- 1 **tablespoon Kahlua (coffee liqueur)**
- 1 **teaspoon almond extract**

### CHOCOLATE LAYER

- 2 **cups (12 ounces ) semisweet chocolate chips, finely chopped**
- ½ **cup heavy whipping cream**
- 1 **tablespoon butter**
- 2 **tablespoons Kahlua (coffee liqueur)**
- 1½ **teaspoons instant coffee granules**
- 1 **teaspoon almond extract**

### DECORATIONS

- 6 **Pirouette cookies, cut crosswise in half**
  **Additional white baking chocolate, melted or white chocolate shavings**

**1.** In a small bowl, combine the wafer crumbs, sugar and butter; press onto the bottom of a greased 9-inch springform pan. Bake at 350° for 5-7 minutes or until set. Cool on a wire rack.

**2.** Place white baking chocolate in a small bowl. In a small saucepan, bring cream and butter just to a boil. Pour over white chocolate; whisk until smooth. Stir in Kahlua and almond extract; spoon into crust. Place in freezer while preparing chocolate layer.

**3.** Place the chocolate chips in a small bowl. In a small saucepan, bring cream and butter just to a boil. Pour over chocolate; whisk until smooth. Stir in the Kahlua, coffee granules and almond extract; spoon over white chocolate layer. Refrigerate for 2 hours or until set.

**4.** To serve, carefully run a knife around the edge of pan to loosen; remove sides. Cut tart into 12 wedges; place on individual plates. Insert a halved Pirouette into the wide end of each slice. Decorate with white chocolate to resemble Christmas trees.

# Chocolate-Caramel Chiffon Cake

While attending pastry school, I learned how to prepare this fluffy, luscious cake. My family just can't get enough of the smooth chocolate cream and caramel sauce.

—ALEXA KRUSHEL WINNIPEG, MANITOBA

**PREP:** 45 MIN. + CHILLING  **BAKE:** 20 MIN. + COOLING
**MAKES:** 12 SERVINGS

- 6 **eggs, separated**
- ¾ **cup baking cocoa**
- ¾ **cup hot water**
- 1¾ **cups sugar**
- 1⅛ **cups all-purpose flour**
- 1⅛ **teaspoons baking soda**
- ½ **cup canola oil**
- 1½ **teaspoons vanilla extract**
- ½ **teaspoon cream of tartar**

**CARAMEL SAUCE**
- ½ **cup butter, cubed**
- 1 **cup packed brown sugar**
- ½ **cup heavy whipping cream**

**CHOCOLATE CREAM**
- 2 **cups heavy whipping cream**
- 1 **cup confectioners' sugar**
- 2 **tablespoons baking cocoa**
- ½ **teaspoon vanilla extract**
  **Chocolate curls, optional**

**1.** Let the egg whites stand at room temperature for 30 minutes. In a small bowl, combine baking cocoa and hot water until smooth; cool for 20 minutes. Line three greased 8-in. round baking pans with parchment paper; grease paper.

**2.** In a large bowl, combine sugar, flour and baking soda. In another bowl, whisk the egg yolks, oil and vanilla; add to the dry ingredients along with the cocoa mixture. Beat until well blended.

**3.** Add the cream of tartar to egg whites; beat with clean beaters until stiff peaks form. Fold into the batter. Gently transfer to prepared pans.

**4.** Bake at 350° for 16-20 minutes or until top springs back when lightly touched. Cool for 10 minutes before removing from pans to wire racks; remove paper. Cool completely.

**5.** For caramel sauce, in a small saucepan, melt butter. Stir in brown sugar and whipping cream. Bring to a boil. Reduce heat; simmer for 3-4 minutes or until thickened. Refrigerate until thickened to spreading consistency.

**6.** For chocolate cream, beat cream, confectioners' sugar, cocoa and vanilla until stiff peaks form.

**7.** Place one cake layer on a serving plate; spread with ½ cup caramel sauce and 1 cup chocolate cream. Repeat layers. Top with remaining cake layer. Spread remaining caramel sauce over the top. Spread remaining chocolate cream over top and sides of cake. Garnish with chocolate curls if desired. Refrigerate leftovers.

# Nutty Chocolate Muffins

The popular mix of peanut butter and chocolate transforms muffins into extra-special treats. Guests gobble them up!

—LISA SPEER PALM BEACH, FLORIDA

**PREP:** 30 MIN.  **BAKE:** 25 MIN. + COOLING
**MAKES:** 16 SERVINGS

- 1¾ **cups all-purpose flour**
- 1¼ **cups plus 2 tablespoons packed brown sugar**
- ⅔ **cup baking cocoa**
- 1 **teaspoon baking soda**
- 1 **teaspoon baking powder**
- ½ **teaspoon salt**
- 2 **eggs**
- 1 **cup buttermilk**
- ½ **cup butter, melted**
- 2½ **teaspoons vanilla extract**
- 1 **cup chopped unsalted peanuts**
- 1 **cup semisweet chocolate chips**

**FILLING**
- 1 **cup creamy peanut butter**
- 3 **tablespoons butter, softened**
- ¾ **cup confectioners' sugar**
- ¼ **teaspoon vanilla extract**

**1.** In a large bowl, combine the first six ingredients. In another bowl, whisk eggs, buttermilk, butter and vanilla. Stir into dry ingredients just until moistened. Fold in nuts and chips. Fill paper-lined muffin cups two-thirds full.

**2.** Bake at 350° for 22-25 minutes or until a toothpick inserted near the center comes out clean. Cool for 10 minutes before removing from pans to wire racks to cool completely.

**3.** In a small bowl, beat the peanut butter, butter, confectioners' sugar and vanilla until fluffy. Cut a small hole in the corner of a pastry or plastic bag; insert a large star tip. Fill bag with peanut butter filling. Insert tip into the top of each cupcake; fill with about 2 teaspoons filling, gradually lifting and piping a small amount of filling onto top of muffins. Refrigerate leftovers.

# Gluten-Free Chocolate Cake Cookies

I reworked some of my favorite treats to suit my special diet. No one guesses that these cake-like cookies are gluten-free.

**—BECKI DIMERCURIO** MARTINEZ, CALIFORNIA

**PREP:** 30 MIN. **BAKE:** 10 MIN./BATCH + COOLING
**MAKES:** 2 DOZEN

- 2 cups confectioners' sugar
- ½ cup plus 3 tablespoons Dutch processed cocoa powder
- 2¼ teaspoons cornstarch
- ¼ teaspoon salt
- 2 egg whites
- 2½ teaspoons Kahlua coffee liqueur
- 1 cup chopped walnuts, toasted
  Additional confectioners' sugar

**1.** In a large bowl, combine the confectioners' sugar, cocoa powder, cornstarch and salt. Stir in egg whites and coffee liqueur until batter resembles frosting. Add walnuts.

**2.** Drop by tablespoonfuls 3 in. apart onto parchment paper-lined baking sheets. Bake at 300° for 10-14 minutes or until set. Cool for 2 minutes before removing from pans to wire racks to cool completely. Dust with additional confectioners' sugar.

**Editor's Note:** *This recipe does not use flour.*

# Triple Mousse Torte

The layers of this three-times-as-nice torte include an English toffee recipe that was passed down from my grandmother. For the base, I used a brownie crust—another family favorite.

**—BETH RICHARDS** FAIRBANKS, ALASKA

**PREP:** 1 HOUR **BAKE:** 20 MIN. + CHILLING
**MAKES:** 12 SERVINGS

- 1 package fudge brownie mix (8-inch square pan size)
- ⅓ cup canola oil
- 2 tablespoons water
- 1 egg

**WHITE CHOCOLATE MOUSSE**
- 1 package (8 ounces) cream cheese, softened
- ½ cup confectioners' sugar
- ½ teaspoon vanilla extract
- 1 cup white baking chips, melted
- 1 cup heavy whipping cream, whipped

**CHOCOLATE MOUSSE**
- 1 package (8 ounces) cream cheese, softened
- 1½ teaspoons vanilla extract
- 1 cup sugar
- ½ cup baking cocoa
- ½ cup semisweet chocolate chips, melted
- 1 cup heavy whipping cream, whipped

**TOFFEE MOUSSE**
- 4 ounces cream cheese, softened
- 2 tablespoons butter, softened
- ½ teaspoon vanilla extract
- 1 cup confectioners' sugar
- ¼ cup baking cocoa
- ½ cup milk chocolate English toffee bits
- ½ cup heavy whipping cream, whipped
  Additional milk chocolate English toffee bits, optional

**1.** In a large bowl, beat the brownie mix, oil, water and egg until well mixed. Spread into a greased 9-in. springform pan. Bake at 350° for 20-25 minutes or until a toothpick inserted 2-in. from the edge comes out clean. Cool completely on a wire rack.

**2.** Meanwhile, in a large bowl, beat the cream cheese, confectioners' sugar and vanilla until light and fluffy. Stir in the melted white chips. Fold in whipped cream. Spread over brownie. Cover and refrigerate for 30 minutes.

**3.** For chocolate mousse, beat cream cheese and vanilla until blended. Combine sugar and cocoa; gradually add to cream cheese mixture. Beat until light and fluffy. Stir in chocolate chips. Fold in whipped cream. Spread over torte. Cover and refrigerate for 30 minutes.

**4.** For toffee mousse, beat the cream cheese, butter and vanilla until blended. Combine confectioners' sugar and cocoa; gradually add to cream cheese mixture. Beat until light and fluffy. Stir in toffee bits. Fold in whipped cream. Spread over top.

**5.** Cover and refrigerate for 4 hours or overnight. Garnish with additional toffee bits if desired.

## Frozen Pecan Mocha Dessert

For frosty refreshment after a rich holiday dinner, give this make-ahead dessert from the freezer a try. The eye-catching decorations on top are easy to create with just a few simple ingredients and make an elegant presentation.

**—ANGELA LEINENBACH** MECHANICSVLLE, VIRGINIA

**PREP:** 35 MIN.  **BAKE:** 30 MIN. + FREEZING
**MAKES:** 10 SERVINGS

    4    egg whites
    ½    cup sugar
    ½    cup finely chopped pecans
**MOCHA CREAM**
    4    egg yolks
    ¼    cup strong brewed coffee, room temperature
    3    tablespoons sugar
    4    ounces semisweet chocolate, coarsely chopped
    1    teaspoon vanilla extract
    1½   cups heavy whipping cream
**GARNISHES**
    1    ounce semisweet chocolate, melted
    ½    cup heavy whipping cream
    2    teaspoons sugar

**1.** Place the egg whites in a small bowl; let stand at room temperature for 30 minutes. Beat on medium speed until soft peaks form. Gradually add the sugar, 1 tablespoon at a time, beating on high until stiff glossy peaks form and sugar is dissolved. Fold in pecans. Spread into a greased 9-in. springform pan. Bake at 350° for 30 minutes or until lightly browned. Cool on a wire rack.

**2.** In the top of a double boiler set over simmering water, beat egg yolks, coffee and sugar until thick and mixture reads 160°, about 4 minutes. Remove from the heat; stir in chocolate and vanilla until smooth.

**3.** Quickly transfer to a bowl; place in ice water and stir for 2 minutes. Beat whipping cream until soft peaks form; fold into chocolate mixture. Pour into crust. Cover and freeze for 4 hours or overnight.

**4.** For garnishes, place melted chocolate in a heavy-duty resealable plastic bag; cut a small hole in a corner of bag. Pipe designs onto waxed paper. Chill until firm, about 10 minutes. In a small bowl, beat cream until it begins to thicken. Add sugar; beat until soft peaks form.

**5.** Remove pie from the freezer 10 minutes before serving. Carefully run a knife around the edge of pan to loosen; remove the sides of springform pan. Using a large star tip, pipe whipped cream around edges; add chocolate garnish.

# White Chocolate Pound Cake with Chocolate Sauce

As good as this homemade pound cake is by itself, it's even better draped with a velvety chocolate-orange sauce warm from the stovetop. Every bite is heavenly!

—**MARY ANN LEE** CLIFTON PARK, NEW YORK

**PREP:** 35 MIN.  **BAKE:** 1 HOUR + COOLING
**MAKES:** 16 SERVINGS

4  **ounces white baking chocolate, chopped**
½  **cup water**
1  **cup butter, softened**
1½  **cups sugar**
4  **eggs**
2  **teaspoons vanilla extract**
3  **cups all-purpose flour**
1  **teaspoon baking soda**
½  **teaspoon salt**
1  **cup buttermilk**

**CHOCOLATE ORANGE SAUCE**
⅔  **cup heavy whipping cream**
½  **cup sugar**
4  **ounces semisweet chocolate, chopped**
4  **tablespoons butter, divided**
1  **tablespoon grated orange peel**
1  **tablespoon orange juice**
2  **teaspoons vanilla extract**

**1.** In a small saucepan, combine the white chocolate and water; cook and stir over low heat until melted. Remove from the heat; cool slightly.
**2.** In a large bowl, cream butter and sugar until light and fluffy, about 5 minutes. Beat in white chocolate mixture. Add eggs, one at a time, beating well after each addition. Beat in vanilla. Combine the flour, baking soda and salt; add to the creamed mixture alternately with buttermilk, beating well after each addition.
**3.** Transfer to a greased and floured 10-in. fluted tube pan. Bake at 350° for 60-65 minutes or until a toothpick inserted near the center comes out clean. Cool for 10 minutes before removing from pan to a wire rack to cool completely.
**4.** Meanwhile, in a small heavy saucepan, combine the heavy whipping cream, sugar, semisweet chocolate and 2 tablespoons butter over medium heat until mixture comes to a boil, stirring constantly. Cook 4-5 minutes longer or until sauce thickens slightly, stirring constantly.
**5.** Remove from the heat. Stir in the orange peel, orange juice, vanilla and remaining butter. Serve warm with cake.

# Candied Tangerine Chocolate Ice Cream

Dress up ordinary ice cream for the yuletide season by mixing in bits of cranberry-dotted bark and candied tangerine peel. The unusual flavor combination is delightfully refreshing.

—TASTE OF HOME TEST KITCHEN

**PREP:** 15 MIN. + STANDING  **COOK:** 65 MIN. + FREEZING
**MAKES:** 1½ QUARTS

- 3 tangerines
- 2 cups plus 2 tablespoons sugar, divided
- 1½ cups water

**ICE CREAM**
- 2 cups 60% cacao bittersweet chocolate baking chips
- 1½ cups whole milk
- ¾ cup sugar, divided
- 4 egg yolks
- 1½ cups heavy whipping cream
- 1 teaspoon vanilla extract

**BARK**
- 1 cup dark chocolate chips
- 1 cup dried cranberries

**1.** With a sharp knife, score each tangerine, cutting peel into four wedge-shaped sections. Loosen and remove peel from each with a spoon (save fruit for another use).

**2.** Place the tangerine peels in a large heavy saucepan; cover with cold water. Bring to a boil. Cover and cook for 10 minutes. Drain and repeat. Cool for 5 minutes. Carefully scrape off excess pulp from peel.

**3.** In another saucepan, combine 2 cups sugar and water; cook and stir over medium heat until sugar is dissolved. Add the tangerine peels. Bring to a boil. Reduce the heat; simmer, uncovered, for 30 minutes or until the tangerine pieces are transparent, stirring occasionally.

**4.** Using a slotted spoon, transfer the peel to a wire rack placed over a baking pan. Let stand for 1 hour. Toss peel in remaining sugar. Let stand for 8 hours or overnight.

**5.** Meanwhile, in a microwave, melt baking chips; stir until smooth. Cool to room temperature. In a large heavy saucepan, heat milk and ½ cup sugar until bubbles form around sides of pan. In a small bowl, combine egg yolks, melted chocolate and remaining sugar. Whisk a small amount of milk mixture into chocolate mixture. Return all to the pan, whisking constantly.

**6.** Cook and stir over low heat until mixture is thickened and coats the back of a spoon. Quickly transfer to a bowl; place in ice water and stir for 2 minutes. Stir in the cream and vanilla. Press waxed paper onto surface of custard. Refrigerate for several hours or overnight.

**7.** For bark, line a 15-in. x 10-in. x 1-in. pan with foil; set aside. In a microwave-safe bowl, melt chocolate chips; stir until smooth. Stir in cranberries. Spread into prepared pan. Chill until firm.

**8.** Chop bark into small pieces; finely chop candied peel. Fill cylinder of ice cream freezer two-thirds full; freeze according to the manufacturer's directions. When the ice cream is frozen, transfer to a freezer container; stir in 1 cup chocolate bark and ½ cup candied peel. Freeze for 2-4 hours before serving. Serve with remaining candied peel and bark.

# Chocolate Espresso Martini

After-dinner drinks and dessert come together perfectly in this coffee-flavored cocktail, sure to perk up java lovers. For extra flair, drizzle chocolate syrup on the inside of each glass.

—TASTE OF HOME TEST KITCHEN

**PREP/TOTAL TIME:** 5 MIN.  **MAKES:** 1 SERVING

- Ice cubes
- 2½ ounces chocolate liqueur
- ½ ounce brewed espresso
- ½ ounce vanilla-flavored vodka
- Coarse sugar
- 1 teaspoon chocolate syrup

**1.** Fill a mixing glass or tumbler three-fourths full with ice. Add chocolate liqueur, espresso and vodka; stir until condensation forms on outside of glass.

**2.** Sprinkle sugar on a plate. Moisten the rim of a chilled cocktail glass with water; hold glass upside down and dip rim into sugar. Drizzle chocolate syrup on the inside of glass. Strain vodka mixture into glass.

## Cherry Chocolate Layer Cake

Heads will turn when you bring this showstopper to the table. And the attention will only increase when you start cutting—revealing the luscious, creamy cherry filling.

—**VICTORIA FAULLING** METHUEN, MASSACHUSETTS

**PREP:** 35 MIN.  **BAKE:** 25 MIN. + COOLING
**MAKES:** 12 SERVINGS

- 1 **cup butter, softened**
- 1¼ **cups sugar**
- ¾ **cup packed brown sugar**
- 3 **eggs**
- 2 **teaspoons vanilla extract**
- 2 **cups all-purpose flour**
- 1 **cup baking cocoa**
- 1½ **teaspoons baking soda**
- ½ **teaspoon baking powder**
- ¼ **teaspoon salt**
- 1½ **cups buttermilk**

**FILLING**
- 1 **package (8 ounces) cream cheese, softened**
- 6 **tablespoons butter, softened**
- 1 **teaspoon almond extract**
- 3 **cups confectioners' sugar**
- 1 **tablespoon maraschino cherry juice**
- ⅔ **cup finely chopped pecans**
- ⅔ **cup chopped maraschino cherries**

**FROSTING**
- 3 **cups confectioners' sugar**
- ½ **cup baking cocoa**
- ½ **cup butter, softened**
- ⅓ **cup half-and-half cream**
- 1 **teaspoon vanilla extract**
  **Chocolate curls and maraschino cherry, optional**

**1.** In a large bowl, cream butter, sugar and brown sugar until light and fluffy. Add eggs, one at a time, beating well after each addition. Beat in vanilla. Combine the flour, cocoa, baking soda, baking powder and salt; add to the creamed mixture alternately with buttermilk, beating well after each addition.

**2.** Transfer to two greased and floured 9-in. round baking pans. Bake at 350° for 25-30 minutes or until a toothpick inserted near the center comes out clean. Cool for 10 minutes before removing from pans to wire racks to cool completely.

**3.** In a large bowl, beat the cream cheese, butter and extract until smooth. Add confectioners' sugar and cherry juice; beat until smooth. Stir in the pecans and cherries. In another bowl, combine the frosting ingredients; beat until smooth.

**4.** Cut each cake horizontally into two layers. Place one cake layer on a serving plate; spread with 1 cup filling. Repeat the layers twice. Top with remaining cake layer. Spread frosting over the top and sides of cake. Garnish with chocolate curls and a cherry if desired. Refrigerate until serving.

## Chocolate Orange Fondue

We celebrate New Year's Eve with a dinner of fondue, and my chocolate version is one of the dessert courses. Try a variety of fresh fruit and cubed cake for dipping.

—**CHARLOTTE WARD** HILTON HEAD ISLAND, SOUTH CAROLINA

**PREP/TOTAL TIME:** 30 MIN.  **MAKES:** 4 CUPS

- 18 **ounces 70% cacao dark chocolate, chopped**
- 1 **cup half-and-half cream**
- ½ **cup light corn syrup**
- ½ **cup orange liqueur**
  **Assorted fresh fruit and cubed pound cake**

**1.** In the top of a double boiler or a metal bowl over barely simmering water, heat chocolate, cream and corn syrup; stir until smooth. Remove from heat, stir in liqueur.

**2.** Transfer to a heated fondue pot; keep fondue warm. Serve with fruit and cake for dipping.

# Swirled Chocolate Marshmallow Pie

I love marshmallows so much, I'll eat a handful straight from the bag! Swirling a homemade marshmallow filling with cocoa creates a holiday-worthy pie everyone enjoys.

**—LYNNE AKIKO** HONOLULU, HAWAII

**PREP:** 1 HOUR + CHILLING  **COOK:** 30 MIN. + COOLING
**MAKES:** 8 SERVINGS

- 1¼ **cups all-purpose flour**
- 1 **tablespoon sugar**
- ½ **teaspoon salt**
- ½ **cup cold butter, cubed**
- ¼ **cup heavy whipping cream**
- 1 **egg yolk**
- ½ **cup dark chocolate chips**

**FILLING**

- ¼ **cup baking cocoa**
- ¼ **cup boiling water**
- 4 **teaspoons unflavored gelatin**
- ⅔ **cup cold water, divided**
- 1 **cup sugar**
- ½ **cup light corn syrup**
- 2 **tablespoons plus 1½ teaspoons honey**

**1.** In a small bowl, combine the flour, sugar and salt; cut in the butter until crumbly. Whisk heavy whipping cream and egg yolk; gradually add to flour mixture, tossing with a fork until the dough forms a ball. Wrap in plastic wrap. Refrigerate for 1 hour or until easy to handle.

**2.** Roll out pastry to fit a 9-in. pie plate. Transfer to pie plate. Trim pastry to ½ in. beyond the edge of plate; flute edges. Line unpricked pastry with a double thickness of heavy-duty foil. Fill with dried beans, uncooked rice or pie weights.

**3.** Bake at 400° for 20 minutes. Remove foil and weights; bake 8-10 minutes longer or until golden brown. Cool on a wire rack.

**4.** In a microwave, melt the chocolate chips; stir until smooth. Brush over the bottom and up the sides of pastry shell. Refrigerate.

**5.** Meanwhile, dissolve cocoa in boiling water; set aside. In a large metal bowl, sprinkle gelatin over ⅓ cup cold water; set aside. In a large heavy saucepan, combine the sugar, corn syrup, honey and remaining water. Bring to a boil, stirring occasionally. Cook, without stirring, until a candy thermometer reads 240° (soft-ball stage).

**6.** Remove from heat and gradually add to gelatin. Beat on high speed until the mixture is thick and the volume is doubled, about 6 minutes. Carefully fold in the dissolved cocoa, creating a swirled effect. Pour into prepared pastry. Cover and cool at room temperature for 2 hours.

**Editor's Note:** *Let pie weights cool before storing. Beans and rice may be reused for pie weights, but not for cooking. We recommend that you test your candy thermometer before each use by bringing water to a boil; the thermometer should read 212°. Adjust your recipe temperature up or down based on your test.*

# German Chocolate Pecan Truffles

My sister-in-law, Jennifer, is a big fan of German chocolate. With her in mind, I experimented a bit with that ingredient and came up with rich truffles featuring toasted coconut, coconut extract and pecans. Everyone loved them!

**—LEZLIE GOINS** FRANKLIN, OHIO

**PREP:** 25 MIN. + CHILLING **MAKES:** 4 DOZEN

- 8 ounces German sweet chocolate, chopped
- ½ cup plus 2 tablespoons heavy whipping cream
- 1 tablespoon light corn syrup
- 1 cup flaked toasted coconut, divided
- 1 cup finely chopped toasted pecans, divided
- ¼ teaspoon coconut extract
- ⅛ teaspoon salt

**1.** Place chocolate in a small bowl. In a small saucepan, bring the heavy whipping cream and corn syrup just to a boil. Pour over the chocolate; let stand for 5 minutes (do not stir).

**2.** Whisk the chocolate mixture until smooth. Stir in ¼ cup coconut, ¼ cup pecans, extract and salt. Cover and refrigerate for at least 1 hour or until firm.

**3.** Shape the chocolate mixture into 1-in. balls; roll in the remaining coconut and pecans. Store in an airtight container in the refrigerator.

# Chocolate Rum Balls

These creamy goodies spiked with a little dark rum are on my cookie tray every Christmas season. If you like, prepare them up to three days ahead of time—just store them in an airtight container in the refrigerator until serving.

**—DAUNA HARWOOD** UNION, MICHIGAN

**PREP:** 30 MIN. + CHILLING **MAKES:** 3¾ DOZEN

- ¼ cup dark rum, warmed
- 1 teaspoon instant coffee granules
- 4 ounces cream cheese, softened
- 1 cup confectioners' sugar
- 1 cup ground almonds
- 3 ounces unsweetened chocolate, melted
- ¾ cup Oreo cookie crumbs

**1.** Combine the warmed rum and instant coffee granules until dissolved. In a large bowl, beat the cream cheese, confectioners' sugar, almonds and rum mixture until blended. Stir in melted chocolate. Refrigerate until almost firm, about 1 hour.

**2.** Shape into 1-in. balls; roll in cookie crumbs to coat. Store in an airtight container in the refrigerator.

## Folded Paper Truffle Box

German Chocolate Pecan Truffles (recipe above) make an adorable gift when you present them in a homemade box. Start by raiding your scrapbook supplies to find two 12-in.-square sheets of paper or card stock.

For the box lid, lay one sheet flat and use a ruler and pencil to draw lines connecting opposite corners, crisscrossing in the center. Then fold each corner into the center, forming triangular flaps (Step 1).

Fold each side to the center, then unfold, making a straight crease on each side (Step 2). Completely unfold two opposite sides until they lay flat, then refold the other sides at the straight creases until the sides stand up (Step 3).

Fold up one of the unfolded ends, creasing the corners into inverted triangles (Step 4). Then fold the upward flap inward over the edge, forming a side of the lid (Step 5).

Repeat Steps 4-5 for the remaining unfolded side (Step 6). Use clear tape to secure the flaps in the lid.

For the bottom of the box, trim the second sheet of paper or card stock to 11½ inches square. Then create the bottom in the same way as the lid.

Place the truffles in paper liners, pack them in the box and make someone on your Christmas list smile!

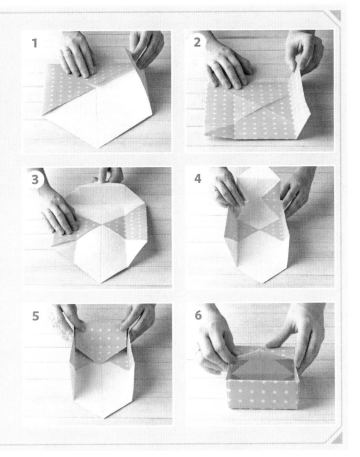

## White Chocolate Terrine with Caramel Sauce

I like to bring this chilled delight to ladies' luncheons and other get-togethers. I prepare the creamy gelatin the night before, then whip up the stovetop sauce the next day.

—AMBER BOURGEOIS BIRMINGHAM, ALABAMA

**PREP:** 20 MIN. + CHILLING **COOK:** 25 MIN.
**MAKES:** 10 SERVINGS (1⅔ CUPS SAUCE)

- 2 teaspoons unflavored gelatin
- ⅓ cup bourbon
- 12 ounces white baking chocolate, chopped
- ¼ cup butter, cubed
- 1½ cups heavy whipping cream, divided
- ½ cup chopped pecans

**CARAMEL SAUCE**
- ½ cup sugar
- 1 cup butter, cubed
- ½ cup heavy whipping cream

**1.** Line an 8-in. x 4-in. loaf pan with plastic wrap; set aside. Sprinkle gelatin over bourbon; set aside.

**2.** In a double boiler or metal bowl over hot water, melt chocolate and butter; stir until smooth. Add 1 cup cream and gelatin mixture; stir until gelatin is completely dissolved. Remove from the heat; cool slightly. Stir in the pecans; cover and refrigerate for 20 minutes.

**3.** In a small bowl, beat remaining cream until stiff peaks form. Fold into the cooled chocolate mixture; transfer to prepared pan. Cover and refrigerate for at least 4 hours or overnight.

**4.** For sauce, in a large heavy saucepan, spread the sugar; cook, without stirring, over medium-low heat until it begins to melt. Gently drag melted sugar to center of pan so sugar melts evenly. Cook, without stirring, until melted sugar turns a medium amber color, about 25 minutes. Gradually stir in butter and cream.

**5.** Lifting terrine with plastic wrap; remove from pan. Remove plastic wrap. Cut terrine into 10 slices; serve with sauce. Refrigerate leftovers.

## Chocolate-Almond Brownie Pizza

Dessert pizza has never been so sophisticated! Featuring a chewy coconut topping and brownie crust, this treat gives traditional holiday pies and cakes some serious competition.

—PAT CASSITY BOISE, IDAHO

**PREP:** 10 MIN. **BAKE:** 35 MIN. + COOLING **MAKES:** 16 SLICES

- 1 package (14 ounces) flaked coconut
- 1 can (14 ounces) sweetened condensed milk
- 2 egg whites
- 1 package fudge brownie mix (13-inch x 9-inch pan size)
- ½ cup sliced almonds
- 1 ounce semisweet chocolate, chopped
- 1 teaspoon canola oil

**1.** In a large bowl, combine the coconut, sweetened condensed milk and egg whites until blended. Set aside.

**2.** Prepare the brownie mix according to the package directions for fudge-like brownies. Spread onto a greased 12-in. pizza pan.

**3.** Bake at 375° for 15-18 minutes or until a toothpick inserted near the center comes out clean. Spread coconut mixture over crust to within ½-in. of the edges. Sprinkle with almonds. Bake 20-25 minutes longer or until topping is golden brown. Cool completely on a wire rack.

**4.** In a microwave, melt the chocolate and oil; stir until smooth. Drizzle over pizza.

# Chocolate Hazelnut Brownies

Toasted nuts, Nutella and liqueur will transform fudgy homemade brownies into a hazelnut-lover's dream. These are perfect for a casual family dinner at Christmastime or any time at all.

**—GENESIS NAVASCA**
SHORELINE, WASHINGTON

**PREP:** 25 MIN. **BAKE:** 30 MIN. + COOLING
**MAKES:** 16 BROWNIES

- ¾ **cup butter, cubed**
- 4 **ounces unsweetened chocolate, coarsely chopped**
- 3 **eggs**
- 2 **cups sugar**
- ⅓ **cup Nutella**
- ¼ **cup hazelnut liqueur**
- 1 **cup all-purpose flour**
- ¾ **teaspoon salt**
- 1¼ **cups coarsely chopped hazelnuts, toasted, divided**

**1.** In a microwave, melt butter and chocolate; stir until smooth. Cool slightly. In a large bowl, beat eggs and sugar. Stir in Nutella and liqueur. Combine the flour and salt; gradually add to the chocolate mixture. Fold in 1 cup nuts.

**2.** Transfer to a greased 9-in. square baking pan. Sprinkle with remaining nuts. Bake at 325° for 30-40 minutes or until a toothpick inserted near the center comes out with moist crumbs (do not overbake). Cool on a wire rack. Cut into bars.

## Holiday Helper

For picture-perfect brownies and bars, bake them in a foil-lined pan and use the foil to lift them out after they're cooled. Trim the edges of the bars and use a ruler to score the lines to cut.

Using a serrated knife, cut downward (not with a sawing motion). For frosted bars, wipe the knife clean between cuts.

## Hazelnut Cream Pie

The key ingredient in this pie is my children's favorite chocolate-hazelnut spread. For the finishing touch, sprinkle on nuts and semisweet chocolate chips.

**—SUSAN BLOCK** CUMMING, GEORGIA

**PREP:** 35 MIN. + CHILLING
**MAKES:** 10 SERVINGS

- 1 **cup graham cracker crumbs**
- ⅓ **cup butter, melted**
- ¼ **cup sugar**
- ¼ **cup finely chopped hazelnuts, toasted**
- 2 **tablespoons Nutella**

**FILLING**
- 1 **package (8 ounces) cream cheese, softened**
- ¾ **cup Nutella**
- 1 **cup plus 2 tablespoons confectioners' sugar**
- 4½ **teaspoons 2% milk**
- 1 **tablespoon hazelnut liqueur**
- 1 **cup heavy whipping cream**
- ⅔ **cup miniature semisweet chocolate chips**

**TOPPING**
- 2 **tablespoons chopped hazelnuts, toasted**
- 1 **tablespoon miniature semisweet chocolate chips**

**1.** In a small bowl, combine the cracker crumbs, butter, sugar and hazelnuts. Press onto the bottom and up the sides of a greased 9-in. pie plate. Bake at 350° for 10 minutes. Cool on a wire rack. In a microwave, heat Nutella until melted; stir until smooth. Spread over bottom of crust. Refrigerate.

**2.** In a large bowl, beat the cream cheese and Nutella until fluffy. Add the confectioners' sugar, milk and hazelnut liqueur; beat until smooth. In another bowl, beat cream until soft peaks form. Gently fold into the cream cheese mixture. Fold in the chocolate chips.

**3.** Spoon into the prepared crust. Sprinkle hazelnuts and chocolate chips over top. Cover and refrigerate at least 2 hours or until chilled.

## Brownie Cheesecake Snickers Pie

What do you get when you combine three sweet treats—rich cheesecake, made-from-scratch brownies and popular Snickers candy bars—in one delectable dessert? Pure bliss!

**—GENISE KRAUSE**
STURGEON BAY, WISCONSIN

**PREP:** 45 MIN.
**BAKE:** 20 MIN. + COOLING
**MAKES:** 10 SERVINGS

- ⅓ **cup butter, cubed**
- 1 **cup sugar**
- 2 **tablespoons water**
- 6 **ounces semisweet chocolate, chopped**
- 1 **teaspoon vanilla extract**
- 2 **eggs**
- ¾ **cup all-purpose flour**
- ¼ **teaspoon baking soda**
- ⅛ **teaspoon salt**

**CREAM CHEESE LAYER**
- 10 **ounces cream cheese, softened**
- ⅓ **cup sugar**
- 1 **egg, beaten**
- 1 **teaspoon vanilla extract**
- 4 **Snickers candy bars (2.07 ounces each), cut into ½-inch pieces**

**GLAZE**
- ½ **cup heavy whipping cream**
- 4 **ounces semisweet chocolate, chopped**

**1.** In a heavy saucepan, bring the butter, sugar and water to a boil, stirring constantly. Remove from the heat. Stir in the semisweet chocolate until melted; cool slightly. Stir in the vanilla.

**2.** In a large bowl, beat the eggs until lightly beaten. Gradually add the chocolate mixture; mix well. Combine the flour, baking soda and salt; gradually add to egg mixture. Spread into a greased 9-in. deep-dish pie plate. Bake at 325° for 20 minutes. Cool on a wire rack for 10 minutes.

**3.** Meanwhile, in a large bowl, beat the cream cheese, sugar, egg and vanilla just until blended. Arrange candy bar pieces over brownie layer; spread cream cheese mixture over top. Bake for 18-20 minutes or until top is set and edges are lightly browned. Cool on a wire rack for 1 hour.

**4.** For the glaze, bring the heavy whipping cream to a simmer; remove from the heat. Add the semisweet chocolate and stir until smooth. Cool for 15 minutes; pour over the pie. Refrigerate until serving.

# Chocolate Hazelnut Puddings

Baked in six-ounce ramekins, these spiced puddings are sized just right for individual servings. They're fun to eat and look pretty with whipped cream and cinnamon on top.

**—DONNA CHILDS** NEW YORK, NEW YORK

**PREP:** 20 MIN. **BAKE:** 40 MIN. + COOLING
**MAKES:** 6 SERVINGS

- 8 eggs, separated
- ¾ cup butter, softened
- ¼ cup plus ¾ cup sugar, divided
- 4 ounces 53% cacao dark baking chocolate, melted and cooled
- ¾ cup all-purpose flour
- ¾ cup ground hazelnuts
- ½ cup graham cracker crumbs
- ¼ teaspoon ground cinnamon
- ¼ teaspoon ground cloves
  Whipped cream
  Additional ground cinnamon, optional

**1.** Place the egg whites in a large bowl; let stand at room temperature for 30 minutes. Grease six 6-oz. ramekins or custard cups; set aside.

**2.** In a large bowl, cream butter and ¼ cup sugar until light and fluffy. Add egg yolks, one at a time, beating well after each addition. Stir in the chocolate, flour, hazelnuts, cracker crumbs, cinnamon and cloves.

**3.** With clean beaters, beat the egg whites on medium speed until soft peaks form. Gradually beat in the remaining sugar, 1 tablespoon at a time, on high until stiff peaks form. Gradually fold into the chocolate mixture.

**4.** Transfer to prepared ramekins. Place in a baking pan; add 1 in. of boiling water to the pan. Bake, uncovered, at 325° for 40-45 minutes or until a toothpick inserted near the center comes out clean. Remove ramekins from water bath. Cool on a wire rack for 20 minutes.

**5.** To unmold, run a knife around the rim of each cup and invert onto dessert plates. Serve warm with whipped cream. Sprinkle with additional cinnamon if desired.

# Dark Chocolate Truffle Tart

Espresso enhances and intensifies the dark chocolate flavor of my truffle tart. I make the crust with toasted walnuts.

**—JOHNNA JOHNSON** SCOTTSDALE, ARIZONA

**PREP:** 20 MIN. + CHILLING
**BAKE:** 20 MIN. + COOLING
**MAKES:** 12 SERVINGS

- ⅓ cup confectioners' sugar
- ⅓ cup walnut halves, toasted
- ½ cup all-purpose flour
- 3 tablespoons baking cocoa
- ⅛ teaspoon salt
- ⅓ cup cold unsalted butter, cubed

**FILLING**

- 8 ounces semisweet chocolate, chopped
- ⅔ cup heavy whipping cream
- 4 tablespoons unsalted butter, cubed
- 1¼ teaspoons instant espresso powder
- 2 eggs, lightly beaten
- 1 egg yolk
- ⅓ cup sugar
- 1½ teaspoons vanilla extract
  Baking cocoa

**1.** Place confectioners' sugar and walnuts in a food processor; cover and pulse until walnuts are finely chopped. Add the flour, cocoa and salt; cover and pulse until blended. Add butter and pulse until mixture resembles coarse crumbs.

**2.** Press dough into the bottom and up the sides of a greased 9-in. fluted tart pan with removable bottom. Refrigerate for 30 minutes. Bake at 350° for 10 minutes.

**3.** Meanwhile, in a double boiler or metal bowl over hot water, melt chocolate, cream, butter and espresso powder; stir until smooth. Remove from the heat; cool slightly. Whisk in eggs, yolk and sugar. Whisk in vanilla.

**4.** Pour filling into the warm crust. Bake for 20-25 minutes longer or until center is just set (mixture will jiggle). Cool completely. Dust tart with cocoa before serving.

## Chocolate Cake Roll with Praline Filling

Here's a recipe that seems complicated but is easier to prepare than you might think. It's worth every bit of effort!

**—JOAN CARRICO** GRAND JUNCTION, COLORADO

**PREP:** 45 MIN.  **BAKE:** 15 MIN. + COOLING  **MAKES:** 10 SERVINGS

| | |
|---|---|
| 4 | eggs |
| ¾ | cup sugar |
| 2 | ounces unsweetened chocolate, melted and cooled |
| 3 | tablespoons water |
| 1 | teaspoon vanilla extract |
| ⅔ | cup all-purpose flour |
| ½ | teaspoon baking powder |
| ¼ | teaspoon baking soda |
| ¼ | teaspoon salt |

**FILLING**

| | |
|---|---|
| ¼ | cup slivered almonds |
| ¼ | cup sugar |
| 1 | cup heavy whipping cream |

**FROSTING**

| | |
|---|---|
| ¼ | cup butter, cubed |
| 2 | ounces unsweetened chocolate, chopped |
| 1¾ | cups confectioners' sugar |
| ¼ | cup 2% milk |
| 1 | teaspoon vanilla extract |

**1.** Line a greased 15-in. x 10-in. x 1-in. baking pan with waxed paper and grease the paper; set aside.

**2.** In a large bowl, beat eggs on high speed for 3 minutes. Gradually add sugar, beating until mixture becomes thick and lemon-colored. Beat in the chocolate, water and vanilla. Combine the flour, baking powder, baking soda and salt; fold into chocolate mixture. Spread evenly into prepared pan.

**3.** Bake at 375° for 10-13 minutes or until the cake springs back when lightly touched. Cool for 5 minutes.

**4.** Invert the cake onto a kitchen towel dusted with confectioners' sugar. Gently peel off waxed paper. Roll up cake in the towel jelly-roll style, starting with a short side. Cool completely on a wire rack.

**5.** Meanwhile, in a small heavy skillet, cook the almonds over medium heat until almost toasted, about 2 minutes. Sprinkle with sugar; cook and stir for 3-5 minutes or until sugar is melted and golden brown. Spread on foil to cool. Crush finely. In a large bowl, beat cream until soft peaks form; fold in crushed praline pieces.

**6.** Unroll the cake; spread the filling evenly over cake to within ½ of edges. Roll up again. Place seam side down on a serving platter.

**7.** For the frosting, melt the butter and chocolate in a microwave; stir until smooth. In a large bowl, combine the confectioners' sugar, milk and vanilla. Add chocolate mixture; beat until smooth. Spread over cake roll.

## Heavenly Drinking Chocolate

Sipping this beverage is like drinking a heavenly blend of dark and milk chocolate. Top it off with a dollop of whipped cream.

**—TASTE OF HOME TEST KITCHEN**

**PREP/TOTAL TIME:** 20 MIN.  **MAKES:** 5 CUPS

| | |
|---|---|
| 4 | cups half-and-half cream |
| 2 | bars (3½ ounces each) 70% cacao dark chocolate, chopped |
| 2 | ounces milk chocolate, chopped |
| 1 | teaspoon vanilla extract |
| ¼ | teaspoon ground nutmeg |
| | Dash salt |
| | Sweetened whipped cream |

In a large saucepan, heat cream over medium heat until bubbles form around sides of pan (do not boil). Remove from the heat; whisk in the chocolates, vanilla, nutmeg and salt until smooth. Return to the heat; cook and stir until heated through. Pour into mugs; top with whipped cream.

133

*yuletide*
# PIES & TARTS

# Dutch Cranberry-Apple Pie

Fresh cranberries bring tongue-tingling tartness and Christmasy red color to classic apple pie. With orange peel, a crumb topping and spices, you'll have a wintry but heartwarming favorite.

**—JERRI GRADERT** LINCOLN, NEBRASKA

**PREP:** 35 MIN. **BAKE:** 50 MIN.
**MAKES:** 8 SERVINGS

| | |
|---|---|
| 3 | **large apples, peeled and thinly sliced** |
| 1 | **tablespoon lemon juice** |
| 2 | **cups fresh cranberries** |
| ½ | **cup raisins** |
| ¼ | **cup chopped walnuts** |
| ¾ | **cup packed brown sugar** |
| ¼ | **cup cornstarch** |
| 1 | **tablespoon grated orange peel** |
| 1 | **teaspoon ground cinnamon** |
| ¼ | **teaspoon ground nutmeg** |
| | **Pastry for single-crust pie (9 inches)** |
| 2 | **tablespoons butter** |

**TOPPING**

| | |
|---|---|
| ½ | **cup all-purpose flour** |
| ¼ | **cup packed brown sugar** |
| 3 | **tablespoons cold butter** |

**1.** In a large bowl, toss the apples with lemon juice; add the cranberries, raisins and walnuts. Combine the brown sugar, cornstarch, orange peel, cinnamon and nutmeg; add to apple mixture and toss gently to coat.

**2.** Roll out the pastry to fit a 9-in. pie plate. Transfer the pastry to pie plate. Trim pastry to ½ in. beyond the edge of plate; flute edges. Fill with apple mixture and dot with butter.

**3.** For the topping, combine the flour and brown sugar; cut in butter until crumbly. Sprinkle over filling. Bake at 350° for 50-60 minutes or until topping is golden brown and filling is bubbly. Cover the edges with foil during the last 15 minutes to prevent overbrowning if necessary.

# Creamy Apple Custard Pie

Treat your family and friends to old-fashioned goodness with this well-used, long-loved recipe. It blends juicy apple slices with a creamy custard in a pastry crust.

**—ELLENA HAND** HUNTSVILLE, ALABAMA

**PREP:** 20 MIN.  **BAKE:** 1 HOUR + CHILLING  **MAKES:** 8 SERVINGS

> **Pastry for single-crust pie (9 inches)**
> 4 **cups thinly sliced peeled apples (such as Gala or Fuji)**
> ¾ **cup sugar, divided**
> ¼ **cup (2 ounces) cream cheese, softened**
> 1½ **cups heavy whipping cream**
> 1 **tablespoon butter, melted**
> ¼ **teaspoon ground nutmeg**
> 3 **eggs**

**1.** Roll out the pastry to fit a 9-in. deep-dish pie plate. Transfer the pastry to the pie plate. Trim pastry to ½ in. beyond edge of plate; flute edges.

**2.** In a large bowl, combine the apples and ½ cup sugar; transfer to pastry shell. Bake at 400° for 15 minutes.

**3.** Meanwhile, in a small bowl, beat the cream cheese and remaining sugar until smooth. Beat in the cream, butter and nutmeg. Add the eggs, one at a time, beating well after each addition.

**4.** Pour cream mixture over apples. Reduce heat to 325°; bake for 45-50 minutes or until the custard is almost set (mixture will jiggle slightly). Cool on a wire rack. Cover and refrigerate for at least 2 hours.

# Ginger-Pear Upside-Down Pie

To showcase the mellow sweetness of pears, I made a spiced filling and streusel. Top the warm pie with vanilla ice cream.

**—MARCY KAMERY** BLASDELL, NEW YORK

**PREP:** 45 MIN. + CHILLING  **BAKE:** 1 HOUR + COOLING
**MAKES:** 8 SERVINGS

**CRUST**
> 1 **cup cake flour**
> 1 **cup all-purpose flour**
> 1½ **teaspoons salt**
> 1 **teaspoon sugar**
> ⅔ **cup cold butter, cubed**
> 1 **teaspoon white vinegar**
> ⅓ **to ½ cup ice water**

**NUT MIXTURE**
> ½ **cup chopped walnuts, toasted**
> ½ **cup chopped pecans, toasted**
> ½ **cup packed brown sugar**
> ¼ **cup butter, melted**

**FILLING**
> 6 **cups sliced peeled fresh pears**
> ½ **cup sugar**

> 3 **tablespoons all-purpose flour**
> ½ **teaspoon ground ginger**
> ¼ **teaspoon ground cinnamon**
> ⅛ **teaspoon ground nutmeg**

**1.** Line bottom and sides of a greased 9-in. deep-dish pie plate with parchment paper; coat with cooking spray. For crust, in a large bowl, combine flours, salt and sugar. Cut in butter until crumbly. Add vinegar; gradually add ice water, tossing with a fork until dough forms a ball.

**2.** Divide the dough in two so that one portion is slightly larger than the other; wrap each portion in plastic wrap. Refrigerate for 15 minutes or until easy to handle.

**3.** Combine the nuts, brown sugar and butter. Spread in prepared pie plate.

**4.** On a lightly floured surface, roll out larger portion of dough to fit prepared pie plate. Place pastry over the nut mixture. Trim pastry even with edge.

**5.** Place filling ingredients in a large bowl; toss. Transfer to pie pastry.

**6.** Roll out remaining pastry to fit top of pie. Place over filling. Trim, seal and flute edges. Cut slits in pastry.

**7.** Bake at 375° for 60-70 minutes or until the crust is golden brown and the filling is bubbly. Cool on a wire rack for 5 minutes.

**8.** Carefully loosen parchment paper around edge of pie; invert pie onto a serving plate. Remove and discard paper. Cool for at least 15 minutes before serving. Serve warm.

## Orange Natilla Custard Pie

After tasting natilla for the first time at a Cuban restaurant in Key West, I knew I had to turn that traditional custard into a pie. For a festive garnish, add curls of orange peel.

—AMY MILLS SEBRING, FLORIDA

**PREP:** 30 MIN. + CHILLING  **BAKE:** 35 MIN. + CHILLING
**MAKES:** 8 SERVINGS

- 1 cup whole milk
- 1 orange peel strip
- 1 lemon peel strip
- 1 whole star anise

**CRUST**
- 1¼ cups all-purpose flour
- ⅛ teaspoon salt
- 7 tablespoons cold butter, cubed
- 5 to 6 tablespoons cold water

**FILLING**
- 4 eggs
- 1 can (14 ounces) sweetened condensed milk
- ½ cup sugar
- ¼ cup orange juice
- 1 teaspoon ground cinnamon
- 1 teaspoon vanilla extract

**FINISHING**
- 1 egg
- 2 tablespoons water
- 2 tablespoons sugar
- ¼ teaspoon ground cinnamon
  Orange peel curls, optional

**1.** In a small saucepan, heat the milk, orange peel, lemon peel and star anise until bubbles form around the sides of pan, stirring occasionally. Remove from the heat. Cool. Cover and steep overnight in the refrigerator.

**2.** In a large bowl, combine the flour and salt; cut in butter until crumbly. Gradually add water, tossing with a fork until dough forms a ball. Wrap in plastic wrap. Refrigerate for 1 hour or until easy to handle.

**3.** Roll out the pastry to ⅛-in. thickness; transfer to a 9-in. pie plate. Trim pastry to ½ in. beyond edge of plate; flute edges.

**4.** Line the unpricked pastry with a double thickness of heavy-duty foil. Fill with dried beans, uncooked rice or pie weights. Bake at 450° for 12 minutes. Remove foil and weights; bake 5 minutes longer or until golden brown. Cool on a wire rack.

**5.** Strain the milk mixture, discarding the orange peel, lemon peel and star anise. In a blender, combine the eggs, sweetened condensed milk, strained milk, sugar, orange juice, cinnamon and vanilla; cover and process until smooth. Pour into crust.

**6.** In a small bowl, whisk the egg and water; brush over the pastry edges. Bake at 400° for 15 minutes. Reduce heat to 350°; sprinkle with sugar. Bake for 18-22 minutes or until the center is almost set. (The pie surface will still jiggle. Custard will set upon cooling.) Cool on a wire rack for 1 hour.

**7.** Cover and refrigerate until chilled. Sprinkle with cinnamon just before serving. Garnish with orange peel curls if desired. Refrigerate leftovers.

**Editor's Note:** *Let pie weights cool before storing. Beans and rice may be reused for pie weights, but not for cooking.*

## Holiday Helper

Rolling out the dough for a pie crust can be tricky. The next time you're making your own crust, try this idea: Place the dough between two pieces of waxed paper and roll out the dough between the pieces. (A little water sprinkled on your countertop will help hold the bottom piece in place as you roll.)

Remove the top piece of waxed paper, lift the bottom piece holding the dough and turn it upside down into your plate. Then peel off the waxed paper. You'll have no messy counter or rolling pin to clean up.

—MRS. J.F. CHAPMAN LAVALETTE, WEST VIRGINIA

# Hand-Held Apple Pies

When I was in high school, my best friend's mom baked these little treats. I was thrilled when she shared the recipe with me!
—**KATIE FERRIER GAGE** HOUSTON, TEXAS

**PREP:** 1 HOUR + CHILLING **BAKE:** 15 MIN. **MAKES:** 2 DOZEN

- 1 **package (8 ounces) cream cheese, softened**
- 1 **cup unsalted butter, softened**
- 2 **cups all-purpose flour**
- ¼ **teaspoon salt**

**FILLING**
- ¼ **cup sugar**
- ¼ **teaspoon ground cinnamon**
- ⅛ **teaspoon ground allspice**
- 2 **cups finely chopped peeled tart apples**
- 2 **tablespoons cold unsalted butter**

**FINISHING**
- 1 **egg yolk**
- 2 **tablespoons water**
  **Coarse sugar and cinnamon-sugar**

1. In a large bowl, beat the cream cheese and butter until smooth. Combine flour and salt; gradually add to butter mixture until well blended.
2. Divide the dough in half. Shape each half into a ball, then flatten into a disk. Wrap in plastic wrap and refrigerate for 1 hour.
3. Combine the sugar, cinnamon and allspice; set aside. Divide each portion of dough into 12 balls. On a lightly floured surface, roll each ball into a 4-in. circle. Place a tablespoonful of chopped apples on one side of each circle. Sprinkle with ½ teaspoon sugar mixture; dot with ¼ teaspoon butter.
4. In a small bowl, whisk egg yolk and water. Brush edges of pastry with egg wash; fold pastry over filling and seal edges well with a fork.
5. Place the pies 2 in. apart on ungreased baking sheets. Brush the remaining egg wash over the tops of pies. Cut slits in the pastry. Sprinkle with coarse sugar and cinnamon-sugar.
6. Bake at 425° for 11-14 minutes or until golden brown. Remove to wire racks to cool.

# Maple-Caramel Walnut Pie

Here's a wonderful twist on traditional nut pies. Flavored with maple syrup, the caramel really complements the walnuts.
—**RUTH EALY** PLAIN CITY, OHIO

**PREP:** 40 MIN. + CHILLING  **BAKE:** 25 MIN. + COOLING
**MAKES:** 10 SERVINGS

- 1¼ **cups all-purpose flour**
- ⅛ **teaspoon salt**
- ¼ **cup cold butter, cubed**
- ¼ **cup shortening**
- 3 **to 4 tablespoons cold water**

**FILLING**

- 1 **cup packed brown sugar**
- ⅔ **cup maple syrup**
- 5 **tablespoons butter, cubed**
- ¼ **cup heavy whipping cream**
- ¼ **teaspoon salt**
- 3 **eggs**
- 2 **teaspoons vanilla extract**
- 2 **cups chopped walnuts**
- 1 **cup walnut halves**

**1.** In a small bowl, combine the flour and salt; cut in the butter and shortening until crumbly. Gradually add the cold water, tossing with a fork until the dough forms a ball. Wrap in plastic wrap. Refrigerate for 2 hours or until easy to handle.

**2.** Roll out pastry to fit a 9-in. pie plate. Transfer pastry to pie plate. Trim pastry to ½ in. beyond edge of plate; flute edges. Line unpricked pastry with a double thickness of heavy-duty foil. Fill with dried beans, uncooked rice or pie weights.

**3.** Bake at 450° for 8 minutes. Remove foil and weights; bake 5 minutes longer. Cool on a wire rack.

**4.** Meanwhile, in a large saucepan, combine the brown sugar, maple syrup, butter, cream and salt; bring to a boil over medium heat, stirring constantly. Remove from the heat; let stand for 10 minutes.

**5.** In a large bowl, beat eggs and vanilla. Gradually add syrup mixture. Stir in chopped walnuts. Pour into crust. Arrange walnut halves over top.

**6.** Bake at 350° for 25-30 minutes or until set. Cool on a wire rack. Refrigerate leftovers.

**Editor's Note:** *Let pie weights cool before storing. Beans and rice may be reused for pie weights, but not for cooking.*

## Praline Sweet Potato Pie

Dress up a Southern-style sweet potato pie by adding crunchy praline crumbles. You can make them up to 2 weeks ahead—just store them in an airtight container.

—CAROL GILLESPIE CHAMBERSBURG, PENNSYLVANIA

**PREP:** 30 MIN. **BAKE:** 45 MIN. **MAKES:** 8 SERVINGS

- ¾ cup sugar
- ¾ cup packed brown sugar
- ¾ cup half-and-half cream
- 3 tablespoons butter
- 1¼ cups chopped pecans
- ½ teaspoon vanilla extract
- 1 sheet refrigerated pie pastry

**FILLING**
- 1¾ cups mashed sweet potatoes
- 3 egg yolks
- 1 cup sugar
- ½ cup whole milk
- ½ cup half-and-half cream
- 6 tablespoons butter, softened
- 2 teaspoons lemon extract
- ½ teaspoon ground cinnamon
- ½ teaspoon ground nutmeg
  Whipped cream

**1.** Line a 15-in. x 10-in. x 1-in. pan with waxed paper; set aside. For the praline crumbles, in a large saucepan over medium heat, combine the sugar, brown sugar, cream and butter. Cook and stir until sugar is dissolved. Stir in nuts.

**2.** Bring to a boil; cook and stir until a candy thermometer reads 238° (soft-ball stage), about 10 minutes. Remove from heat. Add vanilla; stir for 2-3 minutes or until the mixture thickens slightly and begins to lose its gloss. Quickly drop by heaping tablespoonfuls onto prepared pan. Let stand at room temperature until set. Coarsely chop.

**3.** Unroll the pastry into a 9-in. pie plate; flute the edges. Sprinkle 1 cup praline crumbles into pastry. Place sweet potatoes, yolks, sugar, milk, cream, butter, extract and spices in a food processor. Cover and process just until blended. Pour into crust.

**4.** Bake at 450° for 15 minutes. Reduce heat to 350°. Bake 30-35 minutes longer or until center is almost set. Cover the edges with foil during the last 15 minutes to prevent overbrowning if necessary.

**5.** Cool on a wire rack. Garnish with whipped cream and remaining praline crumbles.

## Frozen Maple Mousse Pie

A gingersnap-cookie crust lends spice to this frozen refresher. It's a cool yet comforting finale to a Christmastime meal.

—DEIRDRE DEE COX KANSAS CITY, KANSAS

**PREP:** 25 MIN. + FREEZING **BAKE:** 10 MIN. + COOLING
**MAKES:** 8 SERVINGS

- 1½ cups gingersnap cookie crumbs (about 30 cookies)
- ¼ cup butter, melted
- 2 tablespoons confectioners' sugar

**FILLING**
- ½ cup maple syrup
- 4 egg yolks
- 2 tablespoons dark rum
- 1⅓ cups heavy whipping cream
  Additional gingersnap cookie crumbs

**1.** Combine the cookie crumbs, butter and confectioners' sugar; press onto the bottom and up the sides of a greased 9-in. pie plate. Bake at 350° for 8-10 minutes or until lightly browned. Cool on a wire rack.

**2.** In a double boiler or metal bowl over simmering water, constantly whisk the maple syrup and egg yolks until the mixture reaches 160°. Remove from the heat; beat the mixture for 5 minutes or until thickened. Stir in rum.

**3.** In a large bowl, beat the cream until soft peaks form; fold into maple mixture. Spoon into prepared crust. Cover and freeze for 4 hours or until set. Garnish with cookie crumbs if desired.

## Apple Frangipane Phyllo Tart

An almond-flavored custard, frangipane creates a decadent filling for the bottom layer of my apple tart. Delicate phyllo dough forms the melt-in-your-mouth crust.

**—JESSIE SARRAZIN** LIVINGSTON, MONTANA

**PREP:** 30 MIN.  **BAKE:** 40 MIN.  **MAKES:** 8 SERVINGS

- 10 sheets phyllo dough (14 in. x 9 in.)
  Butter-flavored cooking spray
- 1¼ cups blanched almonds
- ⅓ cup sugar
- 2 tablespoons all-purpose flour
- 2 tablespoons butter, softened
- ⅛ teaspoon salt
- 3 egg yolks
- 1 tablespoon plus 2 teaspoons amaretto
- ⅛ teaspoon almond extract
- 4 small apples, peeled
- 2 tablespoons apple jelly, warmed

**1.** Place one sheet of phyllo dough on a work surface; coat with cooking spray. (Keep remaining phyllo covered with plastic wrap and a damp towel to prevent it from drying out.) Gently press phyllo into a 9-in. tart pan, allowing the ends to extend over edges of pan.

**2.** Layer with remaining phyllo, spraying after each layer; arrange in pan, rotating phyllo so corners do not overlap. Fold in overhanging phyllo to form a pastry shell.

**3.** Place almonds and sugar in a food processor; cover and process until finely ground. Add the flour, butter and salt; pulse until blended.

**4.** Add the egg yolks, amaretto and almond extract; cover and pulse to blend well. Spread filling over the bottom of phyllo shell.

**5.** Halve the apples and thinly slice widthwise. Arrange apples in a pinwheel pattern over filling.

**6.** Bake at 375º for 40-50 minutes or until the apples are tender. Cover edges with foil during the last 15 minutes to prevent overbrowning if necessary. Remove to a wire rack and cool slightly. Brush warmed jelly over apples. Serve warm. Refrigerate leftovers.

## Harvest Pumpkin Pie with Almond Crust

I usually prepare my pumpkin pie with fresh pumpkin, but I've had good results with the canned variety, too.

**—JESSIE GREARSON-SAPAT** FALMOUTH, MAINE

**PREP:** 40 MIN. + CHILLING  **BAKE:** 50 MIN. + COOLING  **MAKES:** 8 SERVINGS

- ¼ cup almonds
- ½ cup all-purpose flour
- ½ cup whole wheat pastry flour
- ½ teaspoon salt
- 6 tablespoons cold butter
- 2 to 3 tablespoons cold water

**FILLING**

- 2 eggs
- 2 cups fresh or canned pumpkin puree
- 1 cup reduced-fat evaporated milk
- ⅓ cup honey
- ⅓ cup packed brown sugar
- 1 tablespoon cornstarch
- 1½ teaspoons ground cinnamon
- 1 teaspoon ground ginger
- ½ teaspoon salt
- ½ teaspoon ground nutmeg
- ¼ teaspoon ground cloves

**1.** In a food processor, process almonds until ground. Add the flours and salt; cover and pulse to blend. Add butter; cover and pulse until mixture resembles coarse crumbs. While processing, gradually add cold water until dough forms a ball. Wrap in plastic wrap. Refrigerate for 1 hour or until easy to handle.

**2.** On a lightly floured surface, roll out the dough to fit a 9-in. pie plate. Trim pastry to ½ in. beyond edge of plate; flute edges.

**3.** In a large bowl, whisk eggs, pumpkin, milk and honey. Combine the brown sugar, cornstarch and spices. Add to egg mixture just until blended. Pour into crust.

**4.** Bake at 425º for 15 minutes; reduce heat to 350º and bake for 35-40 minutes longer or until a knife inserted near the center comes out clean. Cool on a wire rack. Refrigerate leftovers.

# Texas Lemon Chess Pie

Slice into Southern-style comfort food and go back to a simpler time with this classic, feel-good dessert. We consider it a must-have menu item for our family gatherings all year long.

**—CHRISTIAN_ROSE**
TASTE OF HOME ONLINE COMMUNITY

**PREP:** 30 MIN.  **BAKE:** 35 MIN.+ CHILLING
**MAKES:** 8 SERVINGS

| | |
|---|---|
| 1 | **sheet refrigerated pie pastry** |
| 3 | **eggs, separated** |
| ½ | **cup butter, softened** |
| 1½ | **cups sugar** |
| 3 | **tablespoons grated lemon peel** |
| 1 | **tablespoon cornmeal** |
| 1 | **teaspoon vanilla extract** |
| ¼ | **cup evaporated milk** |
| ¼ | **cup lemon juice** |
| | **Whipped cream, optional** |

**1.** Unroll pastry into a 9-in. pie plate; flute the edges. Line unpricked pastry with a double thickness of foil. Fill with dried beans, uncooked rice or pie weights.

**2.** Bake at 400° on lower oven rack for 8 minutes. Remove foil and weights; bake 6-9 minutes longer or until the bottom of crust is light brown. Cool on a wire rack. Reduce heat to 325°.

**3.** In a small bowl, beat egg whites until soft peaks form. Set aside.

**4.** In a large bowl, cream butter and sugar until light and fluffy; beat in the egg yolks, lemon peel, cornmeal and vanilla. Stir in milk and lemon juice. Fold in beaten egg whites. Pour into crust. Cover edges with foil to prevent overbrowning.

**5.** Bake at 325° for 35-40 minutes or until a knife inserted near the center comes out clean. Remove foil. Cool on a wire rack. Refrigerate, covered, for 3 hours or until chilled. Serve with whipped cream if desired.

**Editor's Note:** *Let pie weights cool before storing. Beans and rice may be reused for pie weights, but not for cooking.*

## Fresh Strawberries & Amaretto Cream Pie

As good as traditional strawberry pie is, it's even better when you add a generous layer of amaretto-flavored cream and a toasted almond crust. Keep this recipe in mind whenever you have a bounty of fresh berries, no matter what time of year. You and your family will be glad you did!

**—CHARIS O'CONNELL** MOHNTON, PENNSYLVANIA

**PREP:** 40 MIN.+ COOLING   **BAKE:** 15 MIN. + CHILLING
**MAKES:** 8 SERVINGS

- ¾   cup sliced almonds, toasted
- 1   cup all-purpose flour
- ¼   cup confectioners' sugar
- ⅛   teaspoon salt
- ¼   cup cold butter, cubed
- 2   tablespoons shortening
- 3   to 4 tablespoons ice water

**FILLING**
- 4   cups sliced fresh strawberries, divided
- 1   tablespoon lemon juice
- ½   cup water
- ½   cup sugar
- ¼   cup cornstarch
- 4   to 6 drops red food coloring, optional

**AMARETTO CREAM**
- 1   cup heavy whipping cream
- 2   tablespoons sour cream
- 1   tablespoon confectioners' sugar
- 2   tablespoons amaretto or ½ teaspoon almond extract
    Optional toppings: additional fresh strawberries and toasted almonds

**1.** Place the almonds in a food processor; cover and pulse until almonds are finely ground. Add flour, confectioners' sugar and salt; pulse until blended. Add the butter and shortening; pulse until butter and shortening are the size of peas. While pulsing, add just enough ice water to form moist crumbs. Shape dough into a disk; wrap in plastic wrap. Refrigerate for 30 minutes or until easy to handle.
**2.** On a lightly floured surface, roll dough to a ⅛-in.-thick circle; transfer to a 9-in. deep-dish plate. Trim pastry to ½ in. beyond edge of plate; flute edges. Line unpricked pastry shell with a double thickness of heavy-duty foil. Fill with dried beans, uncooked rice or pie weights.
**3.** Bake at 425° for 8 minutes. Remove foil and weights; bake 5-7 minutes longer or until golden brown. Cool on a wire rack.
**4.** In a large bowl, mash 1 cup strawberries with lemon juice. Add water. In a large saucepan, combine sugar and cornstarch; stir in mashed berry mixture. Bring to a boil over medium heat, stirring constantly. Cook and stir for 2 minutes or until thickened. Transfer to a large bowl; stir in food coloring if desired. Refrigerate for 20 minutes or until cooled slightly, stirring occasionally.
**5.** Fold in the remaining sliced berries; transfer to crust. Refrigerate for at least 3 hours or until set.
**6.** In a small bowl, beat whipping cream until it begins to thicken. Add the sour cream, confectioners' sugar and amaretto; beat until stiff peaks form. Spread over filling. Top with additional strawberries and almonds if desired.
**Editor's Note:** *To toast nuts, spread in a 15-in. x 10-in. x 1-in. baking pan. Bake at 350° for 5-10 minutes or until lightly browned, stirring occasionally. Or, spread in a dry nonstick skillet and heat over low heat until lightly browned, stirring occasionally. When using pie weights, cool before storing. Beans and rice may be reused for pie weights, but not for cooking.*

## Streusel-Topped Cherry Almond Galette

Inspired by French cuisine, this ruby-red galette is a rustic yet elegant dessert everyone will love. The edges of the pastry are folded over the cherry filling before baking.

—**LISA SPEER** PALM BEACH, FLORIDA

**PREP:** 15 MIN. **BAKE:** 30 MIN. **MAKES:** 8 SERVINGS

- 1 sheet refrigerated pie pastry
- 1 package (7 ounces) almond paste
- 1 can (21 ounces) cherry pie filling
- ¼ cup chopped pecans
- ¼ cup packed light brown sugar
- 2 tablespoons all-purpose flour
- 1 tablespoon unsalted butter, melted
- 1 egg
- 1 tablespoon water
- ½ teaspoon sugar
- 1 teaspoon confectioners' sugar

**1.** On a lightly floured surface, roll the pastry into a 12-in. circle. Transfer to a parchment paper-lined baking sheet.
**2.** Shape almond paste into a ball, then flatten into a disk. Roll out between two sheets of waxed paper into a 10-in. circle. Center on the pastry. Spoon cherry pie filling over almond paste.
**3.** In a small bowl, combine the pecans, brown sugar, flour and butter; sprinkle over pie filling. Fold up edges of pastry over filling, leaving center uncovered. Combine egg and water; brush over folded pastry and sprinkle with sugar.
**4.** Bake at 375° for 30-35 minutes or until crust is golden and filling is bubbly. Using the parchment paper, slide galette onto a wire rack to cool completely. Sprinkle with confectioners' sugar.

## Brandied Apricot Tart

Always-available canned apricots make my golden, buttery tart a convenient option for any holiday. I like to top off each glossy slice with a dollop of whipped cream.

—**JOHNNA JOHNSON** SCOTTSDALE, ARIZONA

**PREP:** 25 MIN. **BAKE:** 20 MIN. **MAKES:** 8 SERVINGS

- 1⅓ cups all-purpose flour
- 2 tablespoons sugar
- ½ cup cold butter
- 1 egg yolk
- 4 to 5 tablespoons 2% milk

**FILLING**
- ¾ cup apricot preserves
- 2 tablespoons apricot brandy
- 5 cans (15 ounces each) apricot halves, drained and halved
- 2 tablespoons slivered almonds, toasted
  Whipped cream, optional

**1.** In a large bowl, combine flour and sugar. Cut in butter until crumbly. Add egg yolk. Gradually add milk, tossing with a fork until a ball forms.
**2.** Press the dough onto the bottom and up the sides of an ungreased 11-in. fluted tart pan with removable bottom. Bake at 450° for 8-10 minutes or until lightly browned. Cool on a wire rack.
**3.** In a small saucepan, combine apricot preserves and brandy; cook and stir over low heat until melted. Brush 2 tablespoons over crust. Arrange half of the apricots over crust and brush with ⅓ cup preserve mixture; repeat. Sprinkle with almonds. Bake 18-22 minutes longer or until crust is golden brown. Cool on a wire rack. Serve with whipped cream if desired.

## Making Tarts with Phyllo

The key to working with thin, fragile phyllo dough is handling it quickly and keeping it covered as much as possible so it does not dry out.

**1.** When preparing Baklava Cheesecake Tarts (recipe at right), place 18 sheets of phyllo on a smooth, dry surface and immediately cover them with plastic wrap and a damp towel. Keep the sheets covered until you are ready to work with them.

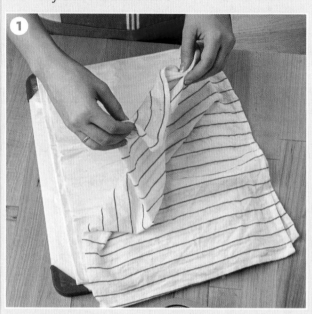

**2.** Working with six sheets of phyllo dough at a time, cut small stacks for the tartlet crusts. Carefully place the stacks in the muffin pan as directed in the recipe, positioning the corners so they do not overlap.

# Baklava Cheesecake Tarts

I love the sticky honey syrup, spices, nuts and crispy phyllo of homemade baklava but don't want the fuss of preparing it in the traditional way. These fun cups offer the classic flavors and textures I crave in the form of little cheesecakes.

—**LAURA CURTIS** HOBOKEN, NEW JERSEY

**PREP:** 30 MIN.  **BAKE:** 20 MIN. + COOLING  **MAKES:** 1 DOZEN

- 2 packages (8 ounces each) cream cheese, softened
- ¾ cup sugar
- 2 eggs, lightly beaten
- 2 tablespoons all-purpose flour
- 2½ teaspoons rosewater, optional
- ¾ cup butter, melted
- 18 sheets phyllo dough (14 inches x 9 inches)

**TOPPING**

- ⅔ cup sugar
- ⅔ cup water
- ⅔ cup honey
- ⅔ cup finely chopped walnuts, toasted
- ⅔ cup finely chopped almonds, toasted
- ⅔ cup finely chopped pistachios, toasted
- ½ teaspoon ground cinnamon
- ¼ teaspoon salt
- ¼ teaspoon ground allspice

**1.** In a large bowl, beat the cream cheese and sugar until smooth. Add the eggs, flour and rosewater if desired; beat on low speed just until combined. Set aside.

**2.** Using two 12-cup muffin tins, brush 12 alternating cups with butter. Layer six sheets of phyllo dough on a work surface, brushing each with butter. Cut the stacked phyllo in half widthwise, then cut in half lengthwise. (Keep remaining phyllo covered with plastic wrap and a damp towel to prevent it from drying out.)

**3.** Carefully place each stack in a greased muffin cup, rotating sheets so corners do not overlap. Repeat twice with remaining phyllo dough and butter, making 12 tarts.

**4.** Fill each with a scant ¼ cup cheesecake mixture. Bake at 350° for 20-22 minutes or until tarts are golden brown and crisp and filling is set. Cool in pan on a wire rack.

**5.** Meanwhile, in a large saucepan, combine the sugar, water and honey; bring to a boil, stirring occasionally. Reduce heat; simmer, uncovered, for 15 minutes, stirring occasionally. Remove from the heat. Stir in the remaining ingredients. Cool. Spoon over tarts just before serving. Refrigerate leftovers.

Combine the flour, nuts, cinnamon, baking powder, salt and cloves; gradually add to the creamed mixture and mix just until moistened.

**2.** Divide the dough in half and flatten each into a thick rectangle. Wrap in plastic wrap and chill until firm, at least 2 hours or overnight.

**3.** Press one portion of the dough onto the bottom and up the sides of a lightly greased 14-in. x 4-in. fluted tart pan with removable bottom. Cover and refrigerate for about 10 minutes.

**4.** Combine preserves and lemon juice; spread over crust. Roll remaining dough between two pieces of parchment paper. Make a lattice crust. Trim edges.

**5.** Bake at 350° for 30-35 min. or until the crust is golden brown and the filling is bubbly. Cool on a wire rack. Dust with confectioners' sugar before serving if desired.

**Editor's Note:** *You may use a greased 9-in. round fluted tart pan with removable bottom instead of a 14-in. x 4-in. pan. Bake as directed.*

## Pineapple Sponge Pie

Here's a home-style delight featuring a fluffy sponge layer on top and a rich custard on the bottom. The tangy pineapple and lemon are refreshing after a big dinner.

—**LOLA BEELER** CHILLICOTHE, OHIO

**PREP:** 25 MIN.  **BAKE:** 35 MIN.  **MAKES:** 8 SERVINGS

- 3  **eggs, separated**
  **Pastry for single-crust pie (9 inches)**
- 3  **tablespoons all-purpose flour**
- ½  **teaspoon plus ⅛ teaspoon salt, divided**
- 1  **cup sugar**
- 1  **cup 2% milk**
- ¼  **cup lemon juice**
- 1  **teaspoon grated lemon peel**
- 1  **cup unsweetened pineapple chunks, drained and chopped**
  **Fresh pineapple wedges and maraschino cherries, optional**

**1.** Place the egg whites in a small bowl; let stand at room temperature for 30 minutes. Roll out pastry to fit a 9-in. pie plate; flute the edges. Combine flour and ½ teaspoon salt; set aside.

**2.** In a large bowl, beat the yolks until slightly thickened. Gradually add the sugar, beating until thick and lemon-colored. Blend in the milk, lemon juice and peel. Add dry ingredients; mix well. Stir in chopped pineapple.

**3.** Beat the egg whites and remaining salt until stiff peaks form; fold into filling. Spoon into pie pastry.

**4.** Bake at 400° for 10 minutes; lower temperature to 325° and bake 25-30 minutes longer or until top is puffed and lightly browned. Cool on a wire rack. Garnish with fresh pineapple and cherries if desired. Refrigerate leftovers.

## Triple Berry Linzer Tart

My grandmother gave me her lattice-topped tart recipe years ago. Now, the bubbling berry preserves, citrus and nuts fill our home with aromas that bring back warm memories.

—**MICHAEL COMPEAN** LOS ANGELES, CALIFORNIA

**PREP:** 30 MIN. + CHILLING  **BAKE:** 30 MIN.
**MAKES:** 12 SERVINGS

- ¾  **cup unsalted butter, softened**
- ⅓  **cup sugar**
- 2  **egg yolks**
- 1  **tablespoon grated orange peel**
- 1½  **teaspoons grated lemon peel**
- 2  **cups all-purpose flour**
- ¼  **cup ground hazelnuts or blanched almonds**
- ¼  **cup ground pecans**
- ¼  **cup ground walnuts**
- 1½  **teaspoons ground cinnamon**
- ½  **teaspoon baking powder**
- ¼  **teaspoon salt**
- ¼  **teaspoon ground cloves**
- 1⅓  **cups triple berry preserves**
- 1  **tablespoon lemon juice**
  **Confectioners' sugar, optional**

**1.** In a large bowl, cream the butter and sugar until light and fluffy. Add the egg yolks and citrus peels; mix well.

# Glazed Fig & Almond Tart

Even people who normally don't care for figs find that they enjoy this. The glazed fruit covers a smooth, luxurious filling of honey-sweetened cream cheese accented with citrus.

**—LORRAINE CALAND** SHUNIAH, ONTARIO

**PREP:** 45 MIN. **BAKE:** 30 MIN.+ COOLING
**MAKES:** 12 SERVINGS

### CRUST
- ⅔ cup sliced almonds, toasted
- 1 cup all-purpose flour
- 6 tablespoons butter, softened
- ¼ cup sugar
- 2 egg yolks

### GLAZED FIGS
- 1 pound dried figs (preferably mission figs), stemmed and halved
- ¾ cup water
- ¼ cup honey
- 2 tablespoons lemon juice
- 2 teaspoons grated lemon peel

### FILLING
- 1 package (8 ounces) cream cheese, softened
- 2 tablespoons honey
- 1 teaspoon grated lemon peel

### OPTIONAL TOPPINGS
- **Sliced almonds, toasted**
- **Confectioners' sugar**

**1.** Place almonds in a food processor; cover and pulse until ground. Add flour; pulse to combine. Set aside.

**2.** In a large bowl, cream butter and sugar until light and fluffy; beat in yolks. Gradually add flour mixture and mix well. Press onto bottom and up the sides of a greased 9-in. fluted tart pan with removable bottom. Bake at 350° for 30-35 minutes or until golden brown. Cool on a wire rack.

**3.** In a large saucepan, combine all ingredients for glazed figs; bring to a boil. Reduce heat; cover and simmer for 25-30 minutes or until the figs are tender. Uncover; cook an additional 5-10 minutes or until the figs are glazed and 3 tablespoons liquid remains. Remove from the heat; cool completely.

**4.** For the filling, in a small bowl, beat the cream cheese, honey and lemon peel until smooth; spread over crust. Arrange the figs over the filling; drizzle with remaining liquid. Serve immediately or cover and refrigerate until chilled. Just before serving, sprinkle with almonds and confectioners' sugar if desired.

**Editor's Note:** *To toast nuts, spread in a 15-in. x 10-in. x 1-in. baking pan. Bake at 350° for 5-10 minutes or until lightly browned, stirring occasionally. Or, spread in a dry nonstick skillet and heat over low heat until lightly browned, stirring occasionally.*

## Mini Coconut Key Lime Pies

Savor the tropical flavor of traditional Key Lime Pie with these miniature goodies. They start with convenient refrigerated cookie dough and bake in a muffin pan.

—LISA SPEER PALM BEACH, FLORIDA

**PREP:** 25 MIN.  **BAKE:** 10 MIN. + COOLING
**MAKES:** 1½ DOZEN

- 1   **tube (16½ ounces) refrigerated sugar cookie dough**
- 1   **can (14 ounces) sweetened condensed milk**
- ½   **cup Key lime juice**
- 3   **egg yolks**
- 2   **teaspoons grated lime peel**
- ½   **cup heavy whipping cream**
- ¼   **cup confectioners' sugar**
- ¼   **teaspoon vanilla extract**
- ⅛   **teaspoon coconut extract**
- ¼   **cup flaked coconut, toasted**

**1.** Slice cookie dough into 18 pieces. With floured fingers, press onto the bottom and ½ in. up the sides of greased muffin cups. Bake at 350° for 8-10 minutes or until edges are lightly browned.

**2.** Meanwhile, in a small bowl, combine the sweetened condensed milk, lime juice, egg yolks and lime peel. Spoon into hot crusts. Bake 7-9 minutes longer or until filling is set. Cool completely in the pans on wire racks. Cover and refrigerate until serving.

**3.** Just before serving, in a small bowl, beat whipping cream until it begins to thicken. Add the confectioners' sugar and extracts; beat until soft peaks form. Remove the pies from the muffin cups. Top with whipped cream and sprinkle with coconut.

### Holiday Helper

Heavy whipping cream is a rich cream that ranges from 36%-40% butterfat and doubles in volume when whipped. It is often labeled as either heavy cream or whipping cream.

Choose a deep bowl for whipping. Before whipping the cream, refrigerate the bowl and beaters for about 30 minutes. Use the chilled bowl and beaters to whip the cream on high as the recipe directs.

150

151

157

*sweet*
# SENSATIONS

## Pistachio Coconut Chews

Fans of coconut will enjoy it in both the top and bottom layer of these nutty, chewy confections. Spiced with a little cardamom, they feature a generous splash of coconut milk, too.

**—TASTE OF HOME TEST KITCHEN**

**PREP:** 20 MIN. + CHILLING
**MAKES:** 2¼ POUNDS

- 8 cups shredded unsweetened coconut
- 3 cups confectioners' sugar
- ½ cup coconut milk
- ⅓ cup light corn syrup
- ½ cup chopped pistachios
- 2 teaspoons matcha (green tea powder)
- ½ teaspoon almond extract
- ¼ teaspoon ground cardamom
   Confectioners' sugar

**1.** In a large bowl, combine the coconut, confectioners' sugar, coconut milk and corn syrup. Press half of the mixture into a greased 9-in. square pan.

**2.** Add the pistachios, matcha, almond extract and cardamom to the remaining coconut mixture and press in an even layer over the top. Cover and refrigerate for 2 hours or until firm. Cut into 1-in. squares. Dip bottoms in confectioners' sugar.

## Honey Caramels

I love whipping up my homemade, honey-sweetened caramels for family and friends. Sometimes I use almonds, filberts or pecans instead of the walnuts.

**—ARLINE HOFLAND** DEER LODGE, MONTANA

**PREP:** 25 MIN.
**COOK:** 30 MIN. + STANDING
**MAKES:** ABOUT 1½ POUNDS

- 1 teaspoon plus ¼ cup butter, divided
- 1 cup heavy whipping cream
- 1 cup honey
- ½ cup sugar
- 1 cup chopped walnuts
- 1 teaspoon vanilla extract

**1.** Line a 8-in. square pan with foil; grease the foil with 1 teaspoon butter and set aside.

**2.** In a large heavy saucepan, combine the cream, honey, sugar and remaining butter. Cook and stir over medium-low heat until a candy thermometer reads 238°.

**3.** Using a pastry brush dipped in cold water, wash down the sides of the saucepan to eliminate the sugar crystals. Cook, stirring constantly, until a candy thermometer reads 255° (hard-ball stage). Stir in the walnuts and vanilla; return the mixture to 255°.

**4.** Remove from the heat. Pour into the prepared pan (do not scrape the saucepan). Let stand until firm, about 5 hours or overnight.

**5.** Using the foil, lift candy out of pan; discard the foil. Cut candy into 1-in. squares. Wrap individually in waxed paper; twist ends.

# Spiced Almond Butter Candy

Roasted almonds and almond butter take center stage in this delectable candy, but the cinnamon, nutmeg and allspice really come through.

—**LAURA MCDOWELL** LAKE VILLA, ILLINOIS

**PREP:** 10 MIN.  **COOK:** 30 MIN. + COOLING
**MAKES:** 3½ POUNDS

 1½ teaspoons butter
 2½ cups almond butter
 2 cups salted roasted almonds, coarsely chopped
 2 teaspoons ground cinnamon
 ½ teaspoon ground nutmeg
 ½ teaspoon vanilla extract
 ¼ teaspoon ground allspice
 2 cups sugar
 1½ cups light corn syrup
 ¼ cup water
 1½ teaspoons baking soda
 1 cup (6 ounces) semisweet chocolate chips or 60% cacao bittersweet chocolate baking chips, melted

**1.** Line a 15-in. x 10-in. x 1-in. pan with foil and grease the foil with butter. In a large bowl, combine almond butter, almonds, cinnamon, nutmeg, vanilla and allspice; set aside.

**2.** In a large heavy saucepan, combine the sugar, corn syrup and water; cook and stir over medium heat until sugar is dissolved. Bring to a boil. Using a pastry brush dipped in water, wash down the sides of the pan to eliminate sugar crystals. Cook, without stirring, until a candy thermometer reads 300° (hard-crack stage).

**3.** Remove from the heat. Immediately stir in the almond butter mixture and baking soda. Spread into prepared pan. Cool completely. Break the candy into pieces. Drizzle with melted chocolate. Let stand at room temperature until set. Store in airtight containers.

**Editor's Note:** *We recommend that you test your candy thermometer before each use by bringing water to a boil; the thermometer should read 212°. Adjust your recipe temperature up or down based on your test.*

# Christmas Mice Truffles

Your guests will say, "Oh, how cute!" not "Eek!" when they spot mouse-shaped truffles on your dessert tray. The little goodies are easy to make with Oreo cookies, cream cheese, maraschino cherries and just a few other ingredients.

**—TASTE OF HOME TEST KITCHEN**

**PREP:** 1½ HOURS **MAKES:** 3 DOZEN

- 1 package (15½ ounces) Oreo cookies
- 4 ounces cream cheese, softened
- 1 jar (16 ounces) maraschino cherries (with stems)
- ½ cup chocolate wafer crumbs
- ½ cup sliced almonds or pine nuts
  Colored nonpareils or pearl dragees

**1.** Place the cookies in a food processor; cover and process until finely crushed. Add the cream cheese; process until blended. (Keep unused mixture covered at all times with a damp cloth.)
**2.** Working with a few at a time, shape 2 teaspoons cookie mixture around a cherry, tapering mixture to resemble a mouse. Sprinkle with wafer crumbs. Add almonds for ears and nonpareils for eyes. Store in an airtight container in the refrigerator.

# Coconut Almond Bark

This yummy bark featuring almonds and coconut is a terrific time-saver when I'm busy but need a treat to share. Sprinkling it with turbinado sugar adds sparkle for the holidays.

**—NIKKI GAGLIARDI** DALLAS, TEXAS

**PREP:** 15 MIN. + CHILLING **MAKES:** 1 POUND

- 2 cups milk chocolate chips
- 1 tablespoon shortening
- 1 package (2¼ ounces) sliced almonds, divided
- 2 teaspoons turbinado (washed raw) sugar or coarse sugar
- ½ cup flaked coconut, toasted

**1.** Line a 15-in. x 10-in. x 1-in. baking pan with waxed paper; set aside.
**2.** In a microwave, melt chocolate chips and shortening; stir until smooth. Stir in ¼ cup almonds. Spread mixture into a 12-in. x 9-in. rectangle on prepared pan.
**3.** Sprinkle with turbinado sugar, coconut and remaining almonds; press lightly into chocolate mixture. Chill for 1 hour or until firm. Break into pieces. Store in an airtight container in the refrigerator.

# Grasshopper Cheesecake

What do you get when you combine a popular mint-chocolate beverage with a cheesecake? Pure bliss! Garnish the top with piped whipped cream and cookie crumbs.

**—MARIE RIZZIO** INTERLOCHEN, MICHIGAN

**PREP:** 25 MIN. + CHILLING **MAKES:** 12 SERVINGS

- 35 chocolate wafers, finely crushed (about 1⅔ cups)
- ¼ cup butter, melted
- 1 tablespoon plus ¾ cup sugar, divided
- 1 envelope unflavored gelatin
- ½ cup cold water
- 1 package (8 ounces) cream cheese, softened
- ⅓ cup green creme de menthe
- 2 cups heavy whipping cream, whipped

**1.** In a small bowl, combine the wafer crumbs, butter and 1 tablespoon sugar. Press half of mixture onto bottom of a greased 9-in. springform pan. Refrigerate until chilled.
**2.** In a small saucepan, sprinkle gelatin over cold water; let stand for 1 minute. Heat over low heat, stirring until gelatin is completely dissolved. Cool.
**3.** In a large bowl, beat the cream cheese and remaining sugar until fluffy. Gradually beat in gelatin mixture. Stir in creme de menthe. Set aside ½ cup whipped cream for garnish. Fold the remaining whipped cream into cream cheese mixture.
**4.** Pour half of the filling over crust. Top with remaining crumb mixture, reserving 2 tablespoons for garnish. Pour remaining filling into pan; garnish with reserved whipped cream. Sprinkle with the reserved crumbs. Chill until set. Remove sides of pan before slicing.

1. In a large bowl, cream the butter and sugar until light and fluffy. Beat in the eggs, egg yolks, vanilla extract and almond extract. Combine the flour, baking powder and salt; gradually add to the creamed mixture and mix well. Divide the cookie dough in half. Shape each half into a ball, then flatten into a disk. Wrap in plastic wrap and refrigerate for 1 hour.

2. On a lightly floured surface, roll one portion of cookie dough to ¼-in. thickness. Cut with floured 2½-in. cookie cutters. Place the cutouts 2 in. apart on greased baking sheets. Repeat.

3. Bake at 350° for 13-16 minutes or until lightly browned. Remove to wire racks to cool completely.

4. For the royal icing, in a large bowl, combine the confectioners' sugar, water, meringue powder, light corn syrup and extract if desired; beat on low speed just until combined. Beat on high for 4-5 minutes or until stiff peaks form. Keep the unused royal icing covered at all times with a damp cloth. If necessary, beat icing again on high speed to restore the texture. Frost the cookies. Let stand until set.

5. To decorate cookies, place the melted candy coating in small resealable plastic bags; cut a small hole in the corner of each bag. Decorate cookies as desired.

**Editor's Note:** *Meringue powder is available from Wilton Industries. Call 800-794-5866 or visit wilton.com.*

# Decorated Sugar Cookie Cutouts

What's the holiday season without cutout cookies? A plate of colorful, fresh-baked bells, trees, wreaths and other shapes always spreads yuletide cheer. This recipe includes directions for preparing royal icing, but feel free to use whatever icing or other decorating techniques you wish.

—**AMANDA RETTKE** SHAFER, MINNESOTA

**PREP:** 1¼ HOURS + CHILLING  **BAKE:** 15 MIN./PER BATCH
**MAKES:** 6 DOZEN

| | |
|---|---|
| 1½ | **cups unsalted butter, softened** |
| 2 | **cups sugar** |
| 2 | **eggs** |
| 2 | **egg yolks** |
| 4 | **teaspoons vanilla extract** |
| 2 | **teaspoons almond extract** |
| 4 | **cups all-purpose flour** |
| 1 | **teaspoon baking powder** |
| 1 | **teaspoon salt** |

**ROYAL ICING**

| | |
|---|---|
| 3¾ | **cups confectioners' sugar** |
| 7 | **tablespoons water** |
| ¼ | **cup meringue powder** |
| 1 | **teaspoon light corn syrup** |
| 1 | **to 2 drops clear vanilla extract, optional** |

**DECORATIONS**

**Assorted candy coating disks, melted**

## Cookie Place Card

Using melted candy coating, pipe your guests' names on frosted rectangular cookies. Let stand until set.

To prop up each cookie, lay a caramel flat and cut it diagonally into two pieces. Using royal icing or melted candy coating, attach two pieces to the back of each cookie, allowing it to stand. Let stand until dry.

# Mini Pumpkin Cakes with Praline Sauce

My family's favorite Christmas dessert is a real Southern treat. A warm praline sauce and sprinkling of pecans make each small pound cake decadent.

—**DIANE ROARK** CONWAY, ARKANSAS

**PREP:** 20 MIN.
**BAKE:** 20 MIN. + COOLING
**MAKES:** 6 LOAVES (3 SLICES EACH)

- 2½ cups all-purpose flour
- 1 teaspoon salt
- 1 teaspoon baking soda
- 1 teaspoon ground cinnamon
- 1 teaspoon ground nutmeg
- ½ teaspoon ground cloves
- ¼ teaspoon ground ginger
- 2 cups canned pumpkin
- 4 eggs
- 2 cups sugar
- ½ cup canola oil
- ½ cup butter, melted

**PRALINE SAUCE**

- 1 cup packed brown sugar
- ¼ cup butter
- ¼ cup heavy whipping cream
- 1 cup chopped pecans

**1.** In a large bowl, combine the first seven ingredients. In another bowl, beat the pumpkin, eggs, sugar, oil and butter until well blended. Gradually stir into the dry ingredients just until blended.

**2.** Transfer to six greased and floured 5¾-in. x 3-in. x 2-in. loaf pans. Bake at 350° for 20-25 minutes or until a toothpick inserted near the center comes out clean. Cool for 10 minutes before removing from pans to wire racks to cool completely.

**3.** For the sauce, in a small saucepan, combine the brown sugar, butter and cream. Cook and stir over medium heat until the sugar is dissolved. Pour over cakes; top with pecans.

# Hazelnut Pots de Creme

White chocolate and toasted ground hazelnuts make a heavenly combination in a rich, silky custard. Your guests are sure to rave about these individual-size treats served in ramekins.

—**ELISE LALOR** ISSAQUAH, WASHINGTON

**PREP:** 30 MIN.
**BAKE:** 25 MIN. + CHILLING
**MAKES:** 6 SERVINGS

| | |
|---|---|
| 2 | **cups heavy whipping cream** |
| 1 | **cup ground hazelnuts, toasted** |
| 4 | **ounces white baking chocolate, chopped** |
| 6 | **egg yolks** |
| ⅓ | **cup sugar** |
| 2 | **tablespoons hazelnut liqueur, optional** |
| | **Chocolate curls** |

**1.** In a small saucepan, heat heavy whipping cream, nuts and chocolate until bubbles form around the sides of the pan and chocolate is melted, stirring occasionally.

**2.** In a small bowl, whisk egg yolks and sugar. Remove cream mixture from the heat; stir a small amount of hot cream mixture into egg mixture. Return all to pan, stirring constantly. Stir in hazelnut liqueur if desired. Strain, discarding nuts.

**3.** Transfer to six 6-oz. ramekins. Place in a baking pan; add 1 in. of boiling water to the pan. Bake, uncovered, at 325° for 25-30 minutes or until the centers are just set (the mixture will jiggle). Remove the ramekins from the water bath; cool for 10 minutes. Cover and refrigerate for at least 2 hours. Garnish servings with chocolate curls.

# Marzipan Squares

With rum-soaked cranberries in sweet homemade marzipan, my chewy bars really suit the Christmas season. I like to dust the cooled squares with confectioners' sugar.

**—AGNES WARD** STRATFORD, ONTARIO

**PREP:** 30 MIN. + CHILLING  **BAKE:** 45 MIN. + COOLING
**MAKES:** 4 DOZEN

**MARZIPAN**
- 1 cup blanched almonds
- 1 cup confectioners' sugar, divided
- 1 teaspoon almond extract
- 1 teaspoon light corn syrup
- 1 tablespoon egg white

**BATTER**
- ¼ cup spiced rum or brandy
- 1 cup dried cranberries
- 1 cup butter, softened
- 2 cups sugar
- 4 eggs
- 3 teaspoons vanilla extract
- ½ teaspoon almond extract
- 2½ cups all-purpose flour
- ½ cup ground almonds
- 2 teaspoons baking powder
- ¼ teaspoon salt
- 1 cup sliced almonds
- 1 tablespoon confectioners' sugar

**1.** For marzipan, place almonds and ¼ cup confectioners' sugar in a food processor; cover and process until blended. Add the extract, corn syrup and remaining confectioners' sugar; cover and process for 1 minute. Add the egg white; process until the mixture forms a ball. Remove and wrap in plastic wrap. Refrigerate for 1 hour or until firm.

**2.** Meanwhile, in a microwave, heat the rum on high until it begins to boil, about 30 seconds. Stir in the cranberries; set aside.

**3.** In a large bowl, cream the butter and sugar until light and fluffy. Add the eggs, one at a time, beating well after each addition. Beat in extracts. Combine the flour, ground almonds, baking powder and salt. Stir into the creamed mixture just until combined. Chop marzipan into ¼-in. pieces; add marzipan, rum mixture and almonds to the creamed mixture.

**4.** Spread into a greased 13-in. x 9-in. baking pan. Bake at 350° for 40-45 minutes or until a toothpick inserted near the center comes out clean. Cool on a wire rack. Dust with confectioners' sugar.

# Iced Coconut Crescents

Cookie crescents get a tropical twist when you add refreshing orange juice and coconut. Bake these little goodies any time of year and decorate them to fit the occasion.

**—MARIA BENBROOK** PORT MONMOUTH, NEW JERSEY

**PREP:** 15 MIN.  **BAKE:** 10 MIN./BATCH  **MAKES:** 4 DOZEN

- ½ cup butter, softened
- ¾ cup sugar
- 3 eggs
- ½ cup orange juice
- 1½ teaspoons vanilla extract
- 3 cups all-purpose flour
- 3 teaspoons baking powder
- 1⅔ cups flaked coconut

**ICING**
- 2 cups confectioners' sugar
- ¼ cup 2% milk
  Assorted sprinkles of your choice

**1.** In a large bowl, cream butter and sugar until light and fluffy. Beat in the eggs, orange juice and vanilla. Combine the flour and baking powder; gradually add to creamed mixture and mix well. Stir in coconut.

**2.** Shape tablespoonfuls of dough into crescent shapes. Place 2 in. apart on ungreased baking sheets. Bake at 350° for 8-10 minutes or until edges are lightly browned. Cool for 1 minute before removing to wire racks to cool.

**3.** In a small bowl, combine the confectioners' sugar and milk. Decorate as desired with icing and sprinkles. Let stand until set.

# Sweet Potato & Marshmallow Swirl Cheesecake

I make a sweet potato souffle that I've always thought tastes like a dessert. I decided to turn that side dish into a sweet treat, and the result was a marshmallow-swirled cheesecake.
—**JESSICA SILVA** EAST BERLIN, CONNECTICUT

**PREP:** 35 MIN. **BAKE:** 1¼ HOURS + CHILLING
**MAKES:** 16 SERVINGS

- 2 pounds sweet potatoes, halved

**CRUST**
- 1 cup crushed gingersnap cookies (about 20 cookies)
- 1 cup finely chopped macadamia nuts
- ¼ cup butter, melted

**FILLING**
- 3 packages (8 ounces each) cream cheese, softened
- ¾ cup sugar
- ¼ cup packed brown sugar
- ⅓ cup sour cream
- ¼ cup heavy whipping cream
- 2 tablespoons butter, softened
- 2 teaspoons vanilla extract
- 1 teaspoon pumpkin pie spice
- 3 eggs, lightly beaten

**MARSHMALLOW SWIRL**
- 1 jar (7 ounces) marshmallow creme
- 4 ounces cream cheese, softened
- 1 egg, lightly beaten
- 4 teaspoons all-purpose flour
- 1 teaspoon vanilla extract

**1.** Place the sweet potatoes on a greased baking sheet, cut side down. Bake at 350° for 25-30 minutes or until tender. Cool slightly. Remove the peel; place the potatoes in a food processor. Cover and process until smooth. (There should be about 2 cups.)

**2.** Place a greased 9-in. springform pan on a double thickness of heavy-duty foil (about 18 in. square). Securely wrap foil around pan.

**3.** In a small bowl, combine the cookie crumbs, macadamia nuts and butter. Press onto the bottom of the prepared pan. Place pan on a baking sheet. Bake at 350° for 15 minutes. Cool on a wire rack. Reduce heat to 325°.

**4.** In a large bowl, beat the cream cheese and sugars until smooth. Beat in the sour cream, whipping cream, butter, vanilla, pie spice and sweet potato puree. Add eggs; beat on low speed just until combined.

**5.** In a small bowl, beat the marshmallow creme, cream cheese, egg, flour and vanilla until smooth.

**6.** Pour half the sweet potato mixture over crust. Pour half the marshmallow mixture over the sweet potato mixture; swirl gently with a knife. Repeat with remaining batters. Place the springform pan in a large baking pan; add 1-in. of hot water to larger pan. Bake at 325° for about 1¼ hours or until center is just set and top appears dull. Remove springform pan from water bath; remove the foil. Cool cheesecake on a wire rack for 10 minutes. Carefully run a knife around edge to loosen; cool 1 hour longer. Refrigerate overnight. Remove sides of pan.

# Cranberry-Pear Cookie Cups

Baking cream-cheese cookie dough in mini muffin tins forms yummy little cups, perfect for holding a spiced fruit filling.
—**ROXANNE CHAN** ALBANY, CALIFORNIA

**PREP:** 30 MIN. + CHILLING **BAKE:** 25 MIN. + COOLING
**MAKES:** 2 DOZEN

- ½ cup butter, softened
- 1 package (3 ounces) cream cheese, softened
- 2 tablespoons sugar
- ¾ cup all-purpose flour
- ¼ cup quick-cooking oats
- ¼ teaspoon ground ginger

**FILLING**
- ½ cup sugar
- ½ cup grated peeled fresh pears
- 1 egg
- 2 tablespoons dried cranberries, chopped
- 1 tablespoon crystallized ginger, finely chopped
- 1 tablespoon pistachios, finely chopped

**1.** In a small bowl, beat the butter, cream cheese and sugar until light and fluffy. Stir in flour, oats and ginger. Cover and refrigerate for 1 hour.

**2.** Meanwhile, in a small bowl, combine the filling ingredients. Shape the dough into 24 balls. With floured fingers, press onto the bottom and up the sides of greased miniature muffin cups. Spoon filling into cups.

**3.** Bake at 350° for 23-25 minutes or until lightly browned. Cool for 10 minutes before removing from pans to wire racks to cool.

## Eggnog Ice Cream with Hot Buttered Rum Sauce

Why save your ice cream maker for summertime? Serve up Christmasy scoops featuring the flavor of eggnog and drizzle them with a delectable buttered rum sauce.

**—DEIRDRE DEE COX** KANSAS CITY, KANSAS

**PREP:** 30 MIN. + CHILLING  **PROCESS:** 20 MIN. + FREEZING
**MAKES:** 1½ QUARTS (1 CUP SAUCE)

| | |
|---|---|
| 6 | egg yolks |
| 1 | cup sugar |
| 3 | cups heavy whipping cream |
| 1 | cup whole milk |
| 1 | vanilla bean |
| ¼ | cup spiced rum |
| ¼ | teaspoon ground nutmeg |

**SAUCE**

| | |
|---|---|
| 6 | tablespoons unsalted butter |
| 1 | cup packed brown sugar |
| ⅓ | cup heavy whipping cream |
| 2 | tablespoons light corn syrup |
| 2 | tablespoons spiced rum |

**1.** In a small bowl, whisk egg yolks and sugar; set aside. In a large heavy saucepan, combine the heavy whipping cream and milk. Split the vanilla bean in half lengthwise. With a sharp knife, scrape the seeds into the pan; add the vanilla bean.

**2.** Heat cream mixture until bubbles form around sides of pan. Whisk a small amount of hot mixture into the egg mixture. Return all to the pan, whisking constantly. Cook and stir over low heat until mixture is thickened and coats the back of a spoon.

**3.** Quickly transfer to a bowl; place in ice water and stir for 2 minutes. Stir in the rum and nutmeg. Press plastic wrap onto the surface of custard. Refrigerate for several hours or overnight.

**4.** Discard vanilla bean. Fill cylinder of ice cream freezer two-thirds full; freeze according to the manufacturer's directions. When ice cream is frozen, transfer to a freezer container; freeze for 2-4 hours before serving.

**5.** For the sauce, in a small saucepan, melt the butter over medium heat. Stir in the brown sugar, heavy whipping cream and light corn syrup; cook and stir until the sugar is dissolved. Remove from the heat; stir in the rum. Serve with ice cream.

# Raspberry-Mocha Chocolate Bark

Give bark a shot of coffee-shop sophistication with espresso beans. Preserves and white chips make it even more special.
—**AYSHA SCHURMAN** AMMON, IDAHO

**PREP:** 10 MIN. + CHILLING  **MAKES:** 1 POUND.

- 1¼ **cups white baking chips**
- 1 **teaspoon shortening, divided**
- ¼ **cup seedless raspberry preserves**
- 4 **tablespoons finely crushed chocolate-covered espresso beans, divided**
- 1 **cup plus 2 tablespoons dark chocolate chips, divided**

**1.** Line a 9-in. square pan with foil; set aside. In a microwave, melt white baking chips and ½ teaspoon shortening; stir until smooth. Spread into prepared pan.
**2.** Microwave preserves in 10- to 20-second intervals until melted; stir until smooth. Drop by teaspoonfuls over the top of white chocolate layer. Cut through layer with a knife to swirl. Sprinkle with 2 tablespoons espresso beans. Refrigerate for 10 minutes or until firm.
**3.** In a microwave, melt 1 cup dark chocolate chips and the remaining shortening; stir until smooth. Spread over the white chocolate layer. Finely chop the remaining dark chocolate chips. Sprinkle chopped chips and remaining espresso beans over the top. Refrigerate until firm. Break into small pieces. Store in an airtight container.

**Editor's Note:** *This recipe was tested in a 1,100-watt microwave.*

# White Chocolate Coconut Flan

Traditional flan gets all dressed up for Christmas when you add a chocolate drizzle, plus a sprinkling of toasted coconut.
—**TYFFANIE PEREZ** SPRINGVILLE, UTAH

**PREP:** 35 MIN.  **BAKE:** 45 MIN. + CHILLING
**MAKES:** 12 SERVINGS

- 1 **cup sugar**
- 2 **tablespoons water**

**FLAN**
- 1 **can (13.66 ounces) coconut milk**
- 1 **cup half-and-half cream**
- 1 **cinnamon stick (3 inches)**
- 1½ **cups white baking chips**
- 4 **ounces cream cheese, softened**
- ½ **cup sugar**
- 3 **eggs**
- 3 **egg yolks**
- 1 **teaspoon vanilla extract**
- ½ **teaspoon coconut extract**

**GARNISHES**
  **Semisweet chocolate and white baking chocolate, melted**
  **Large flaked coconut, toasted**

**1.** In a large heavy skillet, combine sugar and water; stir gently to moisten all the sugar. Cook over medium-low heat until the sugar is dissolved, gently swirling the pan occasionally. Cover and bring to a boil over medium-high heat. Cook for 1 minute.
**2.** Uncover the pan; continue to boil and gently swirl pan until syrup turns a light amber color, about 3 minutes. Immediately remove from the heat and quickly pour into an ungreased shallow 10-in. round baking dish, tilting to coat bottom of dish. Place dish in a large baking pan; let stand for 10 minutes.
**3.** Meanwhile, in a large saucepan, heat the coconut milk, cream and cinnamon until bubbles form around the sides of the pan. Stir in the baking chips until melted. Remove from the heat.
**4.** In a large bowl, beat the cream cheese and sugar until smooth. Add the eggs and egg yolks, one at a time, until blended. Stir 1 cup warm milk mixture into egg mixture; return all to pan, stirring constantly. Add extracts. Slowly pour into prepared dish. Add ¾ in. of boiling water to larger pan.
**5.** Bake, uncovered, at 325° for 45-55 minutes or until the center is just set (mixture will jiggle). Remove baking pan from water bath; cool for 1 hour. Chill overnight.
**6.** To serve, carefully run a knife around edge of pan to loosen; invert onto a rimmed serving dish. Garnish with chocolate; sprinkle with coconut. Refrigerate leftovers.

## Cranberry-Walnut White Fudge

After discovering this nutty white fudge in a church cookbook, I modified the recipe to make it my own. With colorful cranberries, the chunky squares look festive on my Christmas tray.

**—BARBARA CARLUCCI**
ORANGE PARK, FLORIDA

**PREP:** 35 MIN.
**COOK:** 25 MIN. + CHILLING
**MAKES:** ABOUT 1½ POUNDS

| | |
|---|---|
| 1 | teaspoon butter |
| 2 | cups sugar |
| ½ | cup sour cream |
| ⅓ | cup light corn syrup |
| ¼ | teaspoon salt |
| 2 | teaspoons vanilla extract |
| 1 | cup chopped walnuts |
| ¼ | cup dried cranberries |

**1.** Line an 8-in. square pan with foil and grease the foil with butter; set aside. In a large heavy saucepan, combine the sugar, sour cream, corn syrup and salt. Bring to a boil over medium heat, stirring until the sugar is dissolved. Cook, without stirring, until a candy thermometer reads 240° (soft-ball stage).

**2.** Remove from the heat and let stand for 15 minutes, without stirring. Add vanilla. With a wooden spoon, beat until mixture begins to lose its gloss, about 10 minutes. Fold in walnuts and cranberries. Pour into prepared pan; refrigerate until firm.

**3.** Using the foil, lift the fudge out of the pan. Discard the foil; cut fudge into 1-in. squares. Store in an airtight container in the refrigerator.

### Holiday Helper

Cookie cutters filled with fudge make a fun and luscious party favor for guests at a Christmas gathering. Wrap the filled cutters in clear or colored cellophane and tie them with holiday ribbon. Include a copy of the recipe.

## Chocolate-Dipped Almond Macaroons

My mom taught my daughter how to prepare these chocolaty macaroons. When my daughter brought a batch to the county fair, she won a ribbon!

**—TRACI BOOE** VEEDERSBURG, INDIANA

**PREP:** 40 MIN.
**BAKE:** 10 MIN./BATCH + COOLING
**MAKES:** 6 DOZEN

| | |
|---|---|
| 3 | egg whites |
| | Dash salt |
| 1½ | cups confectioners' sugar |
| 2½ | cups unblanched almonds, finely ground |

**CHOCOLATE BUTTERCREAM**

| | |
|---|---|
| 7 | tablespoons sugar |
| 7 | tablespoons water |
| 4 | egg yolks, lightly beaten |
| ⅔ | cup unsalted butter, softened |
| 1 | tablespoon baking cocoa |

**CHOCOLATE DIP**

| | |
|---|---|
| 9 | ounces semisweet chocolate, chopped and melted |

**1.** Place egg whites in a small bowl; let stand at room temperature for 30 minutes. Add the salt; beat on medium speed until soft peaks form. Gradually add confectioners' sugar, 1 tablespoon at a time, beating on high until stiff glossy peaks form and sugar is dissolved. Fold in almonds.

**2.** Drop by rounded teaspoonfuls 2 in. apart onto parchment paper-lined baking sheets. Bake at 350° for 8-12 minutes or until firm to the touch. Cool for 5 minutes before removing to wire racks.

**3.** For buttercream, combine sugar and water in a small heavy saucepan. Bring to a boil; cook over medium-high heat until sugar is dissolved. Remove from the heat. Whisk a small amount of hot mixture into egg yolks; return all to the pan, stirring constantly. Cook for 2 minutes or until mixture is thickened and reaches 160°, stirring constantly. Remove from the heat. Cool to room temperature.

**4.** In a small bowl, beat butter until fluffy, about 5 minutes. Gradually beat in cooked sugar mixture. Beat in the cocoa until smooth. If necessary, refrigerate until buttercream reaches spreading consistency.

**5.** Spread buttercream over bottom of each cooled cookie. Refrigerate until firm, about 15 minutes. Dip the bottom of each cookie in melted chocolate, allowing excess to drip off. Place on waxed paper; let stand until set. Store in an airtight container in the refrigerator.

# Cherry Cannoli Cups

Here's a sweet taste of Italy for the holidays or any time at all. The cute little treats are a cinch to assemble using wonton wrappers. If you like, do some of the prep work the day before—just cover and refrigerate the cherry-cheese filling and store the cooled wonton cups in an airtight container.

—MARIE SHEPPARD CHICAGO, ILLINOIS

**PREP:** 35 MIN.  **COOK:** 5 MIN./BATCH
**MAKES:** 4 DOZEN

| | |
|---|---|
| 48 | **wonton wrappers** |
| ¼ | **cup butter, melted** |
| ¼ | **cup sugar** |
| 2 | **cups chopped hazelnuts, divided** |
| 1 | **carton (15 ounces) part-skim ricotta cheese** |
| 4 | **ounces cream cheese, softened** |
| 3 | **tablespoons confectioners' sugar** |
| 1 | **tablespoon hazelnut liqueur, optional** |
| 1 | **teaspoon vanilla extract** |
| 2 | **jars (one 16 ounces, one 10 ounces) maraschino cherries, drained** |

**1.** Place the wonton wrappers on a work surface; brush with the melted butter. Sprinkle with the sugar. Press into greased miniature muffin cups. Sprinkle each wonton cup with 1 teaspoon hazelnuts.

**2.** Bake at 350° for 5-7 minutes or until lightly browned. Remove to a wire rack to cool completely.

**3.** In a large bowl, beat the ricotta, cream cheese, confectioners' sugar, liqueur if desired and vanilla until smooth. Cut 24 cherries in half and set aside. Chop remaining cherries; fold into cheese mixture.

**4.** Spoon 1 tablespoon filling into each wonton cup. Sprinkle with the remaining hazelnuts. Top with a reserved cherry half.

## Orange-Marmalade Linzer Tarts

These little tarts are almost too pretty to eat! The golden sandwich cookies dusted with confectioners' sugar reveal a colorful, glossy center of orange marmalade.

**—TRISHA KRUSE** EAGLE, IDAHO

**PREP:** 15 MIN. + CHILLING  **BAKE:** 10 MIN. PER BATCH
**MAKES:** 2½ DOZEN

| | |
|---|---|
| 1½ | **cups all-purpose flour, divided** |
| 1 | **cup chopped almonds, toasted** |
| ½ | **teaspoon baking powder** |
| ¼ | **teaspoon salt** |
| ½ | **cup unsalted butter, softened** |
| ⅔ | **cup sugar** |
| 4 | **egg yolks** |
| ½ | **teaspoon almond extract** |
| ½ | **teaspoon grated lemon peel** |
| ¾ | **cup orange marmalade** |
| 2 | **teaspoons confectioners' sugar** |

**1.** In a food processor, combine ½ cup flour and almonds; cover and pulse until the almonds are finely ground. Add the baking powder, salt and remaining flour; cover and process just until combined.
**2.** In a small bowl, cream the butter and sugar until light and fluffy. Beat in the egg yolks, extract and lemon peel. Gradually add almond mixture to creamed mixture and mix well.
**3.** Divide the dough in half. Shape each into a ball, then flatten into a disk. Wrap in plastic wrap and refrigerate for 1 hour.
**4.** On a floured surface, roll out one portion of dough to ⅛-in. thickness. Cut with a floured 2-in. round cookie cutter. Using a floured 1-in. round cookie cutter, cut out the centers of half of the cookies. Place solid and cutout cookies 1 in. apart on greased baking sheets.

**5.** Bake at 350° for 6-8 minutes or until edges are lightly browned. Cool for 5 minutes before removing to wire racks to cool completely. Repeat with remaining dough.
**6.** Spread 1 teaspoon orange marmalade on the bottoms of the solid cookies. Sprinkle the cutout cookies with confectioners' sugar; place on top of marmalade. Store in an airtight container.

## Cranberry-Almond Pound Cake

When you want an extra-special dessert for Christmas, it's hard to beat a seasonal cake. I like to drizzle mine with a simple but elegant glaze flavored with amaretto.

**—JACKIE HOWELL** TUCSON, ARIZONA

**PREP:** 35 MIN.  **BAKE:** 55 MIN. + COOLING
**MAKES:** 12 SERVINGS

| | |
|---|---|
| ½ | **cup dried cranberries** |
| ¼ | **cup amaretto** |
| 4 | **ounces almond paste** |
| 1 | **cup plus 2 tablespoons unsalted butter, softened and divided** |
| 2¼ | **cups sugar, divided** |
| 6 | **eggs** |
| ½ | **teaspoon almond extract** |
| 3 | **cups all-purpose flour** |
| 1¼ | **teaspoons baking powder** |
| ½ | **teaspoon baking soda** |
| ½ | **teaspoon salt** |
| 1 | **cup (8 ounces) sour cream** |
| 2 | **cups fresh or frozen cranberries** |
| **GLAZE** | |
| 1¼ | **cups confectioners' sugar** |
| 5 | **teaspoons 2% milk** |
| 2 | **teaspoons amaretto** |

**1.** In a small saucepan, combine the dried cranberries and amaretto. Bring to a boil. Reduce the heat; simmer, uncovered, for 5 minutes. Set aside to cool.
**2.** In a large bowl, beat almond paste, half of the butter, and ¼ cup sugar until well blended. Add remaining butter and remaining sugar; cream until light and fluffy. Add the eggs, one at a time, beating well after each addition. Beat in almond extract.
**3.** Combine the flour, baking powder, baking soda and salt; add to the creamed mixture alternately with sour cream, beating well after each addition. Fold in the fresh cranberries and dried cranberry mixture. Transfer to a greased and floured 10-in. fluted tube pan.
**4.** Bake at 325° for 55-65 minutes or until a toothpick inserted near the center comes out clean. Cool for 10 minutes before removing from pan to a wire rack to cool completely.
**5.** Combine glaze ingredients; beat until smooth. Drizzle over cake.

# Brandy Alexander Fudge

During the holiday season, we love to indulge in this marbled fudge based on the popular brandy drink featuring creme de cacao. My sister-in-law won first-place honors at our local county fair when she entered this recipe—but in our family, it was already a grand champion!

—**DEBBIE NEUBAUER** PINE CITY, MINNESOTA

**PREP:** 30 MIN. + CHILLING  **MAKES:** ABOUT 3 POUNDS

- 1 **teaspoon plus ¾ cup butter, divided**
- 3 **cups sugar**
- 1 **can (5 ounces) evaporated milk**
- 1 **jar (7 ounces) marshmallow creme**
- 1 **cup (6 ounces) semisweet chocolate chips**
- 2 **tablespoons brandy**
- 1 **cup white baking chips**
- 2 **tablespoons creme de cacao or Kahlua**

**1.** Line an 8-in. square pan with foil and grease the foil with 1 teaspoon butter; set aside. In a large heavy saucepan, combine the sugar, milk and remaining butter. Bring to a full boil over medium heat, stirring constantly; cook and stir for 4 minutes. Remove from the heat and set aside.

**2.** Divide the marshmallow creme between two small heat-resistant bowls. Pour half of the sugar mixture into each bowl. Into one bowl, stir the semisweet chips until melted; stir in brandy. Into the remaining bowl, stir the white chips until melted; stir in creme de cacao.

**3.** Spread chocolate mixture into prepared pan. Top with white mixture; cut through with a knife to swirl. Cool to room temperature. Chill until set completely.

**4.** Using the foil, lift the fudge out of the pan. Discard foil; cut fudge into 1-in. squares. Store in an airtight container in the refrigerator.

**Editor's Note:** *Once you add the chips to the mixture, work fast as the fudge sets up quickly.*

# Orange Crunch Cake

I dressed up a yellow butter cake with a crunchy crumb layer and orange-flavored cream cheese frosting. My inspiration was a specialty I had sampled at a Florida restaurant.

—**BETHANY KINNEY** WYOMING, PENNSYLVANIA

**PREP:** 45 MIN.  **BAKE:** 30 MIN. + COOLING
**MAKES:** 12 SERVINGS

- 1 cup graham cracker crumbs
- ¾ cup slivered almonds
- ½ cup packed brown sugar
- 2 tablespoons all-purpose flour
- ½ teaspoon ground cinnamon
- ½ cup butter, melted

**CAKE**

- ¾ cup butter, softened
- 1½ cups sugar
- 3 eggs
- 1½ teaspoons vanilla extract
- 2½ cups cake flour
- 2½ teaspoons baking powder
- ½ teaspoon salt
- 1½ cups 2% milk

**FROSTING**

- 1 package (8 ounces) cream cheese, softened
- ½ cup butter, softened
- 7 cups confectioners' sugar
- 2 tablespoons orange juice
- 1 tablespoon grated orange peel
- ½ teaspoon orange extract
  Fresh orange wedges

**1.** Grease and flour two 9-in. round baking pans; set aside. In a small bowl, combine the first five ingredients. Add butter; toss to coat. Divide between prepared pans.
**2.** In a large bowl, cream the butter and sugar until light and fluffy. Add the eggs, one at a time, beating well after each addition. Beat in vanilla. Combine the flour, baking powder and salt; add to the creamed mixture alternately with milk, beating well after each addition.
**3.** Transfer to the prepared pans. Bake at 350° for 28-32 minutes or until a toothpick inserted near the center comes out clean. Cool for 10 minutes before removing from pans to wire racks to cool completely.
**4.** In a large bowl, beat the cream cheese and butter until fluffy. Add the confectioners' sugar, orange juice, peel and extract; beat until blended. Place one cake layer crunch side up on a serving plate; spread with 1 cup frosting. Top with remaining cake layer crunch side down. Spread the remaining frosting over top and sides of cake. Just before serving, top with orange wedges.

# Cranberry Persimmon Cookies

At Christmastime, I bake double batch after double batch of these moist drop cookies. Dotted with dried cranberries and pecans, the cake-like treats never last long.

—**CLEO GONSKE** REDDING, CALIFORNIA

**PREP:** 20 MIN.  **BAKE:** 10 MIN./BATCH  **MAKES:** 4 DOZEN

- 1 cup mashed ripe persimmon pulp
- 1 cup butter, softened
- 1 cup sugar
- 2 eggs
- 2 cups all-purpose flour
- 1 teaspoon baking soda
- 1 teaspoon ground cinnamon
- ½ teaspoon salt
- ½ teaspoon ground nutmeg
- ½ teaspoon ground cloves
- 1 cup chopped pecans
- 1 cup dried cranberries or raisins

**1.** Place persimmon pulp in a food processor; cover and process until smooth.
**2.** In a large bowl, cream butter and sugar until light and fluffy. Beat in eggs and persimmon. Combine the flour, baking soda, cinnamon, salt, nutmeg and cloves; stir into persimmon mixture. Stir in pecans and cranberries.
**3.** Drop by rounded teaspoonfuls 2 in. apart onto greased baking sheets. Bake at 375° for 6-8 minutes or until edges begin to brown. Cool for 5 minutes before removing from pans to wire racks.

**Raisin Persimmon Cookies:** *Substitute walnuts for the pecans and raisins for the dried cranberries.*

# Maple Walnut Truffles

Family and friends will be delightfully surprised when they bite into one of these little maple-flavored goodies. The smooth, creamy white layer surrounds a sweet and nutty center.

**—ROXANNE CHAN** ALBANY, CALIFORNIA

**PREP:** 45 MIN. + CHILLING
**MAKES:** 2 DOZEN

- ⅔ **cup ground walnuts**
- 2 **teaspoons maple syrup**
- 1 **teaspoon brown sugar**
- 1 **package (10 to 12 ounces) white baking chips**
- 4 **ounces cream cheese, softened**
- ⅔ **cup butter, softened**
- ¾ **teaspoon maple flavoring**
- 1½ **cups finely chopped walnuts, toasted**

**1.** Place the ground walnuts, syrup and brown sugar in a small bowl; mix well. Scoop teaspoonfuls and form into 24 balls; transfer to a waxed paper-lined baking sheet. Chill.

**2.** Meanwhile, in a microwave, melt chips; stir until smooth. Set aside. In a large bowl, beat cream cheese and butter until smooth. Beat in melted chips and maple flavoring; mix well. Refrigerate for 1 hour or until set.

**3.** Shape tablespoonfuls of cream cheese mixture around each walnut ball. Roll in the chopped walnuts. Refrigerate for 2 hours or until firm. Store in an airtight container in the refrigerator.

## Holiday Helper

I like to dress up pumpkin pies by mixing in a teaspoon or so of maple flavoring. I also add it to whipped topping and baked apples. This addition always gets compliments from guests.

**—ELEANOR RHOADES** WOOSTER, OHIO

164

169

165

To: Jessie
From: Sue

*gifts from the*
KITCHEN

# Mama's Million-Dollar Fudge

My mother-in-law introduced me to her special fudge recipe one Christmas. I was hooked! No other version I've tried comes close to the smooth, rich taste.

**—GLORIA HEIDNER** ELK RIVER, MINNESOTA

**PREP:** 25 MIN. + COOLING   **MAKES:** ABOUT 5½ POUNDS

- 4 teaspoons butter plus ½ cup butter, divided
- 2 jars (7 ounces each) marshmallow creme
- 2 cups chopped walnuts
- 2 cups (12 ounces) semisweet chocolate chips
- 12 ounces German sweet chocolate, chopped
- 1 can (12 ounces) evaporated milk
- 4½ cups sugar
  Pinch salt

**1.** Line a 13-in. x 9-in. pan with foil and grease the foil with 4 teaspoons butter; set aside.

**2.** In a large bowl, place the marshmallow creme, nuts, chocolate chips and chopped sweet chocolate in the order listed; top with remaining butter. Set aside.

**3.** In a heavy saucepan, combine the milk, sugar and salt. Cook over low heat, stirring constantly, until the mixture reaches 235° (soft-ball stage). Pour over mixture in bowl and stir. Immediately spread into prepared pan. Cool.

**4.** Using foil, lift fudge out of pan. Discard foil; cut fudge into 1-in. squares. Store in airtight containers.

# Chocolate-Hazelnut Butter

Store varieties of chocolate-hazelnut butter just can't compete with the homemade kind. Slather it on everything from toast and pretzels to banana chunks and shortbread cookies.

**—CRYSTAL BRUNS** ILIFF, COLORADO

**PREP/TOTAL TIME:** 15 MIN.   **MAKES:** 1½ CUPS

- 2 cups hazelnuts, toasted
- 1¼ cups confectioners' sugar
- 3 to 4 tablespoons baking cocoa
  Dash salt

Place hazelnuts in a food processor; cover and process for 2-3 minutes or until the mixture pulls away from sides of processor. Continue processing while gradually adding confectioners' sugar, cocoa and salt to reach the desired consistency. Store in the refrigerator.

**Editor's Note:** *To toast nuts, spread in a 15-in. x 10-in. x 1-in. baking pan. Bake at 350° for 5-10 minutes or until lightly browned, stirring occasionally. Or, spread in a dry nonstick skillet and heat over low heat until lightly browned, stirring occasionally.*

## Miniature Christmas Fruitcakes

I've found that people who normally don't eat fruitcake make an exception when they sample these treats. Using miniature muffin pans for baking creates fun, single-serving cakes.
—**LIBBY OVER** PHILLIPSBURG, OHIO

**PREP:** 25 MIN. + COOLING  **BAKE:** 25 MIN./BATCH + COOLING
**MAKES:** ABOUT 6 DOZEN

- ½ **cup light molasses**
- ¼ **cup water**
- 1 **package (15 ounces) raisins**
- 1 **pound candied fruit, chopped**
- 1 **teaspoon vanilla extract**
- ½ **cup butter, softened**
- ⅔ **cup sugar**
- 3 **eggs**
- 1 **cup plus 2 tablespoons all-purpose flour**
- ¼ **teaspoon baking soda**
- 1 **teaspoon ground cinnamon**
- 1 **teaspoon ground nutmeg**
- ¼ **teaspoon ground allspice**
- ¼ **teaspoon ground cloves**
- ¼ **cup milk**
- 1 **cup chopped nuts**

**1.** In a small saucepan, combine the molasses and water; add the raisins. Bring to a boil. Reduce heat; simmer for 5 minutes. Remove from heat; stir in the candied fruit and vanilla. Cool.

**2.** Meanwhile, in a large bowl, cream butter and sugar until light and fluffy. Add eggs, one at a time, beating well after each addition. Combine the flour, baking soda and spices; add to the creamed mixture alternately with milk, beating well after each addition. Add the fruit mixture, mixing well. Fold in nuts.

**3.** Fill paper-lined miniature muffin cups almost full. Bake at 325° for 22-24 minutes or until a toothpick inserted near the center comes out clean. Cool for 5 minutes before removing from the pans to wire racks to cool completely. Store in airtight containers.

**Editor's Note:** *To make fruitcakes in regular muffin cups, make the batter as directed and fill 12 paper-lined regular muffin cups. Bake at 325° for 35-40 minutes or until a toothpick inserted near the center comes out clean.*

## Chunky Fruit and Nut Relish

I tuck a jar of this colorful condiment alongside the fudge and cookies in my holiday gift baskets. Packed with pecans, the fruit relish is delicious served with ham or poultry.
—**DONNA BROCKETT** KINGFISHER, OKLAHOMA

**PREP:** 5 MIN.  **COOK:** 10 MIN. + CHILLING  **MAKES:** 6 CUPS

- 2 **packages (12 ounces each) fresh or frozen cranberries**
- 1½ **cups sugar**
- 1 **cup orange juice**
- 1 **can (15¼ ounces) sliced peaches, drained and cut up**
- 1 **cup chopped pecans**
- ¾ **cup pineapple tidbits**
- ½ **cup golden raisins**

**1.** In a large saucepan, bring the cranberries, sugar and orange juice to a boil, stirring occasionally. Reduce heat; simmer, uncovered, for 8-10 minutes or until berries pop.

**2.** Remove from the heat; stir in the peaches, pecans, pineapple and golden raisins. Cool. Cover and refrigerate at least 3 hours.

## Creole Seasoning Mix

When a recipe calls for Creole or Cajun seasoning, I reach for my zippy mix. It's easy to make extra batches and pack them into jars for friends or relatives who like spicy food.

—**MARIAN PLATT** SEQUIM, WASHINGTON

**PREP/TOTAL TIME:** 5 MIN.  **MAKES:** ½ CUP

- 2 **tablespoons plus 1½ teaspoons paprika**
- 2 **tablespoons garlic powder**
- 1 **tablespoon salt**
- 1 **tablespoon onion powder**
- 1 **tablespoon dried oregano**
- 1 **tablespoon dried thyme**
- 1 **tablespoon cayenne pepper**
- 1 **tablespoon pepper**

In a small bowl, combine all ingredients. Store in an airtight container in a cool dry place for up to 1 year. Use to season chicken, seafood, beef and vegetables.

## Pickled Mushrooms for a Crowd

Serve tangy pickled mushrooms alongside a steak entree, as an appetizer with picks, in a salad or as part of an antipasto platter. However you present them, you can't go wrong!

—**JOHN LEVEZOW** EAGAN, MINNESOTA

**PREP:** 15 MIN.  **COOK:** 15 MIN. + CHILLING
**MAKES:** ABOUT 7½ DOZEN (6 CUPS MIXTURE)

- 3 **pounds medium fresh mushrooms**
- 8 **cups water**
- 2 **cups sugar**
- 2 **cups white vinegar**
- 2 **cups dry red wine**
- 3 **tablespoons bitters**
- 1 **teaspoon onion powder**
- 1 **teaspoon garlic salt**
- 1 **teaspoon beef bouillon granules**
- 1 **bay leaf**

**1.** In a large saucepan, combine the mushrooms and water. Bring to a boil; boil for 1 minute. Drain; return the mushrooms to pan.

**2.** In a small saucepan, combine remaining ingredients; bring to a boil, stirring constantly. Pour over mushrooms; cool slightly.

**3.** Transfer the mushroom mixture to glass jars with tight-fitting lids. Cover and refrigerate for at least 2 days. Just before serving, discard bay leaf.

## Creamy Coffee Mix

Cinnamon and sugar perk up the instant coffee in this quick blend. Simply stir a few spoonfuls into boiling water for a change-of pace morning beverage. My mom loved it!

—**JANE FRASER** GIG HARBOR, WASHINGTON

**PREP/TOTAL TIME:** 10 MIN.
**MAKES:** 5 SERVINGS (1 CUP MIX)

- 7 **tablespoons instant coffee granules**
- ¼ **cup powdered nondairy creamer**
- 3 **tablespoons sugar**
- 3 **tablespoons nonfat dry milk powder**
- 1 **teaspoon ground cinnamon**

**ADDITIONAL INGREDIENTS (FOR EACH BATCH)**
- 1 **cup boiling water**
  **Cinnamon sticks, optional**

In a small bowl, combine the first five ingredients; mix well. Store in an airtight container in a cool dry place for up to 2 months. **Makes:** 5 batches (about 1 cup total).

**To prepare coffee:** *Contents of coffee mix may settle during storage. Stir the mix before measuring. Place 3 tablespoons mix in a mug; stir in boiling water until blended. Serve with a cinnamon stick if desired.*

# Almond Tea Bread

One of our favorite holiday traditions is making my aunt's tea bread recipe, which she brought with her from Scotland. Each slice is dotted with Christmasy red cherries.
—**KATHLEEN SHOWERS** BRIGGSDALE, COLORADO

**PREP:** 15 MIN. **BAKE:** 1¼ HOURS + COOLING
**MAKES:** 2 LOAVES (16 SLICES EACH)

| | |
|---|---|
| 1 | **can (8 ounces) almond paste** |
| ¼ | **cup butter, softened** |
| 1 | **cup sugar** |
| 3 | **eggs** |
| 1½ | **cups fresh pitted cherries or blueberries** |
| 3 | **cups all-purpose flour, divided** |
| 4 | **teaspoons baking powder** |
| ½ | **teaspoon salt** |
| ¾ | **cup milk** |

**1.** In a large bowl, combine the almond paste and butter; beat until well blended. Gradually add the sugar, beating until light and fluffy. Add eggs, one at a time, beating well after each addition. In a small bowl, gently toss cherries and 1 tablespoon flour. Set aside.

**2.** Combine the baking powder, salt, remaining flour; add to the creamed mixture alternately with the milk, beating well after each addition.

**3.** Spoon a sixth of the batter into each of two greased and floured 8-in. x 4-in. loaf pans; sprinkle layers with half of the fruit. Cover with another layer of batter and sprinkle with remaining fruit. Top with remaining batter; smooth with spatula.

**4.** Bake at 350° for 1¼ hours or until a toothpick inserted near the center comes out clean. Cool for 10 minutes before removing from pans to wire racks to cool.

# Holiday Eggnog Mix

Eggnog fans will be thrilled to receive this mix. It lasts for up to 6 months, so they can keep enjoying it long after the holidays.
—**TASTE OF HOME TEST KITCHEN**

**PREP/TOTAL TIME:** 10 MIN.
**MAKES:** 18 SERVINGS (6 CUPS EGGNOG MIX)

| | |
|---|---|
| 6⅔ | **cups nonfat dry milk powder** |
| 2 | **packages (3.4 ounces each) instant vanilla pudding mix** |
| 1 | **cup buttermilk blend powder** |
| 1 | **tablespoon ground nutmeg** |

**ADDITIONAL INGREDIENT (FOR EACH BATCH)**

| | |
|---|---|
| ¾ | **cup cold whole milk** |

In a food processor, combine the first four ingredients; cover and pulse until blended. Store in airtight containers in a cool dry place for up to 6 months.

**To prepare eggnog:** *Place ⅓ cup mix in a glass. Stir in ¾ cup milk until blended.*

# Puffed Wheat Balls

My grandmother's cereal balls are perennial favorites with all of her grandchildren and great-grandchildren—including me! The sweet little goodies get snatched up in no time.
—**LUCILE PROCTOR** PANGUITCH, UTAH

**PREP/TOTAL TIME:** 25 MIN. **MAKES:** ABOUT 2½ DOZEN

- 12 **cups unsweetened puffed wheat cereal**
- 2 **cups packed brown sugar**
- 1 **cup light corn syrup**
- 2 **tablespoons butter**
- 1 **cup evaporated milk**
- ⅓ **cup sugar**

**1.** Place the puffed wheat cereal in a large bowl; set aside.
**2.** In a heavy saucepan, bring brown sugar, corn syrup and butter to a boil. In a small bowl, combine evaporated milk and sugar; add to boiling mixture. Cook until candy thermometer reads 240° (soft-ball stage). Pour over the cereal and stir to coat.
**3.** Shape into 2-in. balls. Wrap individually in plastic wrap if desired. Store in airtight containers.

**Editor's Note:** *We recommend that you test your candy thermometer before each use by bringing water to a boil; the thermometer should read 212°. Adjust your recipe temperature up or down based on your test.*

# Caramel Corn

For years, I've taken containers of this yummy snack to our church retreat. Other church members have requested that, if we can't attend, we still send the caramel corn!
—**NANCY BREEN** CANASTOTA, NEW YORK

**PREP:** 10 MIN. **BAKE:** 1 HOUR **MAKES:** 12 QUARTS

- 12 **quarts plain popped popcorn**
- 1 **pound peanuts**
- 2 **cups butter, cubed**
- 2 **pounds brown sugar**
- ½ **cup dark corn syrup**
- ½ **cup molasses**

**1.** Place the popcorn in two large bowls. Add ½ pound peanuts to each bowl. In a Dutch oven, combine the remaining ingredients. Bring to a boil over medium heat; cook and stir for 5 minutes.
**2.** Pour half of the corn syrup over each bowl of popcorn and stir to coat. Transfer to large roasting or 15-in. x 10-in. x 1-in. baking pans. Bake at 250° for 1 hour, stirring every 15 minutes.
**3.** Remove from the oven and break apart while warm. Cool completely. Store in airtight containers.

# Gingerbread-Spiced Syrup

Here's a special treat for the holiday season. Stir a tablespoon into coffee, tea or cider...drizzle it over pancakes, hot cereal or yogurt...or use it as a glaze for chicken or pork chops.
—**DARLENE BRENDEN** SALEM, OREGON

**PREP:** 20 MIN. **COOK:** 30 MIN. + COOLING **MAKES:** 2 CUPS

- 2 **cinnamon sticks (3 inches), broken into pieces**
- 16 **whole cloves**
- 3 **tablespoons coarsely chopped fresh gingerroot**
- 1 **teaspoon whole allspice**
- 1 **teaspoon whole peppercorns**
- 2 **cups sugar**
- 2 **cups water**
- 2 **tablespoons honey**
- 1 **teaspoon ground nutmeg**

**1.** Place the first five ingredients on a double thickness of cheesecloth; bring up corners of cloth and tie with string to form a bag.
**2.** In a large saucepan, combine the sugar, water, honey, nutmeg and spice bag; bring to a boil. Reduce heat; simmer, uncovered, for 30-45 minutes or until syrup reaches desired consistency.
**3.** Remove from the heat; cool to room temperature. Discard spice bag; transfer syrup to airtight containers. Store in the refrigerator for up to 1 month.

## Pink Ice

You'll want to make extra room on your Christmas treat tray for this refreshingly minty candy. With crushed peppermints and a pretty pastel color, the creamy pieces are festive and fun.

**—PHYLLIS SCHEUER** WENONA, ILLINOIS

**PREP:** 10 MIN. + COOLING
**MAKES:** 10 OUNCES

- 10  ounces white candy coating, coarsely chopped
- 2   tablespoons crushed peppermint candies (about 7 candies)
- ¼   teaspoon peppermint extract
- 2   drops red food coloring

**1.** In a microwave, melt white candy coating at 70% power for 1 minute; stir. Microwave in additional 10- to 20-second intervals, stirring until smooth.
**2.** Stir in the crushed peppermint candies, peppermint extract and food coloring. Spread onto waxed paper to cool completely. Break into small pieces; store in an airtight container.

## Peanut Butter Chocolate Pretzels

Chocolate and peanut butter—what's not to love? These dipped, drizzled pretzels in a cheery box or tin will get smiles from everyone on your gift list.

**—MARCIA PORCH** WINTER PARK, FLORIDA

**PREP:** 30 MIN. + STANDING
**MAKES:** ABOUT 3 DOZEN

- 2   cups (12 ounces) semisweet chocolate chips
- 4   teaspoons canola oil, divided
- 35  to 40 pretzels
- ½   cup peanut butter chips

**1.** In a microwave, melt the chocolate chips and 3 teaspoons oil; stir until smooth. Dip the pretzels in melted chocolate; allow excess to drip off. Place on waxed paper-lined baking sheets to set.
**2.** Melt the peanut butter chips and remaining oil; transfer to a small resealable plastic bag. Cut a small hole in a corner of the bag; drizzle over one side of pretzels. Allow to set. Store in airtight containers.

# Crisp Butter Cookies

With just six common ingredients plus colored sugar, you can bake dozens of from-scratch treats in a flash. Bring a plate of crisp, buttery goodies to your next holiday get-together.

**—TAMMY MACKIE** SEWARD, NEBRASKA

**PREP:** 20 MIN. **BAKE:** 10 MIN./BATCH
**MAKES:** 4 DOZEN

| | |
|---|---|
| ½ | cup butter, softened |
| 1 | cup sugar |
| 5 | egg yolks |
| 1½ | teaspoons vanilla extract |
| 2 | cups all-purpose flour |
| ⅛ | teaspoon salt |
| | Colored sugar |

**1.** In a large bowl, cream butter and sugar until light and fluffy. Beat in the egg yolks and vanilla. In a small bowl, combine flour and salt; gradually beat into creamed mixture, mixing well (dough will be very stiff).

**2.** On a well-floured surface, roll out the dough to ⅛-in. thickness. With a sharp knife or pastry wheel, cut the dough into 2½-in. squares, rectangles or diamonds. Place ½ in. apart on ungreased baking sheets. Sprinkle with colored sugar.

**3.** Bake at 375° for 7-8 minutes or until lightly browned. (Watch carefully as cookies will brown quickly.) Remove to wire racks to cool. Store in airtight containers.

## Holiday Helper

Short on time? Here are ideas for dressing up purchased cookies for the holiday season:

- Melt white baking chips and dip gingersnaps halfway into the melted chips.
- Tint vanilla frosting with food coloring and use it to pipe designs on sugar cookies.
- Buy chocolate-covered mint cookies and drizzle them with melted white chocolate.

# Danish Coffee Cakes

I always think that as long as I'm in the kitchen baking, I might as well make enough to share. These three cheese-filled coffee cakes are beautiful and scrumptious.

—**SHERI KRATCHA** AVOCA, WISCONSIN

**PREP:** 45 MIN. + CHILLING  **BAKE:** 20 MIN. + COOLING
**MAKES:** 3 COFFEE CAKES (10 SLICES EACH)

|   |   |
|---|---|
| 1 | package (¼ ounce) active dry yeast |
| ¼ | cup warm water (110° to 115°) |
| 4 | cups all-purpose flour |
| ¼ | cup sugar |
| 1 | teaspoon salt |
| 1 | cup shortening |
| 1 | cup warm 2% milk (110° to 115°) |
| 2 | eggs, lightly beaten |

**FILLING**

|   |   |
|---|---|
| 1 | package (8 ounces) cream cheese, softened |
| ¾ | cup sugar |
| 2 | tablespoons all-purpose flour |
| 1 | egg, lightly beaten |
| 1 | teaspoon poppy seeds |
| 1 | teaspoon vanilla extract |
| ½ | teaspoon lemon extract |

**ICING**

|   |   |
|---|---|
| 1 | cup confectioners' sugar |
| 2 | tablespoons milk |
| ⅛ | teaspoon vanilla extract |

**1.** In a small bowl, dissolve yeast in warm water. In a large bowl, combine the flour, sugar and salt; cut in shortening until crumbly. Add the yeast mixture, milk and eggs; beat until smooth (dough will be soft). Do not knead. Cover and refrigerate overnight.

**2.** In a small bowl, beat the cream cheese, sugar and flour until smooth. Add the egg, poppy seeds and extracts; mix until blended.

**3.** Punch dough down. Turn onto a well-floured surface; divide into thirds. Return two portions to the refrigerator. Roll the remaining portion into a 14-in. x 8-in. rectangle; place on a parchment-lined baking sheet. Spread a third of the filling down center of rectangle.

**4.** On each long side, cut ¾-in.-wide strips, about 2¼ in. into the center. Starting at one end, fold alternating strips at an angle across filling. Pinch ends to seal. Repeat with remaining dough and filling. Cover and let rise in a warm place until doubled, about 45 minutes.

**5.** Bake at 350° for 20-25 minutes or until golden brown. Cool on pans on wire racks. In a small bowl, combine icing ingredients; drizzle over coffee cakes.

## Shaping Coffee Cakes

Use a sharp knife or kitchen shears to cut strips in the dough. A clean, clear plastic ruler may come in handy for measuring and marking the length and width of the strips. After cutting, simply fold alternating strips at an angle as described in the recipe.

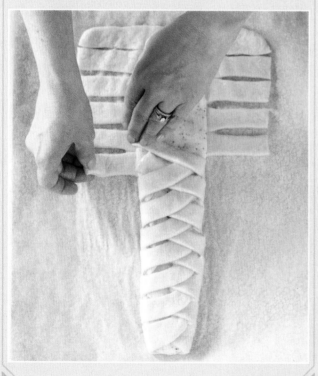

# Creamy Caramels

I discovered this recipe for soft, buttery caramels in a local newspaper. They beat the store-bought version hands-down!
—**MARCIE WOLFE** WILLIAMSBURG, VIRGINIA

**PREP:** 10 MIN. **COOK:** 30 MIN. + COOLING **MAKES:** 2½ POUNDS

- 1 teaspoon plus 1 cup butter, divided
- 1 cup sugar
- 1 cup dark corn syrup
- 1 can (14 ounces) sweetened condensed milk
- 1 teaspoon vanilla extract

**1.** Line an 8-in.-square pan with foil; grease the foil with 1 teaspoon butter and set aside.
**2.** In a large heavy saucepan, combine the sugar, corn syrup and remaining butter; bring to a boil over medium heat, stirring constantly. Boil slowly for 4 minutes without stirring.
**3.** Remove from the heat; stir in the milk. Reduce heat to medium-low and cook until a candy thermometer reads 238° (soft-ball stage), stirring constantly. Remove from the heat; stir in vanilla.
**4.** Pour into prepared pan (do not scrape saucepan). Cool. Using foil, lift candy out of pan. Discard foil; cut candy into 1-in. squares. Wrap individually in waxed paper; twist ends.

**Editor's Note:** *We recommend that you test your candy thermometer before each use by bringing water to a boil; the thermometer should read 212°. Adjust your recipe temperature up or down based on your test.*

# Spicy Chipotle Snack Mix

My family craves anything flavored with chipotle, and this spicy snack fills the bill. It's great for last-minute get-togethers because it takes only 15 minutes to prepare.
—**CHERYL STEWART** CITRUS HEIGHTS, CALIFORNIA

**PREP/TOTAL TIME:** 15 MIN. **MAKES:** ABOUT 2¾ QUARTS

- 5 cups Corn Chex
- 2 cups Rice Chex
- 2 cups Wheat Chex
- 1 cup miniature pretzels
- 1 cup dry roasted peanuts
- ½ cup butter, melted
- 2 teaspoons chipotle chili powder
- 1 teaspoon chili powder
- ½ teaspoon seasoned salt

**1.** In a large microwave-safe bowl, combine the cereals, pretzels and peanuts. In a small bowl, combine the butter and spices; pour over cereal mixture and toss to coat.
**2.** Microwave, uncovered, on high for 5-6 minutes, stirring three times. Spread onto waxed paper to cool. Store in airtight containers.

**Editor's Note:** *This recipe was tested in a 1,100-watt microwave.*

# All-Day Apple Butter

The slow cooker does most of the work for my apple butter. While it cooks, I can turn my attention to all of the other things on my to-do list during the busy Christmas season.
—**BETTY RUENHOLL** SYRACUSE, NEBRASKA

**PREP:** 20 MIN. **COOK:** 11 HOURS **MAKES:** 4 PINTS

- 5½ pounds apples, peeled and finely chopped
- 4 cups sugar
- 2 to 3 teaspoons ground cinnamon
- ¼ teaspoon ground cloves
- ¼ teaspoon salt

**1.** Place the apples in a 3-qt. slow cooker. Combine sugar, cinnamon, cloves and salt; pour over apples and mix well. Cover and cook on high for 1 hour.
**2.** Reduce the heat to low; cover and cook for 9-11 hours or until thickened and dark brown, stirring occasionally (stir more frequently as it thickens to prevent sticking).
**3.** Uncover and cook on low 1 hour longer. If desired, stir with a wire whisk until smooth. Spoon the butter into freezer containers, leaving ½-in. headspace. Cover and refrigerate or freeze.

## Country Bean Soup

Looking for the perfect gift? Put dried beans, peas and lentils in a clear jar and use a festive ribbon to attach the recipe for soup. Big bowlfuls are sure to warm hearts on cold winter days.

**—DONNA HIGBEE** RIVERTON, UTAH

**PREP:** 25 MIN.  **COOK:** 3¼ HOURS  **MAKES:** 10 CUPS PER BATCH

- 1 cup each dried black beans, dried yellow split peas, dried green split peas, dried black-eyed peas, dried pinto beans, dried kidney beans, dried great northern beans and dried lentils

**ADDITIONAL INGREDIENTS (FOR EACH BATCH)**
- 1 smoked ham hock (about ½ pound)
- 1 large onion, chopped
- 2 medium carrots, chopped
- 1 celery rib, chopped
- 1 garlic clove, minced
- 1 to 2 teaspoons salt
- 1 teaspoon chili powder
- ¼ teaspoon pepper
- 1½ quarts water
- 1 can (8 ounces) tomato sauce

Sort the beans, peas and lentils; combine in a large bowl. Divide into four equal batches, 2 cups each. Store in airtight containers in a cool dry place for up to 6 months.
**Makes:** 4 batches.

**To make one batch of soup:** *Rinse the bean mixture with cold water. Place in a large saucepan; add water to cover by 2 in. Bring to a boil; boil for 2 minutes. Remove from the heat; cover and let soak for 1 to 4 hours or until beans are softened.*

*Drain and rinse the bean mixture, discarding liquid. Return bean mixture to pan; add remaining ingredients. Bring to a boil over medium-high heat. Reduce heat; cover and simmer for 3 hours or until beans are tender. Remove ham hock; cut meat into bite-size pieces and return to pan. Heat through.*

176

178

188

*deck the*
HALLS

# Felt Circle Wreath

**CRAFT LEVEL: BEGINNER**

**FINISHED SIZE:** Wreath measures about 14 in. across. Poinsettia measures about 5 in. across.

This fun felt wreath will make any room seem a little warmer and cozier. Use the alternating color scheme shown here, or create your own pattern for a personalized design.

## MATERIALS:
**Patterns on page 177**
**9 sheets each of light, medium and dark green craft felt**
**1 sheet of red craft felt**
**12-in. white Styrofoam wreath**
**About 100 straight pins**
**1-in. rhinestone or button**
**Tacky glue or hot glue**
**1-in.-wide coordinating ribbon for hanging**

## DIRECTIONS:

### WREATH

**1.** Using circle pattern enlarged to 3 in., cut 70 circles from each green color of felt, making a total of 210 circles.

**2.** Using 2 circles of the same color, fold each in half and then in half again, forming triangles. Referring to Photo 1 above, lay triangles flat on inner edge of wreath, point to point, forming a butterfly shape. Pin in place.

**3.** Repeat with 8 more circles of the same color until you have covered a small vertical section of the wreath (see Photo 2 on page 176). Use your fingers to carefully open the triangles slightly. If needed, use another straight pin to hold each triangle open.

**4.** Working close to first felt "stripe," repeat Steps 2 and 3 with a different green color, using 10 more circles. For third stripe, use third green color. Continue alternating the colors as shown in the top photo on page 176. (When wreath is covered, you should have about 21 stripes.)

### POINSETTIA

**1.** Using poinsettia patterns, cut two large poinsettias and one small poinsettia from red felt.

**2.** Layer the two large poinsettias so that the points alternate, then layer the small poinsettia centered on top of the large poinsettias. Glue in place.

**3.** Glue rhinestone or button centered on the small poinsettia. Pin or glue assembled flower to wreath.

### FINISHING

**1.** Cut a 24-in. or desired length of ribbon and fold in half.

**2.** Use pins or glue to secure ends of ribbon to top back of wreath. Let dry. Hang wreath as desired.

**Crafter's Note:** *Want to save time? Instead of cutting the felt circles, look for precut 3-in. circles for purchase online.*

## WREATH AND POINSETTIA PATTERNS

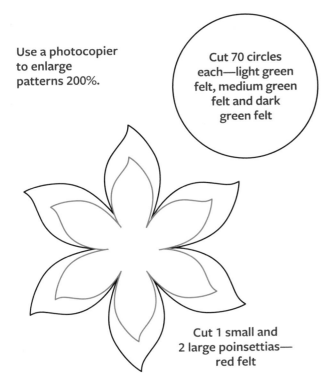

Use a photocopier to enlarge patterns 200%.

Cut 70 circles each—light green felt, medium green felt and dark green felt

Cut 1 small and 2 large poinsettias— red felt

## 'Joy' Wall Letters

**CRAFT LEVEL:** QUICK & EASY

**FINISHED SIZE:** Varies.

Take a cue from Craft Editor Shalana Frisby and turn plain papier-mache letters into a joyous, antique-style accent. Feel free to experiment with the letter size and colors.

### MATERIALS:
**Papier-mache letters spelling "JOY"**
**Multipurpose acrylic sealer**
**Acrylic paint in desired bright color for base**
**Acrylic paint in desired dark color for staining**
**Antiquing medium**
**Polyurethane satin varnish (optional)**
**Flat paintbrush**
**Paper towels or rags**
**Wall-mounting adhesive tabs (optional)**

### DIRECTIONS:
**1.** Use paintbrush to apply acrylic sealer on front and sides of all letters. Let dry.

**2.** Base-coat sealed letters in bright acrylic paint. Apply as many coats as needed for full coverage, letting dry between coats.

**3.** Following manufacturer's instructions, mix antiquing medium with dark acrylic paint. Brush newly mixed staining medium onto painted letters. Use paper towels or rags to wipe off excess paint while still wet. Let remaining paint dry.

**4.** If desired, apply a coat of varnish as a sealer. Let dry.

**5.** For hanging, either use wall-mounting adhesive tabs on each letter or poke a hole in the back of each letter to insert a nail or hook.

# Cinnamon Stick Candle

**CRAFT LEVEL:** BEGINNER

**FINISHED SIZE:** Varies.

Spice up your home in an aromatic way with a flameless candle surrounded by cinnamon sticks. The scented seasonal accent is so easy to create, you'll want to make one for every room.

**MATERIALS:**

**Small flameless pillar candle**
**Cinnamon sticks**
**Clear tape**
**Holiday ribbon**
**Faux berries**

**DIRECTIONS:**

**1.** Line up cinnamon sticks vertically around the outside of the pillar. Secure them around the center with clear tape.

**2.** Wrap a ribbon around the candle and tie in a knot, concealing the tape. Trim ends of ribbon as desired.

**3.** Tuck faux berries into ribbon.

# Advent Treat Jar

**CRAFT LEVEL:** BEGINNER

**FINISHED SIZE:** Varies.

This delightfully different Advent calendar from Craft Editor Shalana Frisby is brimming with fun. Fill a clear jar with small gifts, and your children or grandchildren will enjoy a little treat each day until Christmas.

**MATERIALS:**

**Large square or round glass jar**
**Flexible tape measure**
**Scraps of red and green card stock**
**3-in.-wide coordinating wired ribbon**
**½-in.-wide coordinating ribbon (optional)**
**1- to 3-in.-high sticker numbers and letters**
**Paper punches—3½-in. scallop circle and 3-in. circle**
**25 small boxes or bags**
**Desired ribbon, buttons or sticker embellishments for boxes or bags**
**Desired candy or small presents to place in boxes or bags**
**Glue dots**

**DIRECTIONS:**

**1.** Measure around the center of the jar. Cut a piece of 3-in.-wide ribbon about 1 in. longer than the measurement. Wrap the ribbon tightly around the center of jar. Overlap the ends and secure at the seam with glue dots.

**2.** Punch a scallop circle from the red card stock. Punch a smaller circle from the green card stock. Adhere the green circle centered on the red scalloped circle.

**3.** Use sticker numbers and letters to spell "25 days" on center of green circle. If needed, secure stickers with glue dots.

**4.** Use glue dots to adhere circles centered on top of ribbon seam on side of jar.

**5.** If desired, decorate lid of jar with additional punched circles and adhere ½-in.-wide ribbon around the rim of jar.

**6.** Fill boxes or bags with desired candy or small presents. Decorate with ribbon, buttons or stickers. Place boxes or bags in jar.

# Yarn-Wrapped Trees

**CRAFT LEVEL:** BEGINNER

**FINISHED SIZE:** Varies.

Delve into your stash of leftover yarn to make these cute evergreen trees. A cluster of cozy-looking pines will make a charming decoration on a side table, mantel or shelf.

**MATERIALS (FOR ONE):**
**Low-temperature hot glue gun and glue sticks**
**Solid-color yarn for base color**
**Coordinating metallic yarn or string (optional)**
**Styrofoam cone**
**Coordinating narrow ribbon or strung beads**

**DIRECTIONS (FOR ONE):**
**1.** Using glue to secure, wrap Styrofoam cone with solid-color yarn. Cover cone completely, overlapping the yarn as needed.
**2.** If desired, wrap metallic yarn or string over the base yarn, leaving areas of the base yarn visible to create a two-tone effect.
**3.** Adhere a single spiral of ribbon or beads as a garland.

# Stitched Christmas Tree

**CRAFT LEVEL:** BEGINNER

**FINISHED SIZE:** Design area measures about 5 x 7 in.

Embroiderers of any skill level can make this darling stitched tree, perfect for displaying in a coordinating frame. Craft Editor Shalana Frisby created the pretty pine on a scrap of card stock using just two different stitches.

## MATERIALS:

**Pattern and color key on this page**
**8- x 10-in. photo frame**
**8- x 10-in. mat with 5- x 7-in. opening**
**8- x 10-in. piece of white glitter card stock**
**DMC six-strand embroidery floss in colors listed on**
    **color key**
**Tapestry or embroidery needle**
**⅜-in. green button**
**1-in.-wide red-and-white bow**
**⅜-in.-wide coordinating self-adhesive ribbon**
**Glue dots**

## DIRECTIONS:

### STITCHING

**1.** Lay mat on front of card stock with edges aligned. Trace the interior opening of mat on the card stock to use as a guide. Using the tree pattern, trace the tree, trunk and ornaments inside marked opening.

**2.** Using the needle, poke holes along the tree and trunk outline about every ⅛ in., where stitches will be placed. For the ornaments, poke holes at the ends of each drawn Smryna cross-stitch.

**3.** Refer to color key for all stitching and see Fig. 1 below for all stitch illustrations. To begin stitching, leave a 1-in. tail of floss on back of work and hold it in place while working the first few stitches around it. Using 18-in. lengths of six-strand floss, backstitch the tree and trunk outline. Use a Smyrna cross-stitch for the ornament shapes. To end stitching, run needle under a few stitches in back before clipping the floss close to work.

### ASSEMBLY

**1.** Cut 6 in. of ribbon and adhere it horizontally about ⅛ in. below the base of the tree trunk.

**2.** Use glue dots to adhere red bow to treetop, then adhere button centered on bow.

**3.** Use glue dots to adhere mat centered on top of design area. Place matted design in frame and replace backing.

**TREE PATTERN**

## FIG. 1

Backstitch    Smyrna Cross-Stitch

| COLOR KEY | |
|---|---|
| **DMC Color** | **No.** |
| Dk Rose | 309 |
| Med Brown | 433 |
| Moss Green | 581 |
| Very Dk Raspberry | 777 |

# Muffin Pan Reindeer

**CRAFT LEVEL:** BEGINNER

**FINISHED SIZE:** Decoration measures about
7 in. wide x 10½ in. high, excluding ribbon hanger.

Recycle an old, unwanted muffin pan into Santa's reindeer!
This seasonal sleigh team on a doorknob, wall or window is
sure to get smiles from holiday guests. Plus, the easy project
is great for kids to help with. Don't forget to add one red
pompom nose to represent Rudolph.

## MATERIALS:
**Pattern on this page**
**Muffin pan for six muffins**
**Scraps of light, medium and dark brown card stock**
**Paper punches—⅝-in. circle and 1½-in. circle**
**Five ½-in. dark brown pompoms**
**One ½-in. red pompom**
**Twelve 10 mm wiggle eyes**
**2-ft. length of 1½-in.-wide brown wired ribbon**
**Small permanent glue dots**
**Tacky glue**
**Medium sandpaper and utility mask (if pan is nonstick)**
**Metal primer acrylic paint**
**Brown acrylic paint**
**Flat paintbrush**
**Fine-point brown marker or pen**

## DIRECTIONS:

### MUFFIN PAN
**1.** Clean pan and let dry.
**2.** If the pan is nonstick, sand the surface for better paint
adhesion as follows: Wearing a utility mask and working
in a well-ventilated area, sand entire bottom of pan, using
circular motions to avoid making grooves. Clean with a
damp cloth. Let dry.
**3.** Use paintbrush to apply one even coat of metal primer
to bottom of pan. Let dry.
**4.** Using paintbrush and brown acrylic paint, base-coat
the bottom of pan. Apply as many coats as needed for
complete coverage, allowing to dry between coats.

### REINDEER
**1.** Using the antler pattern, cut 6 left-facing antlers and
6 right-facing antlers from medium brown card stock.
Use the ⅝-in. circle punch to cut 12 small circles for the
background of eyes from dark brown card stock. Use the
1½-in. circle punch to cut 6 circles for muzzles from light
brown card stock.
**2.** Lay pan bottom side up on a flat surface so that the pan
is positioned vertically in front of you. Use tacky glue to
adhere a 1½-in. circle centered at the bottom edge of each
individual cup for the muzzle. Above each muzzle, adhere
two ⅝-in. circles centered side by side for background of
eyes. Let dry.

**3.** Use tacky glue to adhere the red pompom centered on
the top edge of the muzzle on the bottom right reindeer.
In the same way, adhere a dark brown pompom on the
muzzle of each remaining reindeer. Let dry.
**4.** Fold a ¼-in. tab at the bottom of each antler to the
back. Put a few small glue dots on the bottoms of the
folded tabs. Adhere a set of antlers centered on top of each
reindeer face, positioning them about ½ in. back. Bend
antlers up if needed, allowing them to stand.
**5.** Use glue dots to adhere a wiggle eye centered at the
bottom of each small background circle.
**6.** Use brown marker or pen to draw a smiling mouth on
each muzzle.

### FINISHING
Thread ribbon through hole at top of pan. Leaving a 4- to-
5-in. open loop, knot the ends and tie a bow. Trim excess.
(If the pan doesn't have a hole, use tacky glue to adhere a
knotted loop to the top for hanging and let dry.) Hang as
desired.

**Crafter's Note:** *We recommend using a pan without a nonstick
coating. With this type of pan, paint adheres more easily to the
surface without sanding.*

## REINDEER
## ANTLER PATTERN

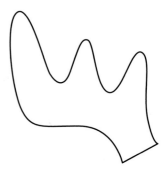

Cut 6 each—
medium brown card stock

Reverse pattern, cut 6 each—
medium brown card stock

## PVC Pipe Snowman

**CRAFT LEVEL:** INTERMEDIATE

**FINISHED SIZE:** Snowman measures about 7 in. wide x 12 in. high.

Visit your local hardware store—or check your garage—to find the supplies for this unique snowman. If you'd like a larger version, simply choose wider pieces of pipe.

### MATERIALS:
**14-in. length of 2-in. white PVC pipe**
**14-in. length of 2½-in. white PVC pipe**
**Low-temperature hot glue gun and glue sticks**
**Two 1-in. wiggle eyes**
**Scraps of black and orange card stock**
**1½-in. circle punch**
**1¾- x 20-in. strip of green fleece**
**White craft glitter**
**Artificial snow (optional)**
**Permanent spray adhesive**
**Kraft paper or large scrap of cardboard**
**Hacksaw (or fine-blade saw) with table vise grip**
**Ruler and permanent marker**

### DIRECTIONS:

#### PIPE CUTTING
**1.** Measure each piece of pipe, marking every 2 in. to create 7 equal segments on each piece.
**2.** Secure a pipe with the table vise grip. Use a handsaw to cut pipe where marked, creating 7 equal 2-in. segments. Repeat with the second pipe, keeping the two different pipe widths separated.

#### BODY ASSEMBLY
**1.** From one set of 7 segments, choose a segment for the center and use hot glue to attach the other 6 segments equally spaced around the center segment with sides

touching. Repeat with the remaining set of 7 segments, creating two separate flower-shaped pieces. Let dry.

**2.** Stack the smaller flower-shaped piece on top of the larger piece and glue in place. Let dry.

**3.** Lay assembled snowman on Kraft paper or cardboard in a well-ventilated area. Coat the entire surface of the snowman with permanent spray adhesive. Sprinkle glitter onto adhesive surface, then shake off the excess.

### FINISHING

**1.** Using the punch, make 2 circles from black card stock. Glue a wiggle eye onto each circle, then glue eyes onto head section of snowman.

**2.** For nose, cut a triangle measuring about 3 in. high and 3 in. wide from orange card stock. Roll into a cone shape and trim the open end. Glue cone in place at the seam, then glue the open end of cone to the face. Let dry.

**3.** If desired, cut fringe along the ends of the fleece. For scarf, wrap fleece around snowman where the head and body sections meet. Tie in front below the nose.

**4.** Display snowman and add artificial snow around the bottom if desired.

**Crafter's Note:** *Don't want to cut the pipe yourself? Ask someone at the hardware store where you buy it to do the cutting. Most offer cutting services for free or for a nominal fee. Or, ask a handy friend or neighbor to help with the cutting.*

# Santa Suit Planter

**CRAFT LEVEL:** QUICK & EASY

**FINISHED SIZE:** Varies.

A purchased red planter will really suit the season when you dress it up for the holidays. Inspired by the jolly old elf himself, Craft Editor Shalana Frisby added a ribbon belt and foam buckle. Use artificial foliage or a real poinsettia as filler.

### MATERIALS:
**Red planter (we used a 5-in.-wide x 10-in.-high planter)**
**2½-in.-wide black satin ribbon**
**Gold glitter 2-mm-thick foam**
**Ruler**
**Glue dots or hot glue (optional)**
**Holiday foliage or stems**
**Floral foam to fit planter (optional)**

### DIRECTIONS:
**1.** Cut a length of ribbon a few inches longer than the circumference of the planter. Set aside.

**2.** Cut a 3-in. square of gold glitter foam. To make two slits for the belt, use the ruler to mark a parallel line along two opposite sides of the square, positioning each line about ½ in. from the edge. Leaving about ½ in. at each end of each line uncut, cut along each marked line.

**3.** Thread the ribbon through one slit from back to front, then thread from front to back through the other slit.

Center the foam square on the ribbon length.

**4.** Position assembled belt horizontally around center of planter. Wrap ribbon tightly around planter and tie the ends in a knot to secure. If desired, use glue dots or hot glue to tack ribbon down on the sides and let dry.

**5.** If desired, insert floral foam in planter. Fill with holiday foliage or stems.

# Pink Poinsettia & Evergreen Swag

**CRAFT LEVEL:** QUICK & EASY

**FINISHED SIZE:** Swag measures about 10 in. wide x 36 in. long.

Want your Christmas decor to go beyond traditional reds and greens? Add a pop of hot pink! Craft Editor Shalana Frisby dressed up a plain evergreen swag with vibrant poinsettias.

## MATERIALS:

**36-in.-long evergreen swag**
**5 large artificial hot pink poinsettias**
**½-in.-wide silver ribbon**
**Silver metallic or glittered pinecones of various sizes**
**Low-temperature hot glue gun and glue sticks**

## DIRECTIONS:

**1.** Lay swag flat on tabletop facing up. Straighten and shape evergreen branches as desired.

**2.** Beginning in the center of the swag and working outward, glue the five poinsettias evenly spaced across the length of the swag.

**3.** Glue one end of silver ribbon on the underside of one end of swag. Spiral ribbon around swag every 6-8 in. to the opposite end of swag, then glue the remaining end of ribbon on underside of swag.

**4.** Glue pinecones of various sizes as desired along length of swag. Let dry.

**Crafter's Note:** *If you can't find metallic or glittered pinecones at the craft store, make your own. Either spray-paint pinecones or apply tacky glue to the edges and dip them in glitter, shaking off the excess.*

# Paper Pinecone Ornaments

**CRAFT LEVEL:** INTERMEDIATE

**FINISHED SIZE:** Varies.

Pretty on a tree or as trims on gift packages, these paper charmers are also lovely strung together in a garland or arranged in a bowl as a centerpiece.

## MATERIALS (FOR ONE):

**12-in. paper trimmer**
**12-in.-square scrapbook paper (not card stock)**
**Bone folder or sturdy plastic knife**
**Styrofoam egg**
**¾-in. appliqué pins**
**Metal thimble (optional)**
**6-in. length of coordinating ribbon**
**Low-temperature hot glue gun and glue sticks**
**Artificial leaves, berries or other embellishments**

## DIRECTIONS (FOR ONE):

**1.** With paper trimmer, cut scrapbook paper into 1-in. x 2-in. rectangles.

**2.** Along one length of each rectangle, fold in the opposite corners, forming a triangle. Use the bone folder or back of plastic knife to make all folds lie flat.

**3.** Pin the short point of each of four triangles (seam side down) to the center of the narrow end of the foam egg, forming a square. Pin each long point of the four triangles to the egg so that the triangles lie flat against the egg (the points will overlap slightly).

**4.** Pinning the long points and leaving the short points hanging free, pin a row of triangles around the narrow end of egg, positioning the triangles side by side with long points slightly overlapping. Continue pinning rows in the same way, making the short points of triangles align with the joining seams of the previous row, until about a 1-in. square of the foam egg shows at the top.

**5.** Fold the 6-in. piece of ribbon to form a hanging loop and pin the ends to the center of the open area on top of egg. Glue if needed.

**6.** Glue artificial leaves, berries or other embellishments around the base of hanging loop, covering the open area of foam egg completely. Let dry.

# Embroidered Holly Napkins

**CRAFT LEVEL:** BEGINNER

**FINISHED SIZE:** Design area measures about 2 in. square.

Using a simple pattern, you can add stitched holly leaves and beaded berries to a plain cloth napkin in no time. Create a matching set for your Christmas dinner table and tie each one with coordinating red ribbon for extra flair.

## MATERIALS (FOR ONE):

**Pattern on this page**
**White cloth napkin**
**DMC six-strand embroidery floss in green**
**Tapestry needle**
**Sewing needle**
**Red all-purpose thread**
**4- to 6-in. embroidery hoop**
**Three 6 mm red crystals or beads**
**Iron and pressing cloth**
**⅛-in.-wide red ribbon (optional)**

## DIRECTIONS (FOR ONE):

**1.** Wash and dry napkin. Iron napkin flat using a pressing cloth to protect the fabric.
**2.** Using a pencil, very lightly trace holly leaves pattern onto one corner of napkin, positioning the holly leaves about 1½ in. above the corner point and about 1 in. from each side.
**3.** Place embroidery hoop tightly on napkin over the traced pattern.
**4.** Using all 6 strands of green embroidery floss and the tapestry needle, backstitch holly leaves pattern, referring to Fig. 1 for stitch illustration. When finished, run end of floss under a few stitches on back, tie off and trim end.
**5.** Use red thread and sewing needle to sew crystals or beads in a triangular bunch at the base of the leaves.
**6.** Fold napkin and tie with red ribbon if desired.

## HOLLY LEAVES PATTERN

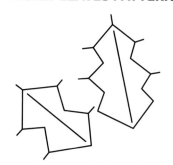

Trace 1—cloth napkin

**FIG. 1**

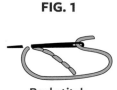

Backstitch

# Paper Decoupage Frames

**CRAFT LEVEL:** BEGINNER

**FINISHED SIZE:** Varies.

Here's an inexpensive way to spruce up your holiday decor while keeping special memories close at heart. You can easily match colors and themes to any style.

**MATERIALS:**
**Unfinished wooden photo frame**
**Fine sandpaper and cloth**
**Patterned card stock**
**Small foam brush**
**Decoupage glue (we used Mod Podge)**
**Paper tape or adhesive-backed ribbon**
**Stickers, paper borders or other embellishments (optional)**
**X-Acto knife and cutting mat**
**Photo to fit frame opening**

**DIRECTIONS:**

**1.** Remove the backing and glass from the wood frame. Sand the surface of frame and wipe with dry cloth.

**2.** Using the small foam brush, apply a thin layer of decoupage glue to the front of frame. Adhere the sheet of card stock to the front of frame so that the card stock covers the entire front of frame, including the photo opening. Let dry.

**3.** Using X-Acto knife and cutting mat, trim excess card stock from around the outer edge and inner opening of frame. If desired, apply a thin coat of decoupage glue to card stock to seal.

**4.** Cover the narrow outer edge of frame with paper tape or adhesive-backed ribbon to conceal the wood. Repeat on the narrow edge around the inner opening.

**5.** If desired, add stickers, paper borders or other embellishments to front of frame.

**6.** Insert glass, photo and backing in frame.

# Stamped Clay Ornaments

**CRAFT LEVEL:** BEGINNER

**FINISHED SIZE:** Varies.

Even if you've never used polymer clay, you'll enjoy making these versatile ornaments. Hang them on your Christmas tree...attach one to a gift package as a festive trim...or drape them around a wine bottle as a hostess gift.

## MATERIALS:

**Pearl or white polymer clay (we used Sculpey Premo in Pearl)**
**1½-in. circle cookie cutter (optional)**
**1-in. or smaller snowflake stamps**
**Plastic mat or waxed paper**
**Clay roller**
**Standard oven or toaster oven**
**Foil-lined baking tray**
**Blue acrylic paint**
**Sponge brush**
**Rags or paper towels**
**Toothpicks**
**Blue embroidery floss**

## DIRECTIONS:

**1.** Condition clay by kneading it with your hands until it is soft and easy to work with.

**2.** With clay roller, roll out clay to a ¼-in. thickness on plastic mat or waxed paper.

**3.** Use cookie cutter or a toothpick to cut out desired number of ornaments in desired shapes.

**4.** Using desired stamp, make indentations centered on each clay shape.

**5.** Use a toothpick to make a hole at the top of each stamped ornament.

**6.** Place ornaments right side up on a foil-lined baking sheet. Bake following clay manufacturer's instructions. Let cool.

**7.** Use sponge brush to coat the front of each ornament with a layer of blue acrylic paint. With a rag or paper towel, immediately wipe excess paint off surface, leaving paint only in the stamped indentations. If necessary, repeat process until all stamped indentations are coated with paint. Let dry.

**8.** Following the clay manufacturer's temperature recommendation, put ornaments back in the oven for 5-10 minutes to set the paint. Let cool. Wipe off surface to buff.

**9.** Cut a 6-in. length of floss for each ornament. Add a hanger to each by threading a length of floss through the hole and knotting the ends.

# Illuminated Corner Floral Arrangement

**CRAFT LEVEL:** QUICK & EASY

**FINISHED SIZE:** Varies.

Set the mood with this glowing vase from Craft Editor Shalana Frisby. She used LED branches to illuminate the arrangement.

## MATERIALS:

**Tall metallic vase**
**4-6 white or silver floral stems**
**2 white LED lighted branches**
**Floral foam to fit vase interior**

## DIRECTIONS:

**1.** Place floral foam snugly in the vase. The foam top should stop a few inches below the top of vase.

**2.** Place the tallest floral stem in the center of the floral foam, inserting the end a few inches into the foam.

**3.** Insert an LED branch on either side of the center stem. Place the battery packs on the outer edges of stem bases between the foam and top of vase. If needed, use wall putty or glue dots to hold battery packs in place.

**4.** Fill in foam with the remaining white or silver stems until arrangement is full. Turn on LED light switches.

# Antiqued Mirror

**CRAFT LEVEL:** BEGINNER

**FINISHED SIZE:** Varies.

Celebrate Christmases past with this easy idea. In a few steps, you can transform a modern glass mirror into a beautifully antiqued base for your favorite centerpiece.

## MATERIALS:

**Tabletop mirror**
**Latex or other protective gloves**
**Plastic putty knife**
**Paint stripper (we used Citristrip spray-on paint stripper)**
**Modern Masters Metal Effects Green Patina Aging Solution**
**Spray bottle**
**Metallic paint (we used a dark silver acrylic paint)**
**Flat paintbrush**
**Kraft paper or card stock slightly larger than mirror**
**Spray adhesive**
**Scrap cardboard**
**Cork or rubber adhesive rounds**

## DIRECTIONS:

**1.** In a well-ventilated area, turn mirror face down on cardboard. Wearing gloves, apply a thick layer of paint stripper to back of mirror. Let sit for several hours.

**2.** Use plastic putty knife to scrape the paint off the back of mirror. After paint has been removed, wash the entire mirror and let dry.

**3.** In well-ventilated area, turn mirror face down on cardboard. Wearing gloves, put a small amount of patina aging solution in the spray bottle. Lightly spray around the edges of mirror (the reflective surface will quickly begin to dissolve).

**4.** After no more than 1-2 minutes, carefully rinse the back of the mirror with water, washing away the patina aging solution. (If needed to age the mirror more, repeat the spraying and washing process until the desired effect is achieved.) Let dry.

**5.** In well-ventilated area, turn mirror face down on cardboard. Using flat paintbrush and metallic paint, base-coat the entire back of mirror, painting over the reflective surface and applying the paint thickly. Let dry at least 24 hrs.

**6.** Apply a thin layer of spray adhesive on back of mirror. Adhere Kraft paper or card stock to back of mirror, trimming paper or card stock along the edges of mirror.

**7.** Place cork or rubber adhesive rounds at each corner of the mirror. Turn mirror over and arrange desired centerpiece on top.

# 'Celebrate' Paper Flag Banner

**CRAFT LEVEL:** BEGINNER

**FINISHED SIZE:** Banner measures about 54 in. long.

This fun-to-create banner will make any holiday party more festive. Just round up basic paper-crafting supplies, and you'll be well on your way to displaying one of your own.

**MATERIALS:**

Paper punches—3½-in. scallop-edge circle and 2½-in. circle

2- to 3-in.-high white chipboard letters spelling "CELEBRATE"

Scraps of coordinating red and green patterned card stock

Scraps of solid red card stock

3 letter-size sheets each of solid light blue and striped card stock

Paper trimmer

Ruler

Permanent glue dot adhesive

Dimensional foam adhesive

⅛-in.-wide red grosgrain ribbon

⅛-in. hole punch

**DIRECTIONS:**

### SQUARE SWALLOWTAIL FLAGS

**1.** Use paper trimmer to cut five 4½-in.-wide x 5-in.-high rectangles of striped card stock, cutting them so that the stripes run horizontally across the width.

**2.** To make a swallowtail, lay a rectangle vertically in front of you. Use ruler to find the midpoint of the width and mark this point about 1 in. up from the bottom, then cut from each bottom corner to the marked point. Create a swallowtail on remaining rectangles in the same way.

**3.** On the short straight end of each rectangle, use hole punch to make a hole about ⅛ in. from each corner.

### TRIANGLE PENNANT-SHAPE FLAGS

**1.** Use paper trimmer to cut five 4-in.-wide x 8-in.-high rectangles of solid light blue card stock.

**2.** To make a triangle, use ruler to find the midpoint of one short end of a rectangle and mark the point. Cut a diagonal line from each corner on the opposite end to the marked point. Create a triangle with each remaining rectangle in the same way.

**3.** On the short straight end of each triangle, use hole punch to make a hole about ⅛ in. from each corner.

### 'CELEBRATE' CIRCLES

**1.** Use scallop-edge circle punch to make 5 red patterned card stock circles and 4 green card stock circles. Use smaller circle punch to make 4 solid red card stock circles.

**2.** Using glue dots, adhere one solid red circle centered on each green patterned circle.

**3.** Beginning with a red patterned circle, lay out alternating red and green patterned circles from left to right on a flat surface. Use glue dots to adhere one letter to each circle, spelling "CELEBRATE."

### ASSEMBLY

**1.** Cut a 6-ft. length of ribbon. Thread ribbon through holes on the top corners of a light blue triangle pennant flag, leaving about a 1-ft.-long tail. Continue adding flags to ribbon, alternating triangle flags and swallowtail flags. If needed, use a glue dot on ribbon to secure each flag.

**2.** Trim ribbon at end of banner, leaving about a 1-ft.-long tail of ribbon.

**3.** Using glue dots, adhere "CELEBRATE" circles along the top edge of banner, positioning them so that they overlap the top corners of the flags.

# Birch Bark Garland

**CRAFT LEVEL:** QUICK & EASY

**FINISHED SIZE:** Varies.

The beauty of nature will enhance any decor...so why not bring it indoors? Using strips of bark from a birch tree, assemble a rustic garland to adorn a tabletop, mantel, staircase or tree.

**MATERIALS:**

**1½- x 11-in. strips of dried birch bark**
**Low-temperature hot glue gun and glue sticks**

**DIRECTIONS:**

**1.** Form a ring with a strip of birch bark, overlapping the ends about 1 in. Glue the ends to secure.
**2.** Insert another strip of birch bark through the first ring and repeat Step 1, forming linked rings.
**3.** Continue adding rings to the garland until it reaches the desired length. Let dry.

**Crafter's Note:** *Sheets and strips of dried birch bark are available for purchase online. The dried bark can easily be cut with scissors to the desired length and width. If you wish, adjust the size of the bark strips to make the garland rings larger or smaller.*

# Festive Yarn Balls

**CRAFT LEVEL:** QUICK & EASY

**FINISHED SIZE:** Varies.

These versatile balls will use up your stash of leftover yarn. Hang them from the ceiling...arrange them along the center of a table...add them to the Christmas tree as ornaments...the possibilities are endless!

**MATERIALS:**

**Disposable wide-mouth plastic container**
**Disposable stir stick**
**Tacky glue or craft glue**
**Yarn**
**Round balloons**
**Waxed paper**

**DIRECTIONS:**

**1.** Blow up the desired number of round balloons to about 4 to 6 in. in diameter and set aside.
**2.** In plastic container, mix a solution of equal parts water and tacky glue or craft glue, stirring well to dissolve glue evenly.
**3.** Place about 1 yd. of yarn in the glue and water mixture, coating the yarn completely.
**4.** Tie the end of coated yarn around tied end of balloon, then wrap coated yarn randomly around balloon. Continue coating yarn with the glue mixture and wrapping the balloon until balloon is mostly covered, with only small cracks between the yarn strands. Tie yarn off at the tied end of balloon and trim yarn.
**5.** Place wrapped balloon on waxed paper. Let dry for 24-48 hrs. or until stiff to the touch, rotating the balloon a few times during the first few hours.
**6.** Use a pin or knife to pop the balloon and remove it from inside the stiffened wrapped yarn. If the yarn collapses in places when the balloon pops, gently reshape the ball with your hands.

# Stenciled Fabric Place Mat

**CRAFT LEVEL:** BEGINNER

**FINISHED SIZE:** Varies.

Create your own card stock stencil to turn an inexpensive place mat into a cheery tabletop decoration. All it takes is a little fabric paint, your favorite extra-large paper punch and a few other basic supplies. Craft Editor Shalana Frisby chose a snowflake design for a wonderfully wintry look.

**MATERIALS (FOR ONE):**

**Blue fabric place mat**
**White fabric paint**
**Round sponge or brush pouncer**
**3-in.-wide snowflake paper punch**
**12-in.-square sheet of card stock**
**Ruler**
**Spray adhesive**

**DIRECTIONS (FOR ONE):**

**1.** Along one edge of the card stock sheet, use a ruler to mark the center point. Punch one snowflake at this point and punch another snowflake on each side of the first one along the edge of the card stock, making three evenly spaced snowflakes for the stencil.

**2.** Apply a thin layer of spray adhesive on back of stencil. Place stencil, adhesive side down, on place mat so that the snowflakes are spaced along one edge of place mat as desired. Press firmly into place.

**3.** Dab round sponge or brush pouncer into paint, then pat straight up and down onto the open snowflake areas of stencil, applying paint to place mat. Continue until all open areas are covered with paint.

**4.** Let dry for a several hours. Remove stencil from place mat and discard. Let dry for at least 24 hrs. before using place mat. Wash place mat according to fabric paint manufacturer's instructions.

## 'Winter' Snowflake Blocks

**CRAFT LEVEL:** BEGINNER

**FINISHED SIZE:** Varies.

A bare mantel, tabletop or shelf will get an instant boost when you add these cute little embellished blocks. Choose a shorter or longer word depending on the size of your space.

### MATERIALS:

**Six Styrofoam or floral foam blocks of different sizes, about 3½-in. wide by 4- to 8-in. high**
**Six 12-in.-square sheets of snowflake-patterned card stock**
**Chipboard or card stock glitter letters spelling "WINTER"**
**Small snowflake punch or snowflake stickers**
**Ultrafine white glitter**
**Clear-drying decoupage or tacky glue**
**Dimensional foam adhesive**
**Clear tape**
**Sponge brush**

### DIRECTIONS:

**WRAPPING BLOCKS**

**1.** Lay each block in the center of a card stock sheet so that the front of the block is facing down and the bottom is closest to you. Center taller blocks lower on the sheet so that enough card stock is above it to cover the top.
**2.** Trace the outline of the block front onto the card stock. Then roll the block once in each direction, tracing the top, bottom, left side and right side of the block around the center outline. Draw lines to connect the shapes, forming triangles. (See Block Diagram at right.)
**3.** For each block, cut out entire drawn shape, leaving flaps at the top, bottom and sides as shown on Block Diagram if desired. Cut a slit through each triangle, cutting from the center of outer line to the inside point.
**4.** Fold and crease all marked lines. Wrap corresponding paper piece around each block, tucking the cut triangle areas underneath as needed. (If desired, add additional paper to cover any exposed areas on the back or bottom of blocks.) Secure paper on the back with tape.

**GLITTERING BLOCKS**

**1.** Using sponge brush, apply decoupage or tacky glue to the edges of each block's front side. Sprinkle glitter onto glue and shake off excess. Let dry.
**2.** If needed, reapply glue and glitter until desired look is achieved.

**FINISHING BLOCKS**

**1.** Use dimensional foam adhesive to apply one chipboard glitter letter to the front of each block.
**2.** Arrange the blocks to spell "WINTER."

**BLOCK DIAGRAM**

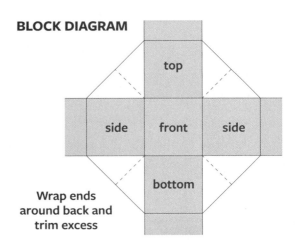

Wrap ends around back and trim excess

# Painted Medallion Wreath

**CRAFT LEVEL: QUICK & EASY**

**FINISHED SIZE:** Wreath measures about 14 in., excluding ribbon.

Bring easy elegance to your home with this simple wreath from Craft Editor Shalana Frisby. She used a lightweight ceiling medallion, available in a variety of sizes at hardware stores. For outdoor use, coat the medallion with a clear acrylic spray sealer after painting.

## MATERIALS:

**14-in. ceiling medallion**
**Light blue spray paint**
**White acrylic craft paint**
**Flat paintbrush**
**Paper towels or rags**
**2½-in.-wide white wired ribbon**
**Kraft paper or large scrap of cardboard**
**Low-temperature hot glue gun and glue sticks**

## DIRECTIONS:

**1.** In a well-ventilated area, lay the medallion face up on Kraft paper or cardboard.
**2.** Spray-paint medallion according to paint manufacturer's instructions. Apply as many coats as needed for complete coverage. Let dry.
**3.** Coat the flat paintbrush with white paint, then wipe off the excess, leaving only a small amount on the bristles. Use brush to highlight raised areas on medallion. Continue to coat brush and wipe off excess before adding paint to medallion as desired. Let dry.
**4.** Cut a 2-ft. length of ribbon. Insert through hole in wreath and glue ends together. Let dry.
**5.** Cut another length of ribbon and tie into bow. Glue bow at ends of looped ribbon. Let dry.

## Angel Wings

**CRAFT LEVEL: BEGINNER**

**FINISHED SIZE:** Angel wings decoration measures about 11 in. wide x 11 in. high.

How divine! These cherubic wings trimmed with shimmering scrapbook paper make a heavenly accent at Christmastime. Customize the design by using a different color scheme, such as a combination of silvers, blues and greens...or by replacing the word "Joy" with a treasured family photo.

### MATERIALS:
**Pattern on this page**
**Scrapbook paper—cream, tan, matte gold and shiny gold**
**Paper punch—1- to 1½-in.-high flower petal or leaf shape**
**Low-temperature hot glue gun and glue sticks**
**Straight pins (optional)**
**Dimensional foam adhesive**
**Compass**
**5⅞- x 1⁵⁄₁₆-in. Styrofoam circle**
**11-in.-square x 1⁵⁄₁₆-in.- thick or larger Styrofoam block**
**Serrated knife or craft knife**
**Decorative scallop-edge scissors**
**3-in.-high chipboard letters spelling "Joy"**

### DIRECTIONS:

**FOAM BASE**

**1.** Trace wing pattern onto foam block. Reverse pattern and trace again for a set of wings.

**2.** Using serrated knife or craft knife, cut out foam wings.

**3.** Using compass, draw an 8-in. circle on matte gold paper and cut out. Glue the foam circle centered on the back of the paper. Create flaps in the gold paper by cutting a slit about every inch in the excess paper around the edge. Glue the flaps over the edge of foam circle, covering exposed foam.

**4.** Lay foam wings side by side about 1 inch apart. Place foam circle, paper side up, on top of wings so that the circle is centered about an inch from the top of wings. Apply a liberal amount of glue between the overlapping foam areas and press together until dry.

**5.** Cut several 1-in.-wide strips of matte gold paper. Use glue or straight pins to attach the strips along the narrow side edges of each wing, covering the exposed foam and following the shape of the wings as closely as possible.

**ASSEMBLY**

**1.** Using flower petal or leaf punch, create several shapes from cream, tan and gold papers.

**2.** Starting at the bottom of each wing and working upward, use glue or straight pins to attach overlapping rows of punched shapes, covering all exposed foam and alternating the colors of shapes.

**3.** Using compass, draw a 4½-in. circle on shiny gold paper. Use decorative scissors to cut around the edge. Glue circle centered on the paper-covered foam circle.

**4.** Spell "Joy" with chipboard letters centered on the shiny gold circle. Use dimensional foam adhesive to adhere letters. Let dry.

**WING PATTERN**

Use a photocopier to enlarge pattern 200%.

Cut 1—Styrofoam block. Reverse and cut 1 more.

# Glass Bottle Luminaria

**CRAFT LEVEL:** QUICK & EASY

**FINISHED SIZE:** Varies.

Wondering what you can do with old glass bottles or mason jars? Using a little glitter paint, Craft Editor Shalana Frisby transformed them into sparkling luminaria to light up the holiday season. Fill a cluster of them with glittery artificial foliage or small battery-powered candles.

## MATERIALS (FOR ONE):

**Glass bottle or jar**
**Ultra-fine glitter paint (we used DecoArt Glamour Dust Ultra-Fine Glitter Paint)**
**Disposable container for mixing paint**
**Paper plates**

## DIRECTIONS (FOR ONE):

**1.** In disposable container, combine 1 tablespoon of water with a few tablespoons of glitter paint. Mix well until the consistency is runny.
**2.** Pour thinned paint into a clean, dry bottle. Swirl paint around bottom of bottle, then rotate bottle on its side, letting paint cover interior of bottle completely.
**3.** When interior of bottle is covered with a thin layer of paint, pour excess paint back into disposable container to reuse if desired.
**4.** Turn bottle upside down on a paper plate and leave upside down for about 1 hour, allowing additional excess paint to drain. If needed, replace paper plate and continue draining paint for another hour.
**5.** When paint is tacky and stops running, turn bottle right side up and let dry.

# Quilted Table Runner

**CRAFT LEVEL:** BEGINNER

**FINISHED SIZE:** Runner measures about 11½ in. wide x 36 in. long.

Even novice quilters can easily make this heartwarming accent from Craft Editor Shalana Frisby and contributing crafter Diane Coates of West Allis, Wisconsin. The lightweight runner is also simple to wash and store when not in use.

## MATERIALS:

**6 different fat quarters in coordinating cotton prints—**
   **3 light colors and 3 dark colors**
**½ yd. cotton fabric for backing**
**45- x 60-in. piece of low-loft polyester or cotton batting**
**Extra-wide double-fold bias tape to coordinate with fabric**
**Standard sewing supplies**
**Thirty 1-in. curved safety pins for basting**
**Rotary cutter and cutting mat**
**Quilting ruler**
**Sewing machine**
**¼-in. pressure foot for sewing machine (optional)**
**Iron and ironing board**

## DIRECTIONS:

### CUTTING

Using the rotary cutter, cutting mat and quilting ruler, cut the backing fabric and batting so that each measures 38 x 14 in. Cut each fat quarter into two 3½- x 14-in. strips, making a total of 12 strips.

### PIECING TOP

Sew the long edges of the fabric strips together with ¼-in. seams, alternating light and dark fabric strips, until you have a 36- x 14-in. top piece. Press seams toward the darker fabrics.

## ASSEMBLY

**1.** Lay the backing fabric wrong side up on a flat surface. Place the batting centered on top of backing fabric. Place the sewn top piece, right side up, centered on top of batting. (The backing and batting are slightly larger than the top; the backing will shrink as the runner is quilted.)

**2.** To pin-baste, pin every 3-4 in., avoiding seam lines.

**3.** Keeping the fabric smooth, quilt the layers by stitching in the ditch where the fabric strips meet, starting at the center of the runner and working out to the ends. (Stitches will disappear into seam.) Remove safety pins.

**4.** Trim table runner to measure 36 x 12 in.

## BINDING

**1.** Fold under ¾ in. on the short end at the beginning of the bias tape and overlap at the end. Unfold the long folded edge (slightly shorter than the other) and place on table runner with right sides together and raw edges even.

**2.** Stitch the bias tape to the table runner with a ⅜-in. seam allowance. To miter corners, stop stitching ⅜ in. from each corner as you approach it, then backstitch. Remove runner from sewing machine and fold binding strip upward, creating a diagonal fold. (See Fig. 1.) Holding the fold in place, bring binding strip down in line with the next edge, creating a horizontal fold at top. (See Fig. 2.)

**3.** Begin sewing again at the top of the horizontal fold, stitching through all layers.

**4.** Refold bias tape to encase the raw edge of table runner.

**5.** Use straight pins to pin from the right side in the ditch of the bias tape seam. Check the back to make sure the pins catch the tape on the back.

**6.** Carefully stitch in the ditch, removing pins as you go.

**Crafter's Note:** *Instead of stitching in the ditch, you can hand-stitch the binding in place in the back, or zigzag-stitch from the front side to stitch down the bias tape in the back.*

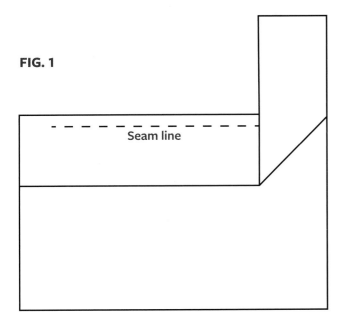

**FIG. 1**

Seam line

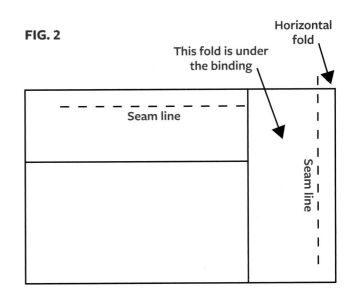

**FIG. 2**

Horizontal fold

This fold is under the binding

Seam line

Seam line

## Footstool Cube with Pockets

**CRAFT LEVEL:** INTERMEDIATE

**FINISHED SIZE:** Footstool measures about 16½ in. long x 13½ in. wide x 11½ in. high.

Kids and adults alike are sure to appreciate this useful and stylish gift created by Craft Editor Shalana Frisby and contributing crafter Diane Coates of West Allis, Wisconsin. They turned a plastic storage crate into a fun footstool featuring a handy pocket on each side.

### MATERIALS:

**Plastic storage crate measuring 16½ in. long x 13½ in. wide x 10½ in. high**
**1-in.-thick high-density foam chair pad**
**⅞ yd. print fabric for sides**
**½ yd. print coordinating fabric for top**
**½ yd. coordinating solid-color fabric for pockets**
**Standard sewing supplies**
**Rotary cutter and cutting mat**
**Sewing machine**

### DIRECTIONS:

#### CUTTING

**1.** Cut the foam chair pad to 16½ x 13½ in. to fit the top of the crate.
**2.** Cut a 17½- x 14½-in. rectangle of print fabric for the top of crate.

**3.** From side print fabric, cut two 17½- x 14-in. rectangles for the long side panels and two 14½- x 14-in. rectangles for the short side panels. (This includes a ½-in. seam allowance for the tops and sides, 1 in. for the chair pad height and an additional 2 in. for the hem at the bottom.)
**4.** Cut two 14½- x 15-in. rectangles of solid-color fabric for the pockets.

#### SEWING

**1.** Fold each solid fabric piece wrong sides together to make 14½- x 7½-in. pocket front pieces. Press in place, creasing the fold. Topstitch ½ in. down from the fold. Place each pocket front piece on a short side panel with right sides up and bottom edges matching. Baste or pin in place on bottom and sides.
**2.** With right sides together and edges matching, pin the four side panels together (the two with pockets at opposite ends). Use a ½-in. seam allowance and straight stitch to sew as pinned from the bottom up, stopping and backstitching ½ in. from the upper edge, forming a box shape. Press seams open.
**3.** With right sides together, pin the top fabric panel to the side panels' top raw edges. Using a ½-in. seam allowance and straight stitch, sew the top panel to the sides, pivoting at the corners.
**4.** For hem around bottom, fold fabric under 2 in. all around with wrong sides together and press in place. Turn edge of fabric under 1 in. Press, pin and topstitch hem all the way around, staying close to inner fold.

#### ASSEMBLY

**1.** Flip crate upside down.
**2.** Place foam on crate.
**3.** Slide fabric cover over crate and foam.

**Crafter's Note:** *Feel free to use a larger or smaller crate. Measure the length, width and height of each side. For the four side panel pieces, add a ½-in. seam allowance to the top and side edges, then add 3 in. to the bottom edges to accommodate the 1-in. chair pad and a 2-in. hem allowance. For the top piece, add a ½-in. seam allowance to all four sides.*

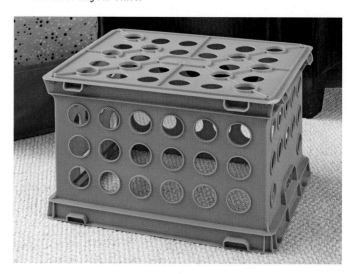

204

220

217

*gifts to* GIVE

# Cookie Sheet Checkerboard

**CRAFT LEVEL:** BEGINNER

**FINISHED SIZE:** Game measures about 11 in. wide x 17 in. long.

Both kids and adults will enjoy this yuletide checkerboard set that pits Santa against Rudolph. Challenge a friend or relative to a game and use chalk to keep score.

## MATERIALS:

**11- x 17-in. metal cookie sheet**
**Medium-grade sandpaper (if cookie sheet is nonstick)**
**Bottle caps—12 silver and 12 white**
**Twenty-four 1-in. clear epoxy dome circle stickers**
**1-in. circle punch**
**Paper trimmer**
**Patterned card stock—holly leaf, Santa and Rudolph**
**12-in.-square solid card stock—light green and dark green**
**12-in.-square red chalkboard specialty card stock**
**Clear-drying all-purpose permanent glue**
**Dry scrapbook adhesive**
**Matte decoupage glue and sealer**
**White acrylic paint**
**Metal primer paint**
**Sponge brushes**
**Utility mask**
**Toothpicks**
**Ruler**

## DIRECTIONS:

### BOTTLE CAPS

1. Use 1-in. circle punch to cut out 12 Santa images and 12 Rudolph images from patterned card stock.

2. Adhere a circle epoxy sticker centered on top of each image (avoid touching the adhesive and transferring fingerprints). Press firmly in place.

3. Use permanent glue to adhere each Santa image face up on the interior of a white bottle cap. In the same way, adhere Rudolph images to silver bottle caps. If needed, use toothpicks to remove excess glue from the edges of the images. Let dry.

### COOKIE SHEET

1. Clean cookie sheet and let dry.

2. If cookie sheet is nonstick, sand the surface for better paint adhesion as follows: Wearing a utility mask and working in a well-ventilated area, sand entire front of cookie sheet, using circular motions to avoid making marked grooves. Clean well with a damp cloth and let dry.

3. Use sponge brush to apply one even coat of metal primer to cookie sheet. Let dry.

4. Using sponge brush, paint cookie sheet white. Apply as many coats as needed for complete coverage, allowing to dry between coats.

### CHECKERBOARD

1. Use paper trimmer to cut thirty-two 1¼-in. squares from dark green card stock and one 10-in. square from light green card stock.

2. Use ruler and pencil to measure and lightly mark a 1¼-in.-square grid on front of the light green square, creating 8 rows of squares. Following the grid as a guide and using dry scrapbook adhesive, adhere the dark green squares in a checkerboard pattern on the light green square, placing a dark green square in every other marked square and staggering the rows.

3. Press each dark green square firmly in place. Erase any visible pencil marks.

### ASSEMBLY

1. Use paper trimmer to cut a 5- x 10-in. rectangle of holly leaf patterned card stock and a 3½- x 8½-in. rectangle of chalkboard card stock.

2. Apply a thin coat of decoupage glue to the interior of the cookie sheet and to the back of both the holly leaf card stock and the checkerboard card stock pieces. Adhere the holly leaf card stock and checkerboard side by side onto the interior of the cookie sheet and press firmly in place, smoothing out any bubbles. Let dry.

3. Apply a thin coat of decoupage glue to the entire surface of checkerboard, holly leaf card stock and cookie sheet sides as a sealer. Apply as many coats as needed for complete coverage, allowing to dry between coats.

4. Use decoupage glue to adhere the chalkboard card stock centered on the holly leaf card stock (do not coat the front of the chalkboard card stock with decoupage glue). Let dry. Use assembled bottle caps to play checkers.

**Crafter's Note:** *We recommend using a cookie sheet without a nonstick coating. With this type of cookie sheet, paint adheres more easily to the surface without sanding.*

# Ribbon Tree Hair Clip

**CRAFT LEVEL:** QUICK & EASY

**FINISHED SIZE:** Small measures about 2½ in. x 2 in. Large measures about 2½ in. square.

Does that special little girl in your life love to dress up? Make her smile with a Christmasy hair accessory she'll want to wear thoughout the holiday season. All you need to create it is a metal clip, ribbon, rhinestones and glue.

## MATERIALS:
- ⅜-in.-wide metal hair clip —1¾-in. long for small size or 2¼-in. long for large size
- Green ribbon—¼ in. wide for small or ⅜ in. to ½ in. wide for large
- ⅜-in.-wide brown ribbon
- ⅛-in.- to ¼-in.-wide red ribbon for bow
- **Small red rhinestones**
- **Low-temperature hot glue gun and glue sticks**

## DIRECTIONS:
**1.** Glue a piece of brown ribbon to the front surface of the metal hair clip, wrapping the ribbon ends around to the back at each end.

**2.** Cut one piece of green ribbon in each of the following lengths: 6 in., 5 in., 4 in., 3 in. and 2 in.

**3.** Place the hair clip vertically in front of you with the base at the bottom. Beginning about ⅜ in. above the base, glue the ends of the longest green ribbon at a slight angle across the front of the hair clip, forming a loop. Continue in descending-size order to glue the ribbons to hair clip, forming a column of angled loops.

**4.** Holding the center of the unglued area on the bottom loop, slightly twist the loop to form a narrow figure eight shape, then glue the center of the loop to front of hair clip. Glue each remaining loop in a figure eight shape in the same way.

**5.** Cut a 5-in. length of red ribbon. Tie in a bow and glue to top of tree. Trim ends as desired.

**6.** Glue rhinestones to ribbon tree for ornaments. Let dry.

## Barn Animal Puppet Set

**CRAFT LEVEL:** BEGINNER

**FINISHED SIZE:** Varies.

Made with wooden candle cups, this cute-as-can-be puppet play set is perfect for little fingers. Use your imagination and a little creativity to add even more animals.

### MATERIALS:

Patterns on page 207
Acrylic craft paint—very dark brown, medium brown, very
   light brown, porcelain, white, green, yellow and pink
Flat paintbrush
Craft foam scraps—gray, black, very dark brown, medium
   brown, orange, dark pink and blue
Ten 5 mm wiggle eyes
Quick-drying tacky glue or super glue
Toothpicks
Premade unfinished wooden toy barn

Five 1¼-in.-high wooden candle cups
Five 1-in. wooden doll heads
1½-in. wooden block
2-in. wooden block
Two 1½-in.-wide wooden circles
Two 2-in.-wide wooden circles
Two ⅜-in. wooden buttons
Fine-point black permanent marker
Compass

### DIRECTIONS:

**FINGER PUPPETS**

**1.** For each finger puppet, glue the flat edge of a doll head onto the bottom of a candle cup. Let dry.

**2.** Base-coat each finger puppet with acrylic paint, using white paint for the sheep, yellow paint for the chick, very light brown paint for the bull, pink paint for the pig and porcelain paint for the farmer. Apply as many coats as needed for full coverage, letting dry between coats.

**3.** Trace black outlines of patterns onto foam as directed on patterns. Cut out pieces. Glue gray nose and black ears onto sheep's head. Glue beak and feathers onto chick's head. Glue horns, medium brown nose and medium brown ears onto bull's head. Glue dark pink nose and ears onto pig's head. Glue mustache onto farmer's head.

**4.** Cut a 3½- x ¾-in. strip from blue foam, then cut the ends at an angle. Glue around farmer's body for vest, overlapping the ends to form a slight V shape at the neck.

**5.** Cut a 3- x ½-in. strip of very dark brown foam. Roll into a circle, overlap ends about ¼ in. and glue in place. On very dark brown foam, use compass to draw a 1½-in. circle, then draw a ¾-in. circle in the center, making a doughnut shape. Cut out shape for hat brim. Glue rolled circle centered on top of brim. Glue hat on farmer's head.

**6.** Glue a set of wiggle eyes centered above the nose on each animal and above the mustache on the farmer.

**7.** Referring to the patterns, use marker to draw mouths and noses on puppets.

**BARN AND TRACTOR**

**1.** Base-coat the wooden barn with medium brown paint. Apply as many coats as needed for full coverage, letting dry between coats.

**2.** Base-coat the remaining wooden pieces, using green paint for the blocks, very dark brown paint for the circles and yellow paint for the buttons. Apply as many coats as needed for full coverage, letting dry between coats.

**3.** For tractor body, center and glue the small block on one side of the large block, making one side of small block flush with one side of large block. (Flush sides are bottom of tractor.) Glue buttons centered, side by side, on front of small block for lights. Glue a small circle on each side of the small block for front wheels. Glue a large circle on each side of the large block for back wheels. Let dry.

**FINGER PUPPET PATTERNS**

**BULL, SHEEP AND PIG EARS**
Cut 2 each—medium brown, black and dark pink foam

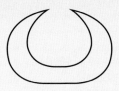

**BULL HORNS**
Cut 1—very dark brown foam

**BULL NOSE**
Cut 1—medium brown foam

**SHEEP NOSE**
Cut 1—gray foam

**PIG NOSE**
Cut 1—dark pink foam

**CHICK FEATHERS AND BEAK**
Cut 1 each—orange foam

**FARMER'S MUSTACHE**
Cut 1—very dark brown foam

# Elf Hat Wine Bottle Topper

**CRAFT LEVEL:** BEGINNER

**FINISHED SIZE:** Bottle topper measures about 3½ in. wide x 4½ in. high.

Bringing wine to a holiday dinner party? Dress up the bottle for the occasion with this elfish topper. For an added gift, attach a loop of ribbon or thread at the top of the hat so it can be reused by the host or hostess as a tree ornament.

## MATERIALS (FOR ONE):

**Patterns on this page**
**Scraps of fleece in two solid colors**
**Sewing machine (optional)**
**Standard sewing supplies**
**⅜-in.-wide coordinating ribbon**
**¾-in. jingle bell**
**Low-temperature hot glue gun and glue sticks (optional)**

## DIRECTIONS (FOR ONE):

### CUTTING

**1.** Using hat pattern, cut two pieces from the desired color of fleece, cutting one piece from the right side of fleece and the other piece from the wrong side of fleece.

**2.** Using trim pattern, cut two pieces from remaining color of fleece, cutting one piece from the right side of fleece and the other piece from the wrong side of fleece.

### SEWING

**1.** Aligning the long straight edges, pin a piece of trim to the bottom of each hat with the wrong side of trim facing the right side of hat.

**2.** Using a ¼-in. seam allowance, machine- or hand-stitch the bottom edge of one hat/trim set, joining the pieces. Repeat for second set.

**3.** Matching the edges, put assembled hat/trim pieces right sides together (trim on the inside). Pin in place.

**4.** Using a ¼-in. seam allowance, machine- or hand-stitch the outer edges of hat/trim pieces, leaving the bottom edge open.

**5.** Turn hat right side out. If needed, trim inside edges of seam so fabric isn't visible at bottom sides of hat.

### FINISHING

**1.** Sew jingle bell on tip of hat.

**2.** Hand-sew or glue ribbon along stitch line on trim.

**3.** Place hat on top of wine bottle.

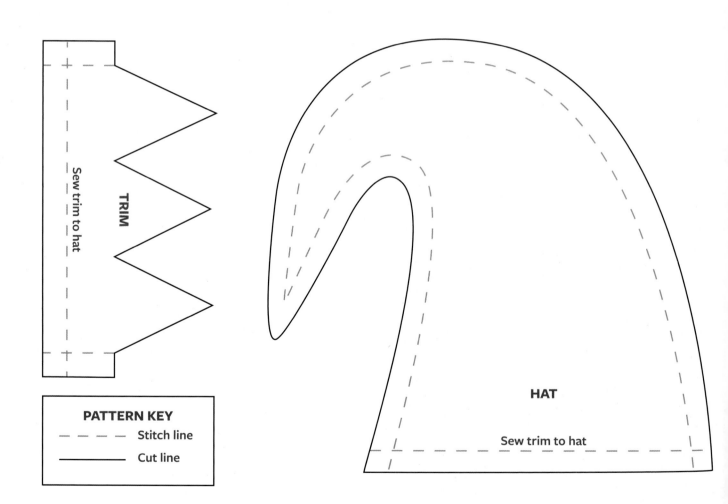

Sew trim to hat

**TRIM**

### PATTERN KEY

– – – – –  Stitch line

——————  Cut line

**HAT**

Sew trim to hat

# Photo Jewelry

**CRAFT LEVEL:** INTERMEDIATE

**FINISHED SIZE:** Varies.

A necklace or bracelet with the image of someone close at heart makes a treasured keepsake. Accent your pieces with letters, photos or other images cut from magazines or scrapbook paper for truly one-of-a-kind creations.

**MATERIALS:**

Bezel pendant blank with chain, or bracelet blank

Desired number of photos or other images

Laminate or clear packing tape

Dry scrapbook adhesive

UV curing resin (we used Magic-Glos)

Toothpicks

Lighter or matches

UV lamp or direct sunlight (we used a fluorescent black light in a desk lamp)

**DIRECTIONS:**

**1.** Cut photo or photos to fit inside pendant or bracelet blank. For bracelet, cut all pieces needed to fill entire length.

**2.** Use laminate or clear packing tape to cover each photo (this protects the colors in the photos from the resin). Trim any excess laminate or tape so it is flush with the edges of photo.

**3.** Affix each photo in desired blank with a dab of dry scrapbook adhesive. (Do not use liquid or tacky glue, which may not dry completely under the resin.) Press firmly into place.

**4.** Following resin manufacturer's instructions, fill the indented bezel area on top of each photo with resin, spreading it evenly with a toothpick. If bubbles form, wave a lit match or lighter over them.

**5.** Harden the resin by placing it in direct sunlight or under a UV lamp for 20 to 60 minutes, following resin manufacturer's suggestions for time. (Do not touch to see if resin is dry because fingerprints will mar it.)

**6.** When resin has hardened, place the pendant on chain.

# Metal Stamped Pendant

**CRAFT LEVEL:** INTERMEDIATE

**FINISHED SIZE:** Varies.

Personalize your handmade jewelry with the technique of metal stamping. Using a few tools, Craft Editor Shalana Frisby turned a pendant blank into an extra-special gift.

## MATERIALS:

**Metal pendant blank**
**Scrap sheet metal or blanks (for practice)**
**⅛-in. alphabet metal stamp set**
**⅛-in. heart or other metal stamp symbol (optional)**
**Hammer**
**Jeweler's anvil or metal bench block**
**Metal hole punch**
**Long-nose pliers**
**Round-nose pliers**
**Wire cutters**
**Jeweler's polishing pad**
**Permanent fine-point black marker**
**6 mm or larger metal jump rings**
**Head pins**
**Small beads or crystals**
**Necklace chain**

## DIRECTIONS:

### PREPARATION

**1.** Clean the surface of the pendant blank and any practice sheet metal or blanks.

**2.** For a centered word design, count the number of letters in the word and divide in half, identifying the center letter or letters. (If the design contains a symbol, count it as a letter.) On front of the pendant blank, use permanent black marker to mark small dots for each letter or symbol position, marking from the center letter outward and leaving about ⅛ in. of space between each mark. (If random placement of letters or symbols is desired, no marking is necessary.)

### STAMPING

**1.** Before stamping desired pendant blank, practice using the alphabet metal stamps a few times on scrap sheet metal or blanks.

**2.** Lay pendant blank flat on jeweler's anvil or metal bench block.

**3.** Using the marked dots for placement and beginning with the center letter, align the alphabet stamp vertically on top of mark. Holding stamp in place against surface, use hammer to firmly strike top of stamp. (If possible, do not strike more than once to avoid a double image. If one strike does not make a complete impression, be sure the stamp is aligned before striking a second time.)

**4.** Repeat Step 3 for each letter, working outward from the center mark.

### COLORING

**1.** Use permanent black marker to color in the recessed areas of each stamped letter. (It's OK to get marker slightly outside recessed areas.)

**2.** Use jeweler's polishing pad to gently rub the surface of the pendant, removing excess marks. (The color should remain in recessed areas. If needed, use marker to lightly fill in areas that are not dark enough.) Wipe metal clean.

### DANGLING CHARMS

**1.** Place bead or crystal onto a head pin.

**2.** With bead or crystal firmly in place at bottom of head pin, bend head pin wire at a 90° angle against the top of the bead or crystal. Use wire cutters to clip wire about ¼ in. from bend.

**3.** Placing round-nose pliers at wire end, roll the wire over, forming a closed loop. If needed, reposition pliers mid-roll to complete the loop.

**4.** Repeat Steps 1-3 to create the desired number of dangling charms.

### FINISHING

**1.** If needed, use metal hole punch to make a hole in stamped pendant.

**2.** Use long-nose pliers to open a jump ring by carefully twisting sideways where ring ends meet (do not pull apart). Slip open jump ring through hole on stamped pendant. Place dangling charms onto same jump ring (if large enough) or onto separate jump rings. Use long-nose pliers to twist jump rings closed.

**3.** Slip pendant and charms onto necklace chain.

**Crafter's Note:** *Over time, the black marker may wear off recessed areas. Repeat the coloring process if needed.*

# Green Dangle Earrings

**CRAFT LEVEL:** INTERMEDIATE

**FINISHED SIZE:** Earrings measure about ½ in. wide x 2 in. long.

Christmastime will shine even brighter with these dangling bead earrings from Sarah Farley of Menomonee Falls, Wisconsin. They're easy to make and customize for friends and family members using beads in their favorite colors.

## MATERIALS:

**2 French hook earrings**
**14 green smooth briolette beads**
**Fourteen 2-in. lengths of gold jewelry wire**
**2½-in.-long medium gold chain (Sarah used a chain with alternating large and small links)**
**Wire cutters**
**Round-nose pliers**
**2 pairs of flat-nose pliers**

## DIRECTIONS:

### WIRED BEADS

**1.** Slide a bead about a third of the way onto a 2-in. piece of gold wire. Bend both ends of the wire over the bead, forming a triangle about ⅛ in. from top of bead.
**2.** Using flat-nose pliers, grab the longer end of wire and bend it straight up over the bead. Next, grip the pliers over the wire triangle shape, clasping both sides. With the second pair of flat-nose pliers, grip the shorter end of wire and wrap it around the longer end once. Cut off any excess.
**3.** Using flat-nose pliers, grab the longer end of wire just above the wrapped wire and bend the longer end, making a right angle. Put the round-nose pliers about ⅛ in. away from the right angle with your wrist upside down. Pull the

end of the wire over the pliers until it is parallel with the bead, then roll your wrist forward, forming a rounded hook shape (see Fig. 1). Do not close it off into a loop or cut the end.
**4.** Repeat Steps 1-3 to make 7 wired beads for each earring.

### ASSEMBLY

**1.** To form a chain piece for each earring, use the wire cutters to cut the 2½-in.-long chain in half. If you have two different sized links on the chain, leave the first small link empty.
**2.** To attach a wired bead to the earring chain, string the open loop onto a link. Then clamp onto the loop with flat-nose pliers. With the second pair of flat-nose pliers, grip the end of the loose wire and wrap it around the space between the loop and the bead about 2-3 times, cutting off any excess wire. (This attaches the bead to the chain link.)
**3.** Following the instructions in Step 2 and starting with the top large link on each chain, attach a total of 7 wired beads on each earring chain, spacing the beads evenly along the links. (For bead spacing, Sarah used two beads on the first link, one on the second link, two on the third link, one on the fourth link and one on the fifth link.)
**4.** To attach the French hooks, use flat-nose pliers to pull the loops on each hook slightly open. For each earring chain, slip the first chain link onto a French hook loop. Using flat-nose pliers, close the French hook loop to secure the earring.

**FIG. 1**

# Frame Earring Holder

**CRAFT LEVEL:** QUICK & EASY

**FINISHED SIZE:** Frame measures about 6½ in. wide x 8½ in. high.

Plan to make Sarah Farley's Green Dangle Earrings on page 212? Pair those stylish beaded accessories with her beautifully functional earring holder. The fun and easy framed piece will accommodate several pairs at once.

**MATERIALS:**

**6½- x-8½-in. unfinished wooden photo frame with 4- x 6-in.**
  **opening**
**Acrylic craft paint**
**Flat paintbrush**
**Tacky glue**
**5- x-7-in. piece of white needlepoint canvas in size 10 mesh**
**Tack pins**
**Paper strips, stickers or other embellishments**

**DIRECTIONS:**

**1.** Use the flat paintbrush to base-coat the frame with acrylic paint. Apply as many coats as needed, letting dry between coats.

**2.** Cut slits in each corner of the canvas piece.

**3.** Put a line of tacky glue on one inner lip of the frame, then align one edge of the canvas piece with the glued edge of frame and press into place. Push a tack pin into the canvas piece to secure it while drying.

**4.** Repeat Step 3 for the remaining three sides of the canvas piece. Let dry and remove tack pins.

**5.** Decorate frame with paper strips, stickers or other embellishments as desired.

# Scented Sachets

**CRAFT LEVEL:** QUICK & EASY

**FINISHED SIZE:** Each sachet measures about 4½ in. square.

Craft Editor Shalana Frisby stitched scrap fabric into pretty sachet sets, perfect to give friends and family. Suggest hanging the aromatic pillows in a closet, putting them in drawers or keeping them handy in a sewing room as pincushions.

## MATERIALS:

**Two 5-in.-square or larger scraps of fabric for each sachet**
**Quilter's ruler**
**Rotary cutter with mat**
**Pinking shears**
**Standard sewing supplies**
**½-in.-wide ribbon or rickrack (optional)**
**2 cups dry white rice**
**1 cup dried lavender buds**
**1-gallon sealable plastic bag**

## DIRECTIONS:

### SCENTED MIX (MAKES ABOUT 8 SACHETS)

**1.** Place rice and lavender buds in plastic bag.
**2.** Shake bag to mix well.

### SACHET ASSEMBLY

**1.** Using quilter's ruler and rotary cutter with mat, cut two 5-in. squares of fabric.
**2.** Layer squares with wrong sides together and edges matching. Pin three sides. If desired, fold an 8-in. length of ribbon or rickrack into a loop and insert the ends in the center of one pinned side for a hanger.
**3.** Using a straight stitch, sew ½ in. from the edge on the pinned sides.
**4.** Spoon 6-8 Tbsp. of scented mix into the sachet's open side. Pin open side closed. Using a straight stitch, sew ½ in. from the edge.
**5.** Trim all sides with pinking shears, avoiding the hanger if added.
**6.** Repeat Steps 1-5 for desired number of sachets.

**Crafter's Note:** *Instead of using dried lavender buds, you can use 5-10 drops of the essential oil of your choice mixed directly into the dry white rice. Use 3 cups of rice for this method.*

# Paper Tree Cards

**CRAFT LEVEL:** QUICK & EASY

**FINISHED SIZE:** Varies.

Love to send handmade cards but short on time? This simple but elegant design makes it easy to create your own in a flash. Just round up basic paper crafting supplies and scraps.

**MATERIALS:**

**Blank card with envelope**
**Scraps of card stock or paper**
**Paper trimmer**
**Tacky glue**
**Glue stick**
**Fine glitter**
**Small star-shaped dimensional sticker or chipboard cutout**

**DIRECTIONS:**

**1.** Trace closed card onto back of card stock or paper. Using traced outline as a guide, cut a rectangle 1 in. shorter than the width and 2 in. shorter than the height.

**2.** Mark the center point along one short edge of the rectangle. Cut a straight line from each corner on the opposite end to the marked point, forming an elongated triangle for the tree.

**3.** Cut random diagonal lines across the triangle from the bottom to the top, laying the pieces flat in the correct order as you cut.

**4.** Lay card in front of you with the fold on the left. Use glue stick to adhere the triangle's bottom piece centered on front of card, positioning piece about $1/2$ in. from the bottom. Working upward, continue to adhere triangle pieces in the order they were cut, leaving about $1/8$ in. between pieces.

**5.** Apply a thin layer of tacky glue to the front of the star. Sprinkle fine glitter onto star, shaking off excess. Let dry.

**6.** Make several small dots of tacky glue on tree. Sprinkle fine glitter onto each dot, shaking off excess. Let dry.

**7.** Glue star to top of tree. Let dry.

**Crafter's Note:** *Instead of using tacky glue and glitter for the dot ornaments on the tree, use small buttons, brads, rhinestones or other embellishments.*

# Mini Accordion Album

**CRAFT LEVEL:** BEGINNER

**FINISHED SIZE:** Folded album measures about 4½ in. square.

Unfold heartwarming memories with this miniature photo album. The versatile design makes a special gift filled with family photos from the previous year.

**MATERIALS:**

**Glue stick**

**Two 4½-in. squares of foam board**

**Two 6-in. squares of patterned card stock**

**Solid card stock—one 9-in. x 4½-in. piece and two 10-in. x 4½-in. pieces**

**Desired photos and embellishments**

**12-in. length of ⅜-in.-wide ribbon**

**Chipboard or other letters for album title (optional)**

**DIRECTIONS:**

**1.** Glue each foam board square centered onto the back of a patterned card stock square. Let dry.

**2.** Cut a small square from each corner of patterned card stock. Fold over sides and glue in place.

**3.** Fold the 9-in. rectangle of solid card stock in half, making two 4½-in. squares. Fold a 1-in. flap on one short end of each 10-in. rectangle, then fold each remaining 9-in. section in half, making two 4½-in. squares.

**4.** Glue together the three rectangles of folded card stock, attaching each 1-in. flap to a 4½-in. segment, to make the accordion-style foldout pages.

**5.** Glue each 4½-in. end page to the back of each covered foam board piece. Let dry.

**6.** Glue photos and other embellishments to the inside pages of album as desired. Let dry.

**7.** Attach letters for a title to front of album if desired. Fold closed. Tie ribbon around the center to secure.

# Drawstring Gift Bag

**CRAFT LEVEL:** INTERMEDIATE

**FINISHED SIZE:** Bag measures about 5 in. wide x
5½ in. long.

Your loved ones will treasure both the gift and the packaging
when you give presents in reusable fabric bags. Choose a
straight-edge bottom or a more sophisticated round bottom.

## MATERIALS:

**Cotton fabric—fat quarter or scraps**
**Quilter's ruler**
**Rotary cutter with cutting mat**
**Compass (for round-bottom bag)**
**Standard sewing supplies**
**Iron with pressing cloth**
**⅛- to ¼-in.-wide ribbon**

## DIRECTIONS:

### BAG WITH CASING

**1.** Cut a 10- x 14-in. rectangle from fabric.
**2.** Press a ½-in. hem on one long side and both short sides
of the rectangle. With a ¼-in. seam allowance, stitch hem
on all three sides, mitering the corners if desired.
**3.** Along the long stitched edge, fold fabric over 1¾ in.
with wrong sides facing and press in place. Topstitch on
existing hem stitch to secure fabric together, then stitch
1 in. from the fold (or ½ in. from the topstitched hem) to

form a ½-in.-wide casing along the length of the fabric.
**4.** Fold rectangle in half lengthwise with right sides
facing and edges matching. Beginning at the bottom edge
of the casing, topstitch on the existing hem stitches to
close the side forming the bag base, making sure to leave
the top 1½ in. of casing edge open.

### FOR STRAIGHT-BOTTOM BAG

**1.** With right sides still facing on bag base, pin bottom raw
edges of bag together.
**2.** With a ¼-in. seam allowance, straight-stitch along
bottom of bag base, joining edges. If desired, zigzag-stitch
along outer edges to finish.

### FOR ROUND-BOTTOM BAG

**1.** Using a compass, draw a 4-in. fabric circle and cut out.
**2.** With right sides still facing on bag base, pin fabric
circle wrong side out around bottom raw edge. Match
circle edge to bag base edge, pinning in place about every
inch. If needed, gather excess fabric at seam.
**3.** With a ¼-in. seam allowance, straight-stitch around
circle bottom and bag base, joining edges. If desired,
zigzag-stitch around outer edges to finish.

### FINISHING

**1.** Cut an 18-in. length of ribbon.
**2.** For a ruffled top edge, thread the ribbon through the
bottom casing. For no ruffle, thread ribbon through the
wider top casing.
**3.** Fill bag as desired. Pull ribbon ends tight and tie a bow.

# Knit Cell Phone Cozy

**CRAFT LEVEL:** BEGINNER

Tote your cell phone in this cute little holder created by Jeanie Maier of Missoula, Montana, and Craft Editor Shalana Frisby. Because the knit cozy is felted, you can cut a simple working buttonhole without having to stitch it. For faster access to a ringing phone, use a Velcro strip or snap instead, making the button on the flap purely decorative.

**MATERIALS:**
**100% wool yarn (we used Lion Brand Yarn Alpine Wool)**
**Size 9 knitting needles**
**Two size 9 double-pointed needles**
**Sewing needle and thread to match yarn**
**Velcro strip or snap closure (optional)**
**Coordinating button**

**PRE-FELTED SIZE:** The base is about 5¼ in. wide x 8 in. long. The flap is about 4 in. wide x 3½ in. long.

**FINISHED SIZE:** The base is about 4 in. wide x 5¼ in. long. The flap is about 3 in. wide x 2½ in. long.
   (Overall shrinkage rate is about 30%. We recommend making a felted swatch to check the gauge and shrinkage rate before making the cozy. Different wool yarns may vary in shrinkage rate.)

**SPECIAL STITCHES:** Stockinette stitch:
Row 1 (right side): Knit. Row 2: Purl. Repeat Rows 1 and 2.

## DIRECTIONS:

### BODY (STARTING AT BOTTOM)

**1.** Cast on 30 stitches.

**2.** Row 1: Knit one; slip one (as if to purl) across the row, ending with a slipped stitch. Turn. Continue as in Row 1 for another 55-60 rows (or until about 8 in. long), making an open tube.

### FLAP

Put the slipped stitches onto one double-pointed needle and the knit stitches onto the other double-pointed needle, allowing the tube to open. With No. 9 needle, bind off the first 15 stitches, then work the other 15 stitches in stockinette stitch for 16 rows (or until about 3½ in. long), making the flap. Bind off; weave in ends.

### FELTING

**1.** Set a top-loading washing machine to the smallest capacity on a hot-water wash cycle. Place cozy in a pillowcase or mesh bag for protection, then place protected cozy, liquid detergent and a few old towels or pairs of jeans (to create agitation) in washing machine.

**2.** Wash in hot water for 10-15 minutes to allow shrinkage.

**3.** Stop washer and remove cozy. If needed, gently rub cozy horizontally and vertically to continue felting by hand until desired size is achieved.

**4.** Rinse cozy in lukewarm water to wash out remaining soap. Shape cozy by hand as desired and lay flat to dry. (Do not apply heat to dry.)

### FINISHING

**1.** If a buttonhole closure is desired, cut a buttonhole in the center of the flap (stitching is not necessary; felted wool will not ravel). Sew the button on the corresponding area of the cozy body.

**2.** If a Velcro or snap closure is desired, sew Velcro or snap centered on the underside of flap and the corresponding area of cozy body. Sew button on the outside of flap for decoration.

**Crafter's Note:** *Did you accidentally knit or purl instead of slipping a stitch? There will be a little closed spot in the tube where you did this. Just go ahead and felt it anyway. Once it is felted, you can carefully cut the closed stitch. Felted wool will not ravel.*

## Crocheted Wire Bracelet

**CRAFT LEVEL:** INTERMEDIATE

**FINISHED SIZE:** Bracelet measures 8 in. long.

Intertwined with Sarah Farley's bracelet is a surprisingly simple idea. The Menomonee Falls, Wisconsin, designer crocheted basic stitches with thin wire, adding beads as she went for an intricate, beautiful accessory.

### MATERIALS:
**40 or more assorted small beads**
**2 medium metal beads**
**Clasp with jump rings**
**9 yds. of 26-gauge wire**
**Wire cutters**
**Flat-nose pliers**
**Size J/10 (6 mm) crochet hook**
**Clear tape**

### DIRECTIONS:

**1.** Use wire cutters to cut wire into six 54-in. pieces.

**2.** Tie a slipknot on one end of each wire piece, leaving a 3- to 4-in. tail.

**3.** Use crochet hook to make each wire piece into a chain, making about 3 chains per inch and sliding a small bead onto every fourth chain. Make each of the beaded chains about 6½ in. long with a 3- to 4-in. tail on each end.

**4.** Working just above the first chain on each wire, twist the tails of the wires together tightly a few times. Use tape to hold the twisted ends in place.

**5.** Leaving taped ends together, slightly separate the crocheted wires into 3 groups of 2 wires each. Working with each group as 1 strand, braid the 3 groups together.

**6.** When finished braiding, twist the loose tails together very tightly. Remove the tape from opposite end and twist those tails in the same way.

**7.** Form each twisted end into a flattened loop about ½ in. long. Tightly twist the base of each loop to secure it in place. Push each loop through a medium metal bead. Trim the excess wire at the base of loop.

**8.** Use pliers to open the jump ring on individual parts of the clasp. Place a jump ring on each loop. Use pliers to close rings and secure toggle clasp parts in place.

# Knit Flower and Bag

**CRAFT LEVEL:** INTERMEDIATE

**FINISHED SIZE:** Flower measures about 4½ in. across. Felted bag measures about 9 in. wide x 4½ in. high.

Use these cute pieces from Sarah McFarland of Burdett, New York, as a pair or separately. The flower can make a fun hair clip, brooch or trim on any other accessory you like.

## MATERIALS:

### (FOR FLOWER)

**1 skein of soft worsted-weight acrylic-blend yarn (Sarah used Lion Brand Amazing Yarn 53% wool, 47% acrylic)**
**Coordinating novelty eyelash yarn for flower center**
**1 yd. of scrap yarn (Sarah recommends smooth worsted-weight acrylic or cotton yarn)**
**Set of four size 6 (4 mm) double-pointed needles (or size needed to obtain correct gauge)**
**Stitch marker**

### (FOR FELTED BAG)

**125 yds. of bulky-weight wool yarn (Sarah recommends Bear Farms 2-ply worsted-weight 100% wool or Lamb's Pride Bulky 85% wool, 15% mohair)**
**1 yd. of scrap yarn (Sarah recommends smooth worsted-weight acrylic or cotton yarn)**
**16-in.-long size 10 (6 mm) circular needle**
**Size 10 (6 mm) spare needle for three-needle bind-off**
**Stitch markers**
**Cotton fabric for lining—fat quarter or scrap piece**
**9-in. nylon zipper**
**Sewing machine with zipper foot**
**Standard sewing supplies**

**GAUGE:** For flower, 18 sts and 24 rows = 4 in. For unfelted bag, about 12 sts and 18 rows = 4 in. To save time, take time to check gauge.

## SPECIAL STITCHES:

1. K2tog: Knit 2 sts together (decrease).
2. Seed stitch (worked flat on odd number of sts): All rows: [k1, p1] to final st, k1.
3. Seed stitch (worked in the round): Knit the purls, and purl the knits as they present themselves.
4. Stockinette stitch (worked in the round): Knit all sts.
5. Three-needle bind-off: Place sts to be joined onto 2 separate needles. Hold them with right sides of knitting together. Insert a third needle into first st on each of the 2 other needles and knit them together as one st. *Knit next stitch on each needle in the same way. Pass first st over second st. Repeat from * until 1 st remains on third needle. Cut yarn and pull tail through last st.

## DIRECTIONS:

### FLOWER PETALS

1. With scrap yarn, cast on 8 sts. Switch to main yarn.
2. P-Row 1 (RS): K across row.

3. P-Row 2 (WS): P across row.
4. P-Rows 3-20: Repeat P-Rows 1-2 nine more times.
5. P-Row 21: P across row.
6. P-Row 22: P across row.
7. P-Rows 23-40: Repeat P-Rows 1-2 nine more times.
8. P-Row 41: P across row.
9. P-Row 42: P across row.
10. P-Rows 43-60: Repeat P-Rows 1-2 nine more times.
11. P-Row 61: P across row.
12. P-Row 62: P across row.
13. P-Rows 63-80: Repeat P-Rows 1-2 nine more times.
14. P-Row 81: P across row.
15. P-Row 82: P across row.
16. P-Rows 83-100: Repeat P-Rows 1-2 nine more times. Do not bind off.
17. Give the strip a single twist. Pick up sts from P-Row 81, turning each of the eight purl bumps into a st on the needle. Repeat this process on each purl row, moving toward the first row and distributing the picked-up sts evenly between the double-pointed needles. When you get to the cast-on row, remove the scrap yarn and k the first-row and last-row sts together, joining the ends of the strip.
18. Strip is now a ring with 5 twisted flower petals and 40 sts on double-pointed needles. These sts are worked in the round to create the flower center. Place a marker at the beginning of the round.

### FLOWER CENTER

1. Carry eyelash yarn along with main yarn when knitting as follows:
2. C-Round 1: K2tog 20 times: 20 sts.
3. C-Round 2: K across row.
4. C-Round 3: K2tog 10 times: 10 sts.
5. C-Round 4: K across row.
6. C-Round 5: K2tog 5 times: 5 sts.
7. Cut the yarn and pull it through the remaining sts, drawing the center tight.

### BAG STRAP

1. With scrap yarn, cast on 7 sts. Switch to main yarn for Row 1. Knit back and forth on circular needle.
2. ST-Row 1 (seed stitch): [K1, p1] 3 times, k1.
3. Repeat ST-Row 1 for a total of 40 rows or until strap is 9 in. long.
4. Unravel the cast-on row. As you remove the scrap yarn, fold strap in half and slip each st from ST-Row 1 to circular needle, making sure not to twist strap. (14 sts: 7 sts from each end of strap.)

### BAG SIDES

1. Cast on an additional 24 sts; place first marker. Cast on 23 sts; work the first 7 strap sts (maintaining seed stitch pattern); place second marker. Work 7 remaining strap sts (in seed stitch): 61 sts. Join to start working in the round. Be careful not to twist.
2. SD-Round 1: [K1, p1] to final st, k1 (seed stitch pattern).

**3.** SD-Rounds 2-6: Maintain seed stitch pattern by knitting the purls and purling the knits as they present themselves.

**4.** SD-Round 7: Maintain seed stitch pattern, stopping work at second marker.

**5.** SD-Round 8: Switch to stockinette stitch, knitting all sts in the round.

**6.** SD-Rounds 9-27: Knit until bag is 6 in. long (approximately 27 rounds).

### BAG BOTTOM
Use three-needle bind-off to join the 23 sts from each side. Break the yarn and draw it through the remaining st.

### BAG FELTING
Bag will shrink approximately 25% when felted. Felt bag as follows: Place bag in a pillowcase or laundry bag and close. Place in washing machine and set machine for a small load. Wash with detergent and hot water but do not let wash cycle get to rinse stage; instead, repeat the agitation cycle, checking every 5 to 10 minutes to make sure bag is felting evenly. When bag is sufficiently felted, let the wash cycle complete. Let bag air-dry completely (do not place in dryer).

### BAG LINING
**1.** Cut 2 lining sides from fabric, making them 1 in. larger than the bag all around.

**2.** With the edges aligned and the right side of the lining piece on the wrong side of the zipper tape, sew each lining piece to the zipper, using a zipper foot to stitch close to the zipper teeth.

**3.** Fold and press the lining away from zipper teeth. Fold the lining pieces so that right sides are together and raw edges are aligned. Stitch the lining's sides and bottom with a ½-in. seam allowance. Test the lining's fit inside felted bag; if necessary, stitch again with a wider seam allowance.

**4.** Hand-sew lining in place through the zipper tape, stitching it close to the bag's upper edge.

---

### ABBREVIATIONS

| | |
|---|---|
| k | knit |
| p | purl |
| st(s) | stitch(es) |
| RS | right side |
| WS | wrong side |

*Instructions between asterisks are repeated as directed.

[  ] Instructions between brackets are repeated as directed.

# Upholstery Fabric Stocking

**CRAFT LEVEL:** BEGINNER

**FINISHED SIZE:** Stocking measures about 8 in. wide x 13 in. long.

A handmade Christmas stocking gets a stylish update when you use leftover or recycled upholstery fabric. Filled with a set of kitchen utensils or other small presents, the seasonal sock makes a heartwarming holiday gift.

## MATERIALS:

**Pattern on page 223**
**22- x 16-in. piece of upholstery fabric for stocking**
**22- x 16-in. piece of fabric for lining**
**12- x 6-in. piece of fabric for cuff**
**Quilter's ruler**
**Rotary cutter and cutting mat**
**Standard sewing supplies**
**Sewing machine**
**Iron and pressing cloth**
**⅝-in.-wide coordinating ribbon**
**3-in. tassel (optional)**

## DIRECTIONS:

### BASE WITH LINING

**1.** Fold the upholstery fabric in half with right sides together, forming a double-layered piece of 11- x 16-in. fabric. Fold the lining fabric in half with wrong sides together, forming a double-layered piece of 11- x 16-in. fabric. Iron each piece, creasing the folded edge.

**2.** Place the folded upholstery fabric inside the folded lining fabric, matching the edges and folds. There will be four layers of fabric with the lining fabric (wrong sides together) outside and the upholstery fabric (right sides together) inside.

**3.** Make an enlarged photocopy of stocking pattern and cut out. Pin face up on fabric layers.

**4.** Use rotary cutter to cut around the outer edge of the pinned stocking pattern, making sure to cut through all four layers of fabric. Remove pins and stocking pattern, then pin the layers of fabric together again with edges matching.

**5.** Using a straight stitch and ½-in. seam allowance, sew around stocking, leaving the top straight edge open. If desired, zigzag-stitch the raw edge to prevent raveling. Turn stocking right side out.

### CUFF

**1.** Fold cuff fabric in half with wrong sides together, forming a double-layered piece of 3- x 12-in. fabric. Iron, creasing the folded edge.

**2.** Fold fabric in half again, forming a 3- x 6-in. layered piece, and pin in place. Using a straight stitch and ½-in. seam allowance, sew short side of layered fabric together, forming an open circle for the cuff. If desired, zigzag-stitch the raw seam edge to prevent raveling.

**3.** Turn fabric so seam is on the inside. Insert cuff fabric inside top edge of stocking with all open raw edges and side seams matching.

**4.** Cut a 7-in. length of ribbon and form a loop with ends matching. Insert ends of ribbon loop at the side seam between cuff and stocking layers, matching ribbon ends with raw fabric ends.

**5.** Pin cuff, ribbon and stocking layers together around top edge. Using a heavy-duty sewing machine needle or sewing by hand, sew around the edge with a ½-in. seam allowance, joining all layers together. If desired, zigzag-stitch the raw edge or hand-sew with a whipstitch to prevent raveling.

**6.** Turn the cuff right side out, overlapping the stocking top edge all around. (The ribbon hanger should be sewn between the cuff and stocking layers at the seam.)

**7.** If desired, either slip the hanger end of a tassel over the stocking ribbon loop or stitch the tassel to the top edge of the exterior side seam.

**STOCKING PATTERN**

Use a photocopier to enlarge pattern 200%.

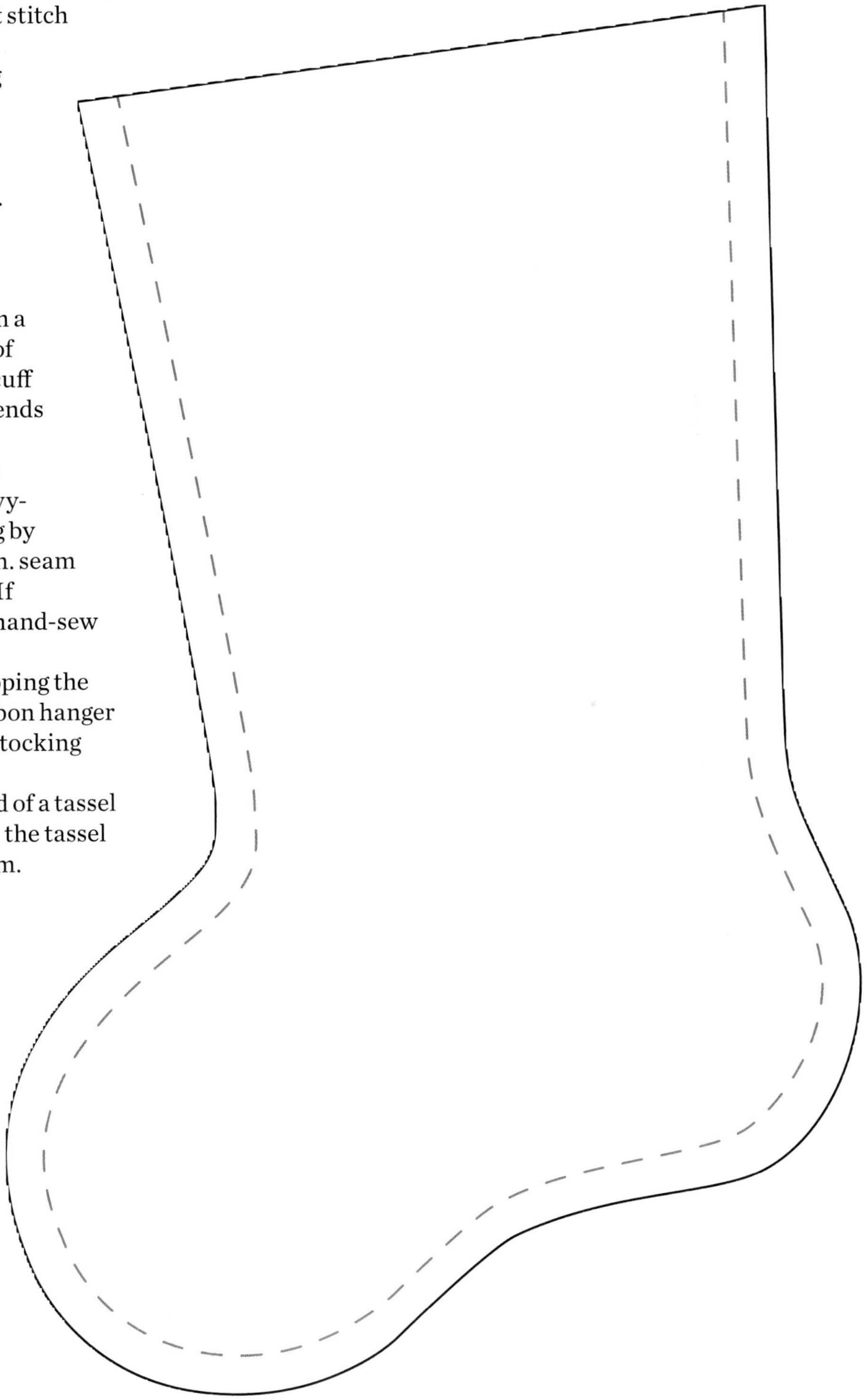

**PATTERN KEY**

– – – – – Stitch line

———— Cut line

## Penguin Card

**CRAFT LEVEL:** BEGINNER

**FINISHED SIZE:** Card measures about 5 in. wide x 7 in. high.

Just wing it this Christmas with handmade cards for everyone on your list. Sandy Rollinger of Apollo, Pennsylvania, created an adorable penguin design you can make in a snap.

### MATERIALS:

Patterns on this page
5- x 7-in. white card with envelope
Card stock—scraps of black, white, green, blue and orange
One sheet or scrap of coordinating snowflake-patterned scrapbook paper
Two small wiggle eyes
Craft glue for paper
Powdered cosmetic blush
Cotton swab
½-in. snowflake paper punch
Paper crimper
Compass
Ruler
Black fine-line marker
Computer and printer (optional)

### DIRECTIONS:

**1.** Cut a 4¾- x 6¾-in. rectangle of snowflake paper. Glue centered onto card front.

**2.** From green card stock, cut two ¾- x 5-in. and two ¾- x 7-in. strips. Run each through paper crimper. Glue short pieces to the top and bottom edges of card front, then glue long pieces to side edges of card front.

**3.** Trace patterns separately and cut out. From blue card stock, cut one hat, two scarf ends and one ⅞- x 2¾-in. rectangle for scarf base.

**4.** From green card stock, cut one ¾- x 3-in. strip for hatband. Use compass to draw a ¾-in. circle on white card stock and cut out.

**5.** Use black marker to make decorative lines around edges of all cutout hat and scarf pieces. Run each piece through paper crimper. Set aside.

**6.** Cut a 2-in. square from black card stock and a 1¼-in. square from white card stock.

**7.** Glue white piece centered on black piece for penguin's face. Glue hat to the top of face and glue scarf base to bottom of face. Glue scarf ends overlapping at an angle on right-hand side of scarf.

**8.** Glue hatband to base of hat and white circle centered on top of hat. Glue wiggle eyes on upper face.

**9.** From orange card stock, cut a small triangle for the beak. Glue onto face, centering beak below eyes.

**10.** Using cotton swab and blush, add a cheek on each side of beak. Using black marker, add eyebrows.

**11.** Glue assembled penguin onto center of card front at a slight angle.

**12.** From white card stock, punch five snowflakes. Glue one to each corner of card front and to the left-hand side of scarf ends.

**13.** Use either black marker or a computer and printer to print "HAVE A COOL YULE!" and "LET IT SNOW!" separately on green card stock. Cut a rectangle around each sentence, creating approximately 2½- x ¾-in. and 1½- x ¾-in. rectangles.

**14.** Use marker to make decorative lines around edges of each printed green piece. Glue each onto card front. Let card dry before placing in envelope.

**CARD PATTERNS**

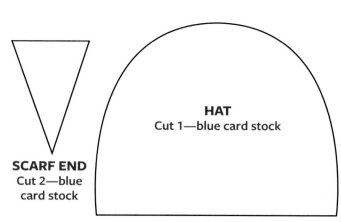

**SCARF END**
Cut 2—blue card stock

**HAT**
Cut 1—blue card stock

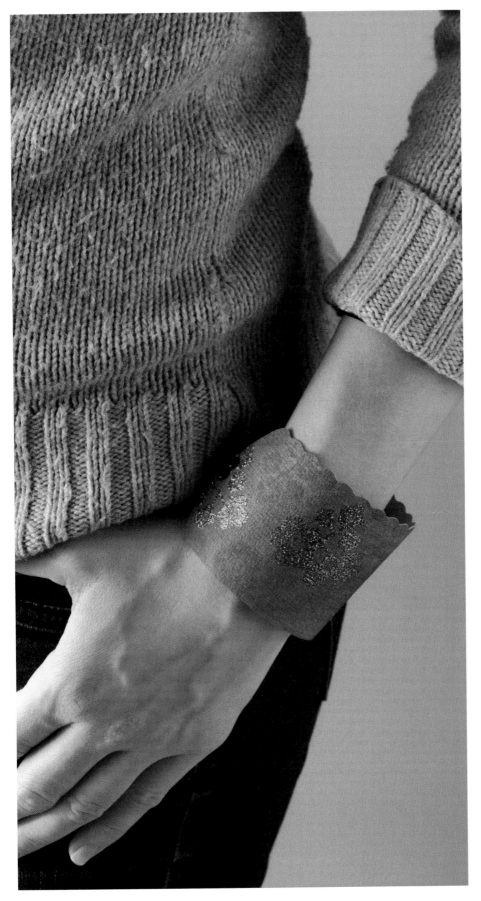

# Cuff Bracelet

**CRAFT LEVEL:** QUICK & EASY

**FINISHED SIZE:** Cuff measures about 2½ in. wide x 8 in. long.

This trendy cuff from Craft Editor Shalana Frisby has the popular look of leather but is actually made of sturdy Grungepaper. Vary the width, color and stamp decorations to fit a friend's or relative's personal style.

## MATERIALS:

**Tim Holtz Idea-ology Grungepaper**
**Two different Tim Holtz Distress Inks**
**Ink-blending tool**
**Stamps**
**Embossing powder**
**Embossing heat tool**
**Decorative-edge scissors or paper cutter (optional)**
**Hook-and-eye clasp**
**Standard sewing supplies**
**Paper towels**

## DIRECTIONS:

**1.** Cut an 8- x 2½-in. piece of Grungepaper. If desired, use decorative scissors or paper cutter to trim one side in a wavy pattern.

**2.** Lay Grungepaper on paper towels. Add ink horizontally along the length of each edge as follows: Dab ink-blending tool onto Distress Ink pad, then rub tool onto Grungepaper in a circular motion, transferring ink. Use inks of different colors along each edge. Let dry.

**3.** Decorate Grungepaper as desired with inked stamps. While the ink is still wet, sprinkle embossing powder on the designs, shaking off excess powder. Following manufacturer's instructions, use heat tool to set embossing powder. If paper edges curl during heating, gently shape flat again while still warm.

**4.** Use standard scissors to round off end corners. Sew hook-and-eye clasp centered on ends of cuff.

## No-Sew Casserole Carrier

**CRAFT LEVEL:** BEGINNER

**FINISHED SIZE:** Carrier fits a standard 9- x 13-in. casserole dish with lid.

You don't have to be a seamstress to make this convenient casserole tote. The sturdy fabric simply folds over your dish and closes with Velcro. Handy straps on each side for carrying make the design even more potluck-perfect.

### MATERIALS:
**20- x 28-in. piece of double-sided fusible ultra-firm stabilizer**
**Two 20- x 28-in. pieces of coordinating cotton fabric**
**⅝-in.-wide peel-and-stick Fabric Fuse permanent adhesive**
**⅝-in.-wide ribbon**
**65-in. length of 1-in.-wide nylon strap**
**Ruler and fabric pen**
**Six 2- x 4-in. strips of industrial-strength Velcro**
**Iron and ironing board**
**Clear tacky glue or Fray Check**

# DIRECTIONS:

## FABRIC BASE

**1.** Iron both pieces of fabric. Place stabilizer between the pieces with edges matching and right sides facing out.

**2.** Following stabilizer manufacturer's instructions, iron layered fabrics and stabilizer, fusing all layers into one piece. Trim ¼ in from all edges, making a 19½- x 27½-in. rectangle.

**3.** Referring to the Assembly Diagram at right, cut a 5- x 7-in. rectangle from each corner.

## ASSEMBLY

**1.** To cover raw fabric edges, apply peel-and-stick Fabric Fuse to the back of the ribbon. Fold sticky side of ribbon centered over raw edge. Covering only one straight edge at a time, trim ends flush to fabric. If needed, use glue or Fray Check to prevent cut ribbon ends from fraying.

**2.** For handle piece, form a loop with the nylon strap. Overlap ends about 1 in., using peel-and-stick Fabric Fuse to secure in place.

**3.** Cut two Velcro strips in half lengthwise, forming four 1- x 4-in. strips. Referring to the Assembly Diagram, measure about 3 in. from the bottom of each 7-in.-long flap and place 2 Velcro strips parallel to one another. Place the remaining 2 Velcro strips centered on opposite sides of the nylon loop. Attach each Velcro strip on loop to a Velcro strip on the fabric, forming handles.

**4.** Referring to the Assembly Diagram, attach 2- x 4-in. strips of Velcro on the exterior top corners of the 7-in.-long end flaps. Attach Velcro on the interior top corners of the 5-in.-long side flaps in the same way.

**5.** Place lidded casserole dish on center of open carrier. Fold over 7-in.-long end flaps, then fold over 5-in.-long side flaps. Secure Velcro to hold casserole dish in place. Wrap handles around sides to carry.

**Crafter's Note:** *If desired, stitch down the edges of the Velcro and handle straps to reinforce them. When needed, spot-clean casserole carrier with a damp cloth. Do not submerge in water.*

## ASSEMBLY DIAGRAM

19½ in.

7 in.

← Velcro closure placement on exterior

Velcro closure placement on interior →

5 in. →

9½ in.

27½ in.

Velcro handle placement

13½ in.

Velcro handle placement

3 in.

**EXTERIOR**

**INTERIOR**

# Wrap It Up Your Way

Why buy costly gift wrap, trims and tags from the store when you can easily make your own? The inexpensive wrapping ideas here will not only save money, but also lend heartwarming handmade touches to all of your Christmas gift boxes, packages and bags.

## 4 MINIATURE PINWHEEL

Paper pinwheels look complicated but take very little time to create. Use a 2-in. square punch to make two squares and glue them back-to-back with the edges even. Fold the glued square in half diagonally and unfold. Repeat, forming crisscrossing fold lines. From each corner, cut on the fold line, stopping ¼ in. from the center point to leave an uncut center area. At each slit, pull the right-hand point down to the center and glue it in place. Finish by gluing on a button.

## 5 FLAG BANNER

Friends and family will cheer for these adorable little pennants. With a 1¼-in. square punch, make one paper square for each flag. Fold each square in half diagonally, forming triangular flags. Leaving a tail for tying the banner if desired, place one end of a strand of string in the creased fold of a flag and glue the flag sides together, attaching it to the strand. Repeat to form a banner.

## 6 MINI CARD & ENVELOPE

It's fun to make holiday cards using 7½- x 4-in. rectangles of card stock. Just fold each in half lengthwise and decorate with stickers, brads and more. For an envelope, lay letter-size card stock vertically in front of you and measure 2 in. from each side, 4 in. from the bottom and 3 in. from the top, marking off the corner sections (see the diagram below). Cut out the corners, fold in the side flaps, then fold the bottom flap up over the sides and glue to secure, forming the envelope. To seal, simply fold down the top flap.

## 1 RECYCLED WRAPPING

Whether you need to wrap a gift in a pinch or just want to cut holiday costs, recycled household items of all kinds can make pretty packaging. Wash food containers such as potato chip cans, then wrap them with extra scrapbook paper, add some baker's twine and glue on a handmade topper. Don't be afraid to use household papers, either! Newspaper, packing Kraft paper and magazine pages all work well as gift wrap. Dress up packages with colorful ribbon, pompoms or scraps of patterned paper.

## 2 BLOOMING FLOWER

It takes just a few minutes to make several of these cute package trims. Using one or more scalloped circle punches, cut 2-3 coordinating circles from card stock or scrapbook paper. Fold the top-layer circle (and a center circle, if desired) in half, then in half again. Unfold the circle, revealing crisscrossing fold lines. Center and stack all paper circles, then insert a brad through the center to secure. Gently crease the folded layers upward on the previously folded lines for a dimensional effect.

## 3 CLOTHESPIN TAG

Gather up scraps of card stock to quickly craft your own gift tags. For each one, cut a rectangular shape and punch several circles of varying sizes. Stack the circles on the tag and secure them with a brad. Use a mini clothespin to attach the tag to a gift box or bag. (Different sizes of clothespins, both unfinished and pre-painted, are sold at craft stores.)

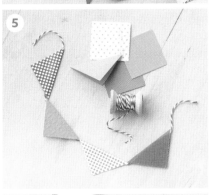

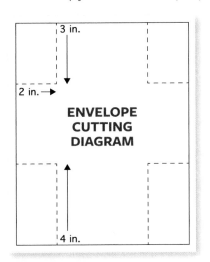

**ENVELOPE CUTTING DIAGRAM**

3 in.

2 in. →

4 in.

## Alphabetical Recipe Index

# General Recipe Index

# Craft Index

## Share the Magic of Christmas

Do you have a favorite recipe that has become part of your family's Christmas tradition? Does your holiday feast include "must-have" yuletide dishes that everyone craves? Those are the types of recipes we'd like to include in future editions of *Taste of Home Christmas*. To submit your special recipes, visit our website, *tasteofhome.com/submit*.